Critical Essays on Eugene O'Neill

Critical Essays on Eugene O'Neill

James J. Martine

G. K. Hall & Co. • Boston, Massachusetts

Library of Congress Cataloging in Publication Data
Main entry under title:

Critical essays on Eugene O'Neill.

(Critical essays on American literature)
Includes bibliographical references and index.
1. O'Neill, Eugene, 1888–1953 — Criticism and interpretation —
Addresses, essays, lectures. I. Martine, James J. II. Series.
PS3529.N5Z62727   1984   812'.52   83–26540
ISBN 0–8161–8683–9

This publication is printed on permanent acid-free paper
MANUFACTURED IN THE UNITED STATES OF AMERICA

CRITICAL ESSAYS ON AMERICAN LITERATURE

This series seeks to anthologize the most important criticism on a wide variety of topics and writers in American literature. Our readers will find in various volumes not only a generous selection of reprinted articles and reviews but original essays, bibliographies, manuscript sections, and other materials brought to public attention for the first time. James J. Martine's volume on Eugene O'Neill is unique in this program in that it consists entirely of original material, including an extensive bibliographical essay in the introduction, the first appearance of O'Neill's letters to Dudley Nichols, as edited by Jackson R. Bryer, and additional essays by Steven E. Colburn, Frank R. Cunningham, Lisa M. Schwerdt, Peter Egri, June Schlueter and Arthur Lewis, Joseph S. Tedesco, Carl E. Rollyson, Jr., Ellen Kimbel, Michael Manheim, Steven F. Bloom, Laurin Roland Porter, B. S. Field, Jr., and Susan Tuck. We are confident that this collection will make a permanent and significant contribution to American literary study.

James Nagel, GENERAL EDITOR

Northeastern University

For three generations:
   Theresa,
   Susan, Louis,
   John, Christopher, and Robert

CONTENTS

INTRODUCTION

If one were to climb the beanstalk of American drama, what would be discovered at the very top is a giant. His name is Eugene O'Neill. He towers above American drama like a colossus, and for many critics — theatrical reviewers and scholars — other playwrights were but petty things to walk under his huge legs and peep about. John McClain, the drama critic of the *New York Journal American*, said at least twice, and as late as 1958, that O'Neill makes today's playwrights look a little silly. One must understand this set of expectations to approach the mass of criticism and scholarship, approbation and disapprobation, on O'Neill. It seems there is no other case in American literature of a reputation towering so alone above others in the field. Hawthorne has Melville as company in American fiction; Emerson and Thoreau are inevitably coupled as one considers their particular corner of that heaven in nineteenth century America. In this country, perhaps only Whitman stands so alone above fellow journeymen in his field. One must appreciate this eminent position allotted to O'Neill if one is to fairly sort out the comments of critics, theatrical and scholarly, on America's second Nobel laureate — the only one in drama.

"Monumental" is the word most often used to describe O'Neill's work, from *Strange Interlude* to *A Touch of the Poet*. This word may be used as well to describe O'Neill and his reputation. But "monumental" describes a monument — and a monument stands on a pedestal. Birds fly over it, and caretakers may buff it — but it remains a monument, impervious to buff and bird. Being a monument, or a giant, is difficult. Viewing either can be neck-straining. Looking up may give a poor perspective. Looking straightforward may present only a view of the ankles.

This towering O'Neill has been measured for the most part and for six decades against O'Neill. It creates problems, to be sure. Even O'Neill's colossal failures must be weighed on the scale of the gargantuan expectations almost everyone had and has of this dramatist — and there were giant killers, to be sure — Jacks and jackasses. Were many of his plays — including some of his best — overwritten? By the mid-1950s, the critics had learned the word "prolix." The terms applied to O'Neill by critics who didn't much like his work are inevitably dinosaur or brontosaurus — giant figures. No one ever accused O'Neill, or his work, of being too small. It would seem the rules that apply to O'Neill apply only to O'Neill. Somewhat the same thing must be said in the compilation of a bibliographic essay on this father of American drama. There is no way to pretend to be comprehensive. One must be selective in seeking a path through the scope and density of scholarship on O'Neill to see what the giant was up to. Climbing the second, scholarly, beanstalk can be slippery business. If O'Neill wrote at length, the same thing must be said concerning what has been written *about* him. There is writing about O'Neill, there is excellent writing about O'Neill, and there is a great deal of both. Necessarily, then, what follows must be selective. To avoid being too long, one must risk being too brief, and, at that, it will be long.

BIBLIOGRAPHY

A basic item for scholars and general readers is John Henry Raleigh, "Eugene O'Neill," in Jackson R. Bryer, ed., *Sixteen Modern American Authors: A Survey of Research and Criticism* (New York: Norton, 1973), pp. 417–43. An update of this volume is promised from Duke University Press in late 1984. A good early study is Ralph Sanborn and Barrett H. Clark, eds., *A Bibliography of the Works of Eugene O'Neill* (New York: Benjamin Blom, 1931) which was reissued in 1965 by Blom by arrangement with Random House. Also included are "The Collected Poems of Eugene O'Neill" which describes O'Neill's early verse and reprints examples. While the editors concede that a perfect bibliography had yet to be compiled and that theirs leaves something to be desired, this volume is interesting because it includes a full collation of items in chronological order beginning with 1912 through 1929, pp. 3–83. Part two, pp. 85–106, contains references to critical matter on O'Neill, then unpublished plays, and anthologies. Part three, pp. 111–61, is devoted to poems by O'Neill, his earliest work. The volume includes 22 illustrations, reproductions of title pages, specimen pages, and front covers.

Jackson R. Bryer made a worthy contribution with "Forty Years of O'Neill Criticism: A Selected Bibliography," *Modern Drama*, 4, No. 2 (Fall 1961), 196–216. See also the same author's *Checklist of Eugene O'Neill* (Columbus: Merrill, 1971), a fundamental checklist of the dramatist's material. The 1970s saw the publication of the two most thorough and important studies in this area. Jordan Y. Miller, *Eugene O'Neill and the American Critic: A Bibliographical Checklist*, rev. 2nd ed. (Hamden, Conn.: Archon Books, 1973) begins with a brief chronology of the playwright's life, pp. 3–14; continues with a chronology of composition, copyright, and domestic publication, pp. 15–43, and major productions of O'Neill's plays, pp. 44–88; and provides a list of miscellaneous letters and other items that O'Neill wrote and that have appeared in print, pp. 89–97. The main portion and real value of the book, however, is the critical bibliography, pp.

98–472, a comprehensive guide to the American critical reception given O'Neill from his earliest days until 1971. Miller lists books, periodicals, and works that include individual references to produced and published versions of the separate plays. The volume lists all critical references under the titles of the plays in alphabetical, rather than chronological order and is handy to use. Charles A. Carpenter, "Parts of Books On O'Neill, 1966–1978: Addenda To Miller," *The Eugene O'Neill Newsletter*, 2, No. 3 (January 1979), 29–31, adds 58 items, many of them published in foreign languages, which was beyond Miller's intention. Another excellent volume is Jennifer McCabe Atkinson, *Eugene O'Neill: A Descriptive Bibliography* (Pittsburgh: Univ. of Pittsburgh Press, 1974). This valuable, impressive guide to O'Neill's writing is a thorough listing of works by O'Neill including reprintings, full descriptions, and locations of materials. A descriptive record of O'Neill's complete published works, this book is significant because it fills a scholarly gap of more than 40 years by updating Sanborn and Clark. Between 1931 and his death in 1953, O'Neill wrote 8 more plays, nearly completed a ninth, and worked on fragments or drafts of eleven others. During this same time, he saw ten more of his plays published and eight others were published posthumously. One must also mention the massive three volume J. Russell Reaver, comp., *An O'Neill Concordance* (Detroit: Gale, 1969) although Miller and others have questioned the scholarly usefulness of a concordance that is not complete since only 28 plays are included. All the major works since 1924 and representative earlier works are analyzed. Worthy of mention is that Louis Sheaffer, Pulitzer Prize biographer of O'Neill, has been awarded a grant-in-aid by the American Council of Learned Societies in connection with his next book, a survey of the major writings on the playwright. For the past half dozen years the best source of information on O'Neill has been *The Eugene O'Neill Newsletter* edited by Frederick C. Wilkins, Suffolk University, Boston, Mass. Containing essays of interest to O'Neill scholars, it includes news, notes, and queries. Readers can also find there abstracts of articles and reviews printed elsewhere. This is now an important and major source.

EDITIONS

In 1973, Raleigh concluded that there was no "established" text by O'Neill according to the practices of modern textual criticism. O'Neill's plays have been published and reprinted too often to catalog here. While there is as yet no complete edition, there are satisfactory collections. The Wilderness Edition, *The Plays of Eugene O'Neill* (New York: Scribner's, 1934–1935) is twelve volumes of the O'Neill canon up to that point. The edition, however, was limited to 770 copies signed by the author. The Wilderness Edition was the source of an edition in three volumes, *The Plays of Eugene O'Neill* (New York: Random House, 1941) which omits only some early one act plays. *The Plays of Eugene O'Neill* (New York: Random

House, 1951) adds *The Iceman Cometh* to volume 3, and it is this which Raleigh considers the standard edition. Supplements to this edition may be found listed in Raleigh, pp. 418–20, Atkinson, and Miller. Especially worthy of note and more readily available is the 3 volume Modern Library Edition, *The Plays of Eugene O'Neill* (New York: Random House, 1982). Although copyright restrictions prohibit completeness, volume 1 contains 13 plays, volume 2 contains 8, and volume 3 contains 9. The reader may want to see *A Moon for the Misbegotten* (New York: Random House, 1952); *Long Day's Journey Into Night* (New Haven: Yale Univ. Press, 1956); *A Touch of the Poet* (New Haven: Yale Univ. Press, 1957); *Hughie* (New Haven: Yale Univ. Press, 1959); and *More Stately Mansions* (New Haven: Yale Univ. Press, 1964), shortened from O'Neill's partly revised script by Karl Ragnar Gierow and edited by Donald Gallup. Also recommended here is Travis Bogard, ed., *The Later Plays of Eugene O'Neill* (New York: Modern Library, 1967) which contains *Ah, Wilderness!*; *A Touch of the Poet*; *Hughie*; and *A Moon for the Misbegotten*. Raleigh, pp. 418–19, describes the circumstances, and problems, of publication of *Thirst and Other One-Act Plays* (Boston: Gorham Press, 1914); *The Lost Plays of Eugene O'Neill* (New York: New Fathoms, 1950); and *Ten "Lost" Plays of Eugene O'Neill* (New York: Random House, 1964). Concerning the controversy over the publication of the New Fathoms edition of the "lost plays," see John Mason Brown, "Finders Keepers, Losers Weepers," *Saturday Review of Literature*, 33 (17 June 1950), 28, 30–31, or Schaeffer, *O'Neill: Son and Artist*, pp. 625–26. Also of interest is Jennifer McCabe Atkinson, ed., *"Children of the Sea" and Three Other Unpublished Plays by Eugene O'Neill* (Washington, D.C.: NCR/A Bruccoli Clark Book, 1972) which reproduces four apprentice works. Travis Bogard, we are told, is presently at work on a complete two volume edition of O'Neill's published plays for the Library of America Series.

From 1922 on, O'Neill's plays have been available abroad. See Horst Frenz, "A List of Foreign Editions and Translations of Eugene O'Neill's Dramas," *Bulletin of Bibliography*, 18, No. 1 (May-August 1943), 33–34, the first attempt to list British, German, Swedish, French, Italian, Rumanian, and South American publication of O'Neill's works. See as well, Frenz, "Eugene O'Neill's Plays Printed Abroad," *College English*, 5, No. 6 (March 1944), 340–41.

While there are O'Neill collections in the New York Public Library and the Dartmouth Library, among others, the major manuscript holdings are located at the Princeton Library and the Yale Library. The manuscript holdings at Princeton are described in Marguerite Loud McAneny, "Eleven Manuscripts of Eugene O'Neill," *Princeton University Library Chronicle*, 4, Nos. 2 and 3 (February-April 1943), 86–89. Walter Prichard Eaton, "The Eugene O'Neill Collection," *Yale University Library Gazette*, 18, No. 1 (July 1943), 5–8, describes the Yale University Library's manuscript material including several of O'Neill's most important plays. The O'Neill Collection at Yale is by far the largest single collection of material. A brief description of the major collections is in Egil Törnqvist, *A Drama of Souls* (New Haven: Yale Univ. Press, 1969), 266–67.

The major work on O'Neill's letters has only recently begun. Earlier pieces include "A Letter From Eugene O'Neill to Arthur H. Quinn," *Arizona Quarterly*, 13, No. 4 (Winter 1957), 293–94; John S. Mayfield, "Eugene O'Neill and the Senator From Texas," *Yale Univ. Library Gazette*, 35, No. 2 (October 1960), 87–93; James Milton Highsmith, "A Description of the Cornell Collection of Eugene O'Neill's Letters to George Jean Nathan," *Modern Drama*, 14, No. 4 (February 1972), 420–25; Highsmith, "The Cornell Letters: Eugene O'Neill on His Craftsmanship to George Jean Nathan," *Modern Drama*, 15, No. 1 (May 1972), 68–88; and William J. Scheick, "Two Letters by Eugene O'Neill," *Resources for American Literary Study*, 8 (1978), 73–80. The 1980s will address the need for editions of the playwright's letters, and the work has fallen to sure and eminent scholarly hands. Jackson R. Bryer, ed., *"The Theatre We Worked For": The Letters of Eugene O'Neill to Kenneth Macgowan* (New Haven: Yale Univ. Press, 1982) collects 157 letters and telegrams of a twenty-nine year correspondence beginning in 1920 with the celebrated theatrical critic and producer. This significant volume is only the harbinger of larger things. Bryer and Travis Bogard have reached an agreement with Yale to edit a larger, more inclusive collection of the dramatist's letters. This badly needed volume will be an important contribution to O'Neill scholarship and is previewed by Bryer's piece in the volume readers presently have before them.

BIOGRAPHY

As the bibliographic situation is better than satisfactory, further scholarly work is forthcoming on manuscript materials, and the future for the letters is promising, the area of biography in an *embarras de richesses*. It is not, however, difficult to be selective here, for there are two major biographies. By almost any measure, Arthur Gelb and Barbara Gelb, *O'Neill* (New York: Harper's, 1962) would be considered a definitive biography. O'Neill's life, from his relationship with his parents and brother, through his sea faring days to his remarkable final years with his last wife, Carlotta Monterey O'Neill, was as dramatic as anything he ever wrote. His life, of course, provided sources of much of his writing. The Gelbs's massive biography captures the drama and torment of his life. It is hardly a funny story, and the Gelbs have brought their man back alive. Well written, rich in detail, the Gelbs's *O'Neill* is an outstanding biography; a new edition (New York: Harper and Row, 1973) adds an "Epilogue," pp. 945–64. The picture is altered somewhat by another excellent biography, this one in two volumes, Louis Sheaffer, *O'Neill: Son and Playwright* (Boston: Little, Brown, 1968) that covers the dramatist's life up to 1920 when *Beyond the Horizon* opened on Broadway. Sheaffer's second volume, *O'Neill: Son and Artist*

(Boston: Little, Brown, 1973) covers O'Neill's rise to celebrity world wide and the period of the decline of his reputation, which ironically is now seen as the time of composition of his greatest, most enduring drama. Sheaffer's massive biography is carefully researched and well presented. While some critics and scholars seem to consider the Sheaffer volumes the most significant, it would serve no purpose here to attempt to choose a standard biography between the work of Sheaffer and the Gelbs. Perhaps it is enough to say that a giant of the proportions of O'Neill deserved two such comprehensive biographies. In any case, the presence of two major biographies must be seen as a happy circumstance for readers. The interviews and years of research (7 for Sheaffer, 5 for the Gelbs) were time well spent for the authors; the pages (1,293 pp. for Sheaffer, 990 for the Gelbs) are time well spent for those interested in the details of O'Neill's life.

There are other, quite worthy, studies of the life. Since O'Neill was a remarkably autobiographical writer, the number of biographical examinations is warranted. The first book published completely devoted to O'Neill is Barrett H. Clark, *Eugene O'Neill* (New York: McBride, 1926). This was revised and reissued in 1929 as *Eugene O'Neill: The Man and His Plays*. Of subsequent editions of this volume, perhaps the most useful is that issued in 1947. This is a pioneer work without the completed canon at its disposal, but it remains a worthwhile reference source. Although not technically a biography, also of interest is Agnes Boulton, *Part of a Long Story* (Garden City: Doubleday, 1958). This memoir by an O'Neill wife and the mother of two of his children is, as the title suggests, only part of a long story, but it is an interesting part, including O'Neill's tales of his attempted suicide, his early alcoholism, and his struggles in Greenwich Village and Provincetown. While the focus of Boulton's story is chronologically narrow, Croswell Bowen, *The Curse of the Misbegotten* (New York: McGraw-Hill, 1959) was the first significant attempt to cover the playwright's life from birth to death. Written with the cooperation of O'Neill's son, Shane, Bowen's account focuses upon the life of the dramatist and the lives of those around him. The O'Neill tragedy is seen as the "curse" of a lack of communication of love that bedeviled both O'Neill's parents' and brother's relationship with him and his with his wives and children. Unhindered by annotation and scholarly apparatus, the narration pauses only briefly on each play; the prose is readable and the story compelling.

Like Sheaffer's first volume, Doris Alexander, *The Tempering of Eugene O'Neill* (New York: Harcourt, Brace and World, 1962) covers the important periods of O'Neill's life up to his earliest success. Alexander centers on that part of his life which was to be the crucible from which he would draw what were later his best plays. This biography is a significant scholarly item. Frederic I. Carpenter, *Eugene O'Neill* (New York: Twayne, 1964; rev. ed. Boston: Twayne, 1979) is an outstanding briefer look at the playwright and his plays. Carpenter's book is intelligent and readable, a good place to begin for those interested in O'Neill. Since O'Neill must be considered an eminently autobiographical dramatist, many of the books listed below treat the biography in one way or another in relation to the plays. As well, there is scarcely a book on American drama that does not include sketches of O'Neill, and reminiscences and recollections abound. One charming sample is Warren H. Hastings and Richard F. Weeks, "Episodes of Eugene O'Neill's Undergraduate Days at Princeton," *Princeton Univ. Library Chronicle*, 29, No. 3 (Spring 1968), 208–15. This piece by classmates and friends of O'Neill during his year at Princeton notes his "intense shyness," and refutes several popular legends about O'Neill while adding fuel for others. Eugene O'Neill's life was the stuff of which legends are made, and it is fortunate that his major biographers have attempted to separate fact from fabrication.

CRITICISM

General Estimates

Books
   Eugene O'Neill is an excellent example of reputation's roller-coaster ride. In June 1920, *Beyond the Horizon* was awarded O'Neill's first of four Pulitzer Prizes. Other Pulitzers were given in May 1922 for *Anna Christie* and May 1928 for *Strange Interlude*. Following tremendous popular, critical, and financial success in the 1920s, O'Neill's reputation, certainly not his artistic powers, declined. In 1923, O'Neill was elected to the National Institute of Arts and Letters and won the gold medal for drama. Ten years later, in November of 1933, the playwright was elected a member of the American Academy of Arts and Letters, and in 1936 he was awarded the Nobel Prize for Literature. The award of the Nobel Prize to O'Neill was ironic in a way, for it marked the passing of his reputation into near oblivion during much of the remainder of his life. Following his death on 27 November 1953, he was restored to critical approval and public favor, and posthumously awarded his fourth Pulitzer Prize, this time for his great play, *Long Day's Journey Into Night*.
   Scholarship and criticism on O'Neill's work is vast and varied, to which the catalog of books in Miller, pp. 105–56, will bear testimony. The Gelbs, Sheaffer, and Carpenter do deal with the plays, and Barrett Clark's 1926 biography was also the first critical book. Other early studies include a brief pamphlet of limited value, Joseph T. Shipley, *The Art of Eugene O'Neill* (Seattle: Univ. of Washington Bookstore, 1928), after Clark's, the first work devoted exclusively to O'Neill. Alan D. Mickle, *Six Plays of Eugene O'Neill* (New York: Liveright, 1929) provides unqualified praise for O'Neill, placing him in the company of the world's greatest playwrights. Quite another matter is William Salisbury, *A Dress Suit Becomes Hamlet. Why Not, If Mourning Becomes Electra?* (New Rochelle: Independent Publ. Co., 1933). This pamphlet is a vicious attack on O'Neill's plays up to that point. Jordan

Miller calls this invective "a low water mark in dramatic criticism." Unlike Mickle's panegyric is Virgil Geddes, *The Melodramadness of Eugene O'Neill* (Brookfield, Conn.: Brookfield Players, 1934). This pamphlet subjects O'Neill to disapproval. Geddes does not think much of O'Neill or his plays, but it is not the scurrilous attack of Salisbury. While not restricted to O'Neill, an early book on the Provincetown Players, Helen Deutsch and Stella Hanau, *The Provincetown: A Study of the Theatre* (New York: Farrar and Rinehart, 1931) will be of interest to those interested in the playwright.

The first major critical book is Sophus Keith Winther, *Eugene O'Neill: A Critical Study* (New York: Random House, 1934). Treating the canon up to the time of the Nobel Prize, this book is an excellent pioneering study, a highly favorable estimation of O'Neill and an interesting approach to his thought. In an enlarged second edition (New York: Russell & Russell, 1961) Winther adds a brief final chapter, "O'Neill and Modern Tragedy," pp. 296–312, on the four plays published since the first edition. A final item worth notice from the 1930s is Richard Dana Skinner, *Eugene O'Neill: A Poet's Quest* (New York: Longmans, Green, 1935). Reissued three decades later (New York: Russell & Russell, 1964), this search for an inner continuity of the plays uses a chronology provided by O'Neill (pp. vii–x) and examines the dramas in chronological order from *Bound East For Cardiff* to and including *Days Without End*.

In the 1940s, the United States went to war, her premier dramatist into withdrawn isolation, his reputation into near total eclipse, and serious scholarship on him into hiding. But the giant did not sleep. Suffering from physical ills and tormented by psychological introspection and reverie, his trembling hand tended the golden eggs that many critics now consider his finest works. With the New York premiere of *The Iceman Cometh* in 1946, revivals of *Anna Christie* and *Desire Under the Elms* in 1952, O'Neill's death in 1953 and the subsequent availability of new materials, the magnificent first American production in 1956 of *Long Day's Journey* directed by Jose Quintero, the 1957 production of *A Moon for the Misbegotten* and the 1958 production of *A Touch of the Poet*, and a profusion of Quintero staged revivals in the 1960s, O'Neill criticism and scholarship once again flourished. An important source of information on O'Neill's association with the Theatre Guild is Lawrence Langner, *The Magic Curtain* (New York: Dutton, 1951). The recollections of this Guild director, O'Neill's close friend, will be of interest to those concerned with either productions or relationships. The first extensive scholarly analysis is Edwin A. Engel, *The Haunted Heroes of Eugene O'Neill* (Cambridge, Mass.: Harvard Univ. Press, 1953). Engel explores recurrent and dominant themes in the plays—dreams, drunkenness, and death—tracing them back to Nietzsche and Jung. The book is of interest precisely because it does not deal with biography but does a close literary analysis, concerned with themes and the merit of the plays themselves. Of special significance is the recent reissue (Staten Island: Gordian Press, 1981) of Doris V. Falk, *Eugene O'Neill and the Tragic Tension:*

An Interpretive Study of the Plays (New Brunswick: Rutgers Univ. Press, 1958). Deliberately narrow in scope, confining itself to the tracing of a single, complex pattern in the plays, this volume examines the plays in order of performance. Psychological in approach, relating the pattern to the mind of the man who wrote the plays, this is a valuable piece of O'Neill scholarship, done with the permission of Carlotta to study and quote from the manuscripts in the O'Neill Collection at Yale.

As the gears of scholarship began to turn in the 1960s, a number of volumes began to appear, including major scholarly contributions. Three brief and inexpensive critical introductions are Clifford Leech, *Eugene O'Neill* (New York: Grove, 1963); John Gassner, *Eugene O'Neill* (Minneapolis: Univ. of Minnesota Press, 1965); and Horst Frenz, *Eugene O'Neill* (New York: Frederick Ungar, 1971). Leech's 120 pages provide a convenient introduction. Gassner's Minnesota pamphlet of 48 pages is a good introduction to the plays and is reprinted in Gassner, *Dramatic Soundings* (New York: Crown, 1968), pp. 254–81. Frenz's 121 page monograph, translated from the German by Helen Sebba, begins with a short introduction on the history of the American theatre then turns quickly to O'Neill. While organized around biographic detail, the focus is on the plays. The drama, Frenz suggests, gives a glimpse of the man behind the experimenter, a man whose suffering and sacrifice distinguish him from any other American playwright or literary movement.

John Henry Raleigh, *The Plays of Eugene O'Neill* (Carbondale: Southern Illinois Univ. Press, 1965) greatly exceeds the ordinary length of volumes in the Crosscurrents/Modern Critiques series and considers the plays not in chronological sequence but as one organic whole made up of a variety of themes, characters, and preoccupations. Raleigh's analysis and evaluation of O'Neill's completed, published plays sees the great late plays not breaking new ground or discovering new themes but demonstrating mastery over similar elements in the earlier plays. Like Engel, Chester Clayton Long, *The Role of the Nemesis in the Structure of Selected Plays by Eugene O'Neill* (The Hague: Mouton, 1968) avoids the biographical in the examination of the plays, and this book is seen by critics as an important piece of O'Neill scholarship.

Perhaps the best scholarly studies of O'Neill are those provided by Timo Tiusanen, Egil Törnqvist, and Travis Bogard. A major critical study on many elements of O'Neill's plays, Timo Tiusanen, *O'Neill's Scenic Images* (Princeton: Princeton Univ. Press, 1968) concludes that the later plays are the great plays and is one of the most significant volumes of O'Neill scholarship. Another volume by an eminent O'Neill scholar is Egil Törnqvist, *A Drama of Souls: Studies in O'Neill's Super-naturalistic Technique* (New Haven: Yale Univ. Press, 1969). This is a valuable and comprehensive study. Another excellent volume is Travis Bogard, *Contour In Time: The Plays of Eugene O'Neill* (New York: Oxford Univ. Press, 1972) which contains outstanding discussions of the individual plays. Concerned with the autobiographical nature of O'Neill's drama, this work by an important scholar is the product of a first rate mind and is among the best comprehensive critical studies of O'Neill.

Also worth mention are Leonard Chabrowe, *Ritual and Pathos: The Theater of O'Neill* (Lewisburg: Bucknell Univ. Press, 1976); Harry Cronin, *Eugene O'Neill, Irish and American: A Study in Cultural Context* (New York: Arno, 1977); and Lennart Josephson, *A Role: O'Neill's Cornelius Melody* (Stockholm: Almqvist & Wiksell, 1977). Drawing on some previously unpublished manuscript material, Jean Chothia, *Forging A Language: A Study of the Plays of Eugene O'Neill* (Cambridge: Cambridge Univ. Press, 1979) centers on the linguistic medium of O'Neill's plays from low-colloquial through Irish dialect, Broadway slang and idiomatic American English to poetic prose. Chothia demonstrates that O'Neill's use of language, often berated, is, in fact, flexible and complex and that his dramatic language is much more poetic and effective than is commonly acknowledged. Another volume that contains much new O'Neill material is Virginia Floyd, ed., *Eugene O'Neill at Work: Newly Released Ideas for Plays* (New York: Ungar, 1981). Normand Berlin, *Eugene O'Neill* (New York: Grove, 1982) is a good introduction several scholars and critics like very much, and John Orlandello, *O'Neill on Film* (Madison, N.J.: Fairleigh Dickinson Univ. Press, 1982) compares nine O'Neill plays with their film adaptations. Michael Manheim, *Eugene O'Neill's New Language of Kinship* (Syracuse: Syracuse Univ. Press, 1982) argues that the early plays are a series of distortions of the autobiographical motifs that will later emerge in *Long Day's Journey*. A sensitive and intelligent volume that demonstrates how O'Neill's career began in greatly disguised autobiography and ends in high tragedy, this fine book includes a useful treatment of motifs in *Long Day's Journey*.

There are a number of nice collections of essays on the dramatist. The entire issue of *Modern Drama*, 3, No. 3 (December 1960) is devoted to O'Neill, featuring an overview by Edwin A. Engel, "O'Neill 1960," pp. 219–23, and including articles by Arthur Nethercot, Doris Alexander, John Shawcross, Horst Frenz, and Sophus Winther, among others. A most substantial collection of essays, critiques, letters, and reviews is Oscar Cargill, N. Bryllion Fagin, and William J. Fisher, eds., *O'Neill and His Plays: Four Decades of Criticism* (New York: New York Univ. Press, 1961) which includes personal memoirs of O'Neill by friends and colleagues, theatrical reviews, and a selection of O'Neill letters and his own essays. While the bulk of the volume reprints items published elsewhere, there is a fine introduction, pp. 1–16, and a good selected bibliography, pp. 487–517. John Gassner, ed., *O'Neill: A Collection of Critical Essays* (Englewood Cliffs, N.J.: Prentice-Hall, 1964) reprints a baker's dozen of articles and includes essays by Raleigh and Bogard published for the first time. Jordan Y. Miller in *Playwright's Progress: O'Neill and the Critics* (Chicago: Scott, Foresman, 1965) reprints over 60 reviews and essays, and Ernest G. Griffin, *Eugene O'Neill: A Collection of Criticism* (New York: McGraw-Hill, 1976) reprints criticism and includes Griffin's "Eugene O'Neill: An Introduction To His Life and Career," pp. 1–20, and a selected bibliography, pp. 139–51. Virginia Floyd, ed., *Eugene O'Neill: A World View* (New York: Ungar, 1979) provides a substantial collection of articles. The volume's first part presents essays with a European perspective including works by Tiusanen, Leech, Törnqvist, Frenz, and Peter Egri, among others. The second section is devoted to six essays, one by Frederick Wilkins and two by Raleigh. The book's final feature is the insights and comments of performers on O'Neill by Florence Eldridge, Geraldine Fitzgerald, Ingrid Bergman, and stage director Arvin Brown. Floyd provides introductions to the three parts.

Considerations of space make even a mere listing of graduate research on O'Neill impossible. To the 76 doctoral dissertations listed in Miller, pp. 473–85, the reader will have to add 38 dissertations done in the decade since.

Articles

Including a valuable letter from O'Neill, Arthur Hobson Quinn, "Eugene O'Neill, Poet and Mystic," *Scribner's Magazine*, 80, No. 4 (October 1926), 368–72, is an early estimation, by a respected scholar, of O'Neill as a great dramatist. While too much a historian not to know that it was too soon for a firm evaluation, Quinn recognizes O'Neill's genius; he is interesting in his view of the playwright as both mystic, a Celtic mystic at that, and poet. Occasioned by the production of *Dynamo*, Ernest Boyd, "Eugene O'Neill And Others," *Bookman*, 69 (April 1929), 179–81, was the first to suggest that O'Neill is best when he deals with simple, elemental emotions and when he attempts to treat ideas dramatically he is lost. Francis Ferguson, "Eugene O'Neill," *Hound & Horn*, 3, No. 2 (January-March 1930), 145–60, is an early evaluation written by one who is no admirer, and the essay focuses upon what Ferguson takes to be O'Neill's failures as a dramatist. Although it points out patterns and the autobiographic nature of the plays up to *Mourning*, H. G. Kemelman, "Eugene O'Neill and the Highbrow Melodrama," *Bookman*, 75, No. 5 (September 1932), 482–91, by reducing characters to stereotypes and plots to their skeletons, reduces everything to absurdity; what might have seemed a devastating satiric attack in 1932 may be read 50 years later as a debunking article that is amusing, funny in places — if one allows for the fact that there is no writer to whom this might not be done. Edd Winfield Parks, "Eugene O'Neill's Symbolism: Old Gods for New," *Sewanee Review*, 43, No. 4 (October-December 1935), 436–51, is an even-handed essay with a misleading title. More emphasis is placed by Parks on the oft-omitted subtitle than the title. Not unmindful of O'Neill's weaknesses and certain of his strengths, in this defense of O'Neill's *Days Without End*, Parks's approach is through O'Neill's language, themes and philosophy; while the cause is *Days*, the article's treatment and importance goes beyond that. Inspired by O'Neill's Nobel, Homer E. Woodbridge, "Eugene O'Neill," *South Atlantic Quarterly*, 37,

No. 1 (January 1938), 22–35, is an appreciative piece dealing with melodrama, naturalism, and symbolism in the plays. Written with the knowledge that O'Neill was at work on his large "cycle" of plays and that the canon was not complete, John Gassner, "The Provincetown's Playwright," in *Masters of the Drama*, 3rd ed. (New York: Dover Publications, 1940), 639–61, 798–800, is a fair, intelligent overview of the plays up to *Days Without End*. Fully aware of O'Neill's imperfections, Gassner points out that O'Neill had produced a greater body of drama that "has stimulated and stirred intelligent audiences in America and abroad than any playwright of his generation." Even higher praise comes from Gilbert Norwood, "The Art of Eugene O'Neill," *Dalhousie Review*, 21 (1941), 143–57, which is interesting because Norwood uses groupings of plays different than anyone before him. This overview of O'Neill's oeuvre up to the end of the 1930s concludes that *Desire* and *Mourning* are his finest plays and that he must be included among the world's greatest playwrights unsurpassed, in some aspects, by Aeschylus or Shakespeare. Centering upon the contrast in O'Neill between dream and reality, Frederic I. Carpenter, "The Romantic Tragedy of Eugene O'Neill," *College English*, 6, No. 5 (February 1945), 250–58, traces the rise and tragic fall of the romantic dream in the major works. This is an excellent essay, very good on *Strange Interlude* and *Mourning* but especially fine on *Lazarus Laughed* which Carpenter calls the most perfect of O'Neill's plays. Like Ernest Boyd, George Jean Nathan, "O'Neill: A Critical Summation," *American Mercury*, 63, No. 276 (December 1946), 713–19, points to O'Neill's emotional rather than intellectual nature. This piece *in piccolo* and in chronological order evaluates the canon up to and including *Iceman*. Among the best general essays, acknowledging both virtues and limitations, is Joseph Wood Krutch, "O'Neill's Tragic Sense," *American Scholar*, 16, No. 3 (Summer 1947), 283–90. Occasioned by the premiere of *Iceman*, this is an important document because its intelligence and moderation place in perspective not only O'Neill but his critics as well and explains, in part, the wide diversity of reaction to the dramatist's works. Rudolf Stamm, "The Dramatic Experiments of Eugene O'Neill," *English Studies*, 28 (1947), 1–15, begins with a brief overview of American drama, comments on the period between the wars relating O'Neill to Mencken and Sinclair Lewis, then gives an adequate synopsis of the plays up to but not including *Iceman*. An attempt to evaluate the best work of O'Neill measured by the standards of the great traditions in tragedy, William Peery, "Does the Buskin Fit O'Neill?," *Univ. of Kansas City Review*, 15, No. 4 (Summer 1949), 281–87, is interesting, but it finds the dramatist lacking mostly because Peery weighs O'Neill's oranges against Aristotle's apples. An important piece, oft cited, oft reprinted, on O'Neill's faults, Eric Bentley, "Trying to Like O'Neill," *In Search of Theater* (New York: Knopf, 1953), 233–47, finds the playwright a victim of his times. In this essay that first appeared in *Kenyon Review*, 14 (July 1952), 476–92, Bentley deals at length with *Iceman*. At O'Neill's death, a number of articles appeared. Three will provide a sample: John Mason Brown, "Eugene O'Neill: 1888–1953," *Saturday Review*, 36 (19 December 1953), 26–28, is an appreciation of O'Neill's greatness; "The Unmarked Casket," *Saturday Review*, 36 (26 December 1953), 28, is from a *Boston Post* news account of O'Neill's burial; N. Bryllion Fagin, "Eugene O'Neill," *Antioch Review*, 14, No. 1 (March 1954), 14–26, objectively, conceding the playwright's faults, places him securely in the contexts of twentieth century world drama and the development of American drama. Also worth brief mention are Roy Walker, "The Right Kind of Pity," *The Twentieth Century*, 155 (January 1954), 79–86, which includes high praise for *Iceman* and *Misbegotten*, and Montagu Slater, "Eugene O'Neill," *Nation*, 178, No. 9 (27 February 1954), 174–75.

With Nietzsche behind O'Neill, pessimism before him, and O'Neill's cynicism of social structures, Doris M. Alexander, "Eugene O'Neill as Social Critic," *American Quarterly*, 6, No. 4 (Winter 1954), 249–363, sees the main trend in the "social criticism" of the writer as being negative. In a pair of essays, Lester Cole and John Howard Lawson, "Two Views on O'Neill," *Masses & Mainstream*, 7, No. 6 (June 1954), 56–63, raising fundamental questions of theory and method in Marxist criticism, Cole, responding to an earlier Lawson piece, buries O'Neill as Lawson in his answer praises him. Two 1957 pieces are of general interest: Stark Young, "Eugene O'Neill: Notes from a Critic's Diary," *Harper's Magazine*, 214, No. 1285 (June 1957), 66–71, 74, supplies recollections of their relationship from Young's journal of 1923 and 1924, plus one entry each from 1928, 1946, and 1956. Also worthy is Malcolm Cowley, "A Weekend With Eugene O'Neill," *Reporter*, 17, No. 3 (September 1957), 33–36. While the Gelbs touch Cowley's recollections of the weekend in November 1923 and O'Neill's subsequent binge and Arthur Nethercot draws on it, Cowley's prose makes this a worthwhile piece that is at once funny and sobering. Bruce Ingham Granger, "Illusion and Reality in Eugene O'Neill," *Modern Language Notes*, 73, No. 3 (March 1958), 179–86, views the attempt to bridge the distance between illusion and reality as tragic and the tension between the two as essential to O'Neill's drama. Jordan Y. Miller, "The Georgia Plays of Eugene O'Neill," *Georgia Review*, 12, No. 3 (Fall 1958), 278–90, sees the two plays (*Ah, Wilderness!* and *Days Without End*) written at Casa Genotta, Sea Island, Georgia as sure signs of decline, even surrender, on the part of O'Neill; Miller uses the later plays *Misbegotten* and *Iceman* as corroborating evidence. If Miller finds decline in the O'Neill canon, Tom F. Driver, "On The Late Plays of Eugene O'Neill," *Tulane Drama Review*, 3, No. 2 (December 1958), 8–20, does not. Driver examines the treatment of time in *Long Day's Journey*, a Freudian basis for *Iceman*, and illusion in *A Touch of the Poet* before restoring the giant to his heavens. Like Driver, Rudolph Stamm, " 'Faithful Realism': Eugene O'Neill and the Problem of Style," *English Studies*, 40 (1959), 242–50, sees in the last plays O'Neill's perfection of a style of his own and calls those plays the culmination of his work. While not restricted to O'Neill, Edward Groff, "Point of View in Modern Drama," *Modern Drama* (hereafter *MD*), 2, No. 3 (December 1959), 268–82, has interesting things to say about O'Neill's techniques. As well, Doris M. Alexander provides two studies of specific influences on the dramatist: "Eugene O'Neill, 'The Hound of Heaven,' and The 'Hell Hole,' " *Modern Language Quarterly*, 20, No. 4 (December 1959), 307–14, describes the relationship of the Francis Thompson poem and the flight from love theme to three apparently dissimilar plays, *Servitude, Welded*, and *Days Without End*; "Eugene O'Neill and *Light on the Path*," *MD*, 3, No. 3 (December 1960), 260–67, makes a case for the influence of a Theosophical Society treatise by Mabel Collins on the confirmed mystic O'Neill, especially on *The Fountain*.

Edd Winfield Parks, "Eugene O'Neill's Quest," *Tulane Drama Review*, 4, No. 3 (March 1960), 99–107, sees the man and the playwright in a quest for a tenable explanation of the meaning of life. Robert F. Whitman, "O'Neill's Search for a 'Language of the Theatre,' " *Quarterly Journal of Speech*, 46, No. 2 (April 1960), 153–70, is a lengthy piece attempting to identify unifying threads in many of the plays. In a volume devoted to translations of Italian criticism of American literature, Nicola Chiaromonte, "Eugene O'Neill (1958)," *Sewanee Review*, 68, No. 3 (July-September 1960), 494–501, examines *Long Day's Journey* and *Misbegotten* and is a mix of comments on O'Neill's weaknesses and a perceptive appreciation of his gifts. In a translation by Barrett Clark, Hugo von Hofmannsthal, "Eugene O'Neill," *Tulane Drama Review*, 5, No. 1 (September 1960), 169–73, Hofmannsthal wraps himself in the cloak of European drama, and the result is a set of supercilious, superficial, hardly perceptive comments on O'Neill. Another case of a misleading title, this essay tells more about Hofmannsthal and his dramatic theories than about the American playwright. Donald Gallup, "Eugene O'Neill's 'The Ancient Mariner,' " *Yale Univ. Library Gazette*, 35, No. 2 (October 1960), 61–86, is, on the other hand, of special interest to serious scholars because it prints the entire text of O'Neill's dramatic adaptation of the Coleridge poem. The same volume of *Modern Drama*, 3, No. 3 (December 1960) that contains Alexander's study of O'Neill and the Theosophists includes several other articles. An outstanding piece is Norman C. Chaitin, "O'Neill: The Power of Daring," pp. 231–41. Powerful and direct, Chaitin's estimate of the man O'Neill and his life reads almost as if it were a Dos Passos biography in *U.S.A.* Drew B. Pallette, "O'Neill and the Comic Spirit," pp. 273–79, suggests that comedy is an important aspect of O'Neill's work, from early satire, inadvertent comedy, and comic relief to a good deal of rowdy comedy in his last plays, and traces the strain of sardonic comedy in the plays. Signi Falk, "Dialogue in O'Neill," pp. 314–25, examines both O'Neill's natural, idiomatic dialogue and his literary, grandiose prose, and the essay reminds us that when his aims were modest he achieved his best work. Also included is Janis Klavsons, "O'Neill's Dreamer: Success and Failure," pp. 268–72.

This same issue contains the first essay of what would eventually amount to a decade and a half sideline for Arthur H. Nethercot. Scholarly in approach, "The Psychoanalyzing of Eugene O'Neill," pp. 242–56, begins with a survey of essays and addresses the question of whether O'Neill was a deep student of psychoanalysis, which the playwright denied. The essay claims it does not psychoanalyze O'Neill, but in its attempts to demonstrate the psychoanalyzing O'Neill did in his plays, Nethercot does both. "The Psychoanalyzing of Eugene O'Neill: Part II," *MD*, 3 (February 1961), 357–72, continues this survey of O'Neill as a psychoanalytical dramatist, citing critics who have pointed out the "presence of psychoanalytical material in O'Neill's plays," and drawing heavily upon Engel and Falk. Whether one is convinced or not, it is certainly clear that literary critics analyze many characters in psychoanalytical terms as a matter of course. This is heady — in both meanings of the word — stuff, both educated and educating. Subsequent to the publication of the Gelbs's biography, Nethercot in "The Psychoanalyzing of Eugene O'Neill: Postscript," *MD*, 8, No. 2 (September 1965), 150–55, finds evidence corroborating his speculations in his earlier essays. Most of this article is devoted to O'Neill's life — not works — and O'Neill's relationships with several psychiatrists. "The Psychoanalyzing of Eugene O'Neill: P. P. S.," *MD*, 16, No. 1 (June 1973), 35–48, raises once again the question of the dramatist's knowledge of psychoanalysis, its influence on him, and his use of it in the plays. This time, Nethercot draws upon Bowen, the Gelbs again, and Cowley's *Reporter* piece. The essence of this P. P. S. is to add the names of two more books on psychoanalysis O'Neill *may* have read. Nethercot then launches into an attack on Sheaffer, Alexander, and especially Falk before concluding that O'Neill would have made an excellent psychoanalyst himself. A separate but related item by Nethercot, "Madness in the Plays of Eugene O'Neill," *MD*, 18, No. 3 (September 1975), 259–79, begins with an attempt to establish O'Neill's unsettled mental condition and proposes that O'Neill's interest in the subject of madness might have been personal rather than clinical. Nethercot concluded his 1973 essay by suggesting O'Neill would have made an excellent psychoanalyst and two years later suggests he may have been a borderline madman. Either Nethercot couldn't make up his mind or thought they are the same thing.

Clifford Leech contributes a two part essay, "Eugene O'Neill and his Plays," *The Critical Quarterly*, 3, Nos. 3, 4 (1961), 242–56, 339–53. Part 1 is unenthusiastic about most of O'Neill, up to *Mourning*, a discussion of which concludes the piece. If praise for O'Neill remains qualified, part 2 is a bit more interesting because it is devoted to anagnorisis or "discovery" and *Iceman* and *Long Day's Journey*.

The first sentence of Max Wylie, "Aspects of E. G. O. (Eugene Gladstone O'Neill)," *The Carrell*, 2, No. 1 (June 1961), 1–12, is "Not much that is dependable has been written about Eugene O'Neill." If that were true, it would have remained so twelve pages later. Appreciative of the talent, Wylie is vicious in his portrayal of the man; not even Lytton Strachey could have done this: there is no "and all," only warts. Conversational and sensational, this is "scholarship" as it might appear in *The National Enquirer*.

The last two sentences of the essay are meant to sum O'Neill's life: "But isn't it interesting? And wasn't it awful?" The sentences actually sum up Wylie's lecture. While not the act of vituperation of Wylie, David Daiches, "Mourning Becomes O'Neill," *Encounter*, 16, No. 6 (June 1961), 74–78, looks at the clay feet of the human model for the colossus. Also unlike Wylie, Daiches is serious, sensitive, and suggestive about O'Neill's relationship with his muse and his art. Written by one who is most often considered one of the giant killers, Mary McCarthy, "American Realists, Playwrights," *Encounter*, 17, No. 1 (July 1961), 24–31, sees O'Neill as the great figure of a school of realists in the American theatre and concludes that *Long Day's Journey* is the closest that realism can get to tragedy.

Eugene M. Waith, "Eugene O'Neill: An Exercise in Unmasking," *Educational Theatre Journal*, 13, No. 3 (October 1961), 182–91, examines the use of literal masks across the O'Neill canon but, even more interesting perhaps, sees the characteristic structure of his plays determined by a movement toward "unmasking," a discovery or revelation or both. Another article on the use of masks is A. Richard Sogliuzzo, "The Uses of the Mask in *The Great God Brown* and *Six Characters In Search of an Author*," *Educational Theatre Journal*, 18, No. 3 (October 1966), 224–29, which compares and contrasts O'Neill's and Pirandello's use of masks, intelligently without attempting to suggest influence either way. Morris Freedman, "O'Neill and Contemporary American Drama," *College English*, 23, No. 7 (April 1962), 570–74, suggests that comparing O'Neill with every other American playwright reveals their shortcomings and his own seem less severe in the shadow that he casts on much of American drama. As the title indicates, Doris V. Falk, "That Paradox, O'Neill," *MD*, 6, No. 3 (Winter 1963), 221–38, deals with paradoxes in O'Neill: his own mix of pity and contempt for his characters and for himself, the suggestion that he hated most what he most longed for, and, ashamed of that longing, he cheapened it. Inspired by the publication of the Gelbs's biography, Thomas P. McDonnell, "O'Neill's Drama of the Psyche," *Catholic World*, 197, No. 1,178 (May 1963), 120–25, examines the entanglement of O'Neill's life with his plays, even those which are not overtly autobiographical. This writer further suggests that O'Neill never ceased to struggle with his Catholic conscience and his drama was the drama of the traumatic loss of belief. Of specialized interest is William H. Davenport, "The Published and Unpublished Poems of Eugene O'Neill," *Yale Univ. Library Gazette*, 38, No. 2 (October 1963), 51–66, a compressed study that offers critical summaries of O'Neill's published poems, inscriptions, poetical fragments, and about 30 unpublished poems.

An interesting, well written essay is James P. Pettegrove, "Eugene O'Neill as Thinker," *Maske und Kothurn*, 10 (1964), 617–24, that, while conceding that O'Neill's approach was artistic or mystical rather than rational, makes some intelligent points about O'Neill as a serious investigator of the religious experience in our time; the essay allows for the negative, accentuates the positive in the plays. Seeking one aspect that would account for O'Neill's universal appeal and promise of immortality, Sophus K. Winther, "Eugene O'Neill — The Dreamer Confronts His Dream," *Arizona Quarterly* (hereafter *ArQ*), 21, No. 3 (Autumn 1965), 221–33, this life-long friend of O'Neill arrives at the notion of the beautiful illusion, a dramatist torn between romantic ideals and the modernist's intellectual scorn of them. Yet another attempted evaluation of O'Neill's dramaturgy in terms of tragedy and the tragic, William R. Thurman, "Journey into Night: Elements of Tragedy in Eugene O'Neill," *Quarterly Journal of Speech*, 52, No. 2 (April 1966), 139–45, concludes that a requisite affirmative quality is never fully achieved. Following Quinn, Alexander, and others who characterize O'Neill as a mystic, Henry F. Pommer, "The Mysticism of Eugene O'Neill," *MD*, 9 (May 1966), 26–39, supplies evidence of his suprarational mysticism and its effects on a handful of plays from *The Fountain* on. Using the plays as evidence, James M. Salem, "Eugene O'Neill and the Sacrament of Marriage," *Serif*, 3, No. 2 (1966), 23–35, sees O'Neill as a moral conservative, especially on the subject of marriage and marital fidelity.

Although it begins by pointing out the same physical similarities of the artist characters that Kemelman identified in 1932, Robert C. Lee, "The Lonely Dream," *MD*, 9, No. 2 (September 1966), 127–35, goes on to point out that few of the fictional dreamers create works of art and concludes that alienation sums up the artist characters. A decade later, Thomas P. Adler, " 'Through A Glass Darkly': O'Neill's Esthetic Theory As Seen Through His Writer Characters," *ArQ*, 32, No. 2 (Summer 1976), 171–83, would narrow Lee's group of artists to those who were specifically writers, and, taken together and studied cumulatively, four very definite motifs are seen to emerge. Three excellent essays of special interest by Egil Törnqvist appeared beginning in 1966. Anyone interested in the use, and meaning, of the surnames or Christian names of O'Neill's characters must see "Personal Nomenclature in the Plays of O'Neill," *MD*, 8, No. 4 (February 1966), 362–73, which is rich, imaginative and suggestive. In "Personal Addresses in the Plays of O'Neill," *Quarterly Journal of Speech*, 55, No. 2 (April 1969), 126–30, Törnqvist extends his 1966 piece to include a consideration of the way O'Neill's characters address one another and the significance of varied addresses, titles, nicknames, appellatives, and pet names. Taken together, the two essays form an intelligent whole by one who has read the canon carefully and thoughtfully. Törnqvist examines the extent to which O'Neill's oeuvre is permeated with religious allusions and symbols in "Jesus and Judas: On Biblical Allusions in O'Neill's Plays," *Etudes Anglaises*, 24, No. 1 (January-March 1971), 41–49. William R. Reardon, "O'Neill Since World War II: Critical Reception In New York," *MD*, 10, No. 3 (December 1967), 289–99, is accurate, and is just what the title suggests it is. Charis Crosse Bowling, "The Touch of Poetry: A Study of the Role of Poetry in Three O'Neill Plays," *CLA Journal*, 12, No. 1 (September 1968), 43–55, deals with the use of the poetry of other writers in the plotting, characterization, and thematic development of *A Touch of the Poet; Ah, Wilderness!;* and *Long*

Day's Journey. Emil Roy, "The Archetypal Unity of Eugene O'Neill's Drama," *Comparative Drama*, 3, No. 4 (Winter 1969–70), 263–74, discusses O'Neill's archetypal motifs, their often ironic implications, and is especially interesting on the quest-motif.

Responding to attacks of past giant killers and anticipating future neglect, David Fedo, "In Defense of Eugene O'Neill," *Boston Univ. Journal*, 18, No. 3 (Fall 1970), 30–35, is an even-handed, balanced defense. Representative of early 1970s women's studies scholarship is Lois S. Josephs, "The Women of Eugene O'Neill: Sex Role Stereotypes," *Ball State Univ. Forum*, 14, No. 3 (Summer 1973), 3–8. Most of what Josephs says may be true, but she damns O'Neill in part for what he did not do or what he did not write about. James Milton Highsmith, " 'The Personal Equation': Eugene O'Neill's Abandoned Play," *Southern Humanities Review*, 8, No. 2 (Spring 1974), 195–212, provides a summary and analysis of an undated typescript O'Neill began prior to May 1915 and never completed which may be of interest to serious scholars for thematic elements that would appear in later plays. Like Pallette in 1960, H. N. Levitt, "Comedy in the Plays of Eugene O'Neill," *Players: Magazine of American Theatre*, 51, No. 3 (February/March 1976), 92–95, is a carefully organized article on comedy in O'Neill. Levitt provides a summary, a chart, and a brief consideration of the importance of comedy in the plays. While Pallette sees some comic elements used as comic relief, Levitt states O'Neill never uses them for comic relief although there is no indication that Levitt has seen the Pallette piece. William T. Going, "Eugene O'Neill, American," *Papers on Language and Literature*, 12, No. 4 (Fall 1976), 384–401, tries to do two things — establish both O'Neill's life and work as representatively twentieth century American *and* demonstrate that O'Neill wished to be linked with the nineteenth century New England tradition in American literature.

Sight and sounds are the topics of two essays by James A. Robinson: "O'Neill's Grotesque Dancers," *MD*, 19, No. 4 (December 1976), 341–49, looks at the thematic use of movement including grotesque motion and dance; "O'Neill's Symbolic Sounds," *Modern Language Studies*, 9, No. 2 (Spring 1979), 36–45, deals with the use of sounds and aural effects from the whining of a wireless and the sound of dripping water to the more famous tom-tom and fog horn. Robinson centers on the use of sound as a structural part of the expressionistic experiments of the Twenties. Beginning with O'Neill's need for privacy and a description of how consumed he was in his work, Egil Törnqvist, "O'Neill's Work Method," *Studia Neophilologica*, 49 (1977), 43–58, as the title suggests, describes the places, and way, O'Neill worked. James R. Scrimgeour, "From Loving to the Misbegotten: Despair in the Drama of Eugene O'Neill," *MD*, 20, No. 1 (March 1977), 37–53, traces O'Neill's treatment of despair, focusing on the unchanging characteristics, and O'Neill's changing treatment, of despairing characters in *Days Without End, The Great God Brown, Lazarus, Iceman, Long Day's Journey*, and *Misbegotten*. With the exception of three pieces written in 1932 for

The American Spectator, O'Neill, by his own admission, had little success, or interest, in the expository essay. In "Eugene O'Neill's Aesthetic of the Drama," *MD,* 21, No. 1 (March 1978), 87–99, Paul Voelker has worked a wonder in piecing together from O'Neill's letters and interviews a coherent aesthetic of dramaturgy. While Going in 1976 places O'Neill in nineteenth century New England tradition, Stephen L. Fluckiger, "The Idea of Puritanism in the Plays of Eugene O'Neill," *Renascence,* 30, No. 3 (Spring 1978), 152–62, seeks the extent of the impact of Puritan ideas by using only internal evidence of the plays, particularly *Desire Under the Elms.* Arnold Goldman, "The Culture of the Provincetown Players," *Journal of American Studies,* 12, No. 3 (1978), 291–310, is well written, perhaps the best account in 50 years of the social, intellectual, and psychological *milieu* that would provide a matrix for O'Neill.

There are, to be sure, a number of comparative essays using O'Neill as either half of a tandem of influence. A representative sample includes: Frederic Fleisher, "Strindberg and O'Neill," *Symposium,* 10, No. 1 (Spring 1956), 84–94; Murray Hartman, "Strindberg and O'Neill," *Educational Theatre Journal,* 18, No. 3 (October 1966), 216–23; Albert Rothenberg, "Autobiographical Drama," *Literature and Psychology,* 17, Nos. 2–3 (1967), 95–114; Egil Törnqvist, *"Miss Julie* and O'Neill," *MD,* 19, No. 4 (December 1976), 351–64; Törnqvist, "Nietzsche and O'Neill: A Study in Affinity," *Orbis Litterarum,* 23, No. 2 (1968), 97–126; Maurice M. La Belle, "Dionysus and Despair: The Influence of Nietzsche upon O'Neill's Drama," *Educational Theatre Journal,* 25, No. 4 (December 1973), 436–42.

Other relationship studies include: Clara Blackburn, "Continental Influences on Eugene O'Neill's Expressionistic Dramas," *American Literature* (hereafter *AL*), 13 (March 1941-January 1942), 109–33; Lester M. Wolfson, "Inge, O'Neill, and the Human Condition," *Southern Speech Journal,* 22, No. 4 (Summer 1957), 221–32; Edward T. Herbert, "Eugene O'Neill: An Evaluation By Fellow Playwrights," *MD,* 6, No. 3 (December 1963), 239–40, which includes brief evaluations by Paul Green, Thornton Wilder, Sean O'Casey, Arthur Miller, and Clifford Odets; William R. Brashear, "O'Neill and Shaw: The Play as Will and Idea," *Criticism,* 8, No. 2 (Spring 1966), 155–69; Mardi Valgemae, "O'Neill and German Expressionism," *MD,* 10, No. 2 (September 1967), 111–23; Ruby Cohn, "Absurdity in English: Joyce and O'Neill," *Comparative Drama,* 3, No. 3 (Fall 1969), 156–61; John H. Stroupe, "The Abandonment of Ritual: Jean Anouilh and Eugene O'Neill," *Renascence,* 28, No. 3 (Spring 1976), 147–54; Lucina P. Gabbard, "At the Zoo: From O'Neill to Albee," *MD,* 19, No. 4 (December 1976), 365–74; and James A. Robinson, "O'Neill and Albee," *West Virginia Univ. Bulletin Philological Papers,* 25 (February 1979), 38–45; Paul D. Voelker, "Eugene O'Neill and George Pierce Baker: A Reconsideration," *AL,* 49, No. 2 (May 1977), 206–20; Joe Weixlmann, "Staged Segregation: Baldwin's *Blues for Mister Charlie* and O'Neill's *All God's Chillun Got Wings,*" *Black American Literature Forum,* 11, No. 1 (Spring 1977), 35–36;

Peter Egri, "The Short Story in the Drama: Chekhov and O'Neill," *Acta Litteraria Academiae Scientiarum Hungaricae*, 20 (1978), 3–28; and Normand Berlin, "Ghosts of the Past: O'Neill and *Hamlet*," *Massachusetts Review*, 20, No. 2 (Summer 1979), 312–23.

O'Neill abroad has been almost exclusively the domain of Horst Frenz. See his articles: "Eugene O'Neill in Russia," *Poet Lore*, 49, No. 3 (Autumn 1943), 241–47; "Eugene O'Neill on the London Stage," *Queen's Quarterly*, 54 (Summer 1947), 223–30. "Eugene O'Neill on the German Stage," *Theatre Annual*, 11 (1953), 24–34; "Notes on Eugene O'Neill in Japan," *MD*, 3, No. 3 (December 1960), 306–13; Frederic Fleisher and Frenz, "Eugene O'Neill and the Royal Dramatic Theater of Stockholm: The Later Phase," *MD*, 10, No. 3 (December 1967), 300–11; and Lewis W. Falb, "The Critical Reception of Eugene O'Neill on the French Stage," *Educational Theatre Journal*, 22, No. 4 (December 1970), 397–405.

Studies of Individual Works

The reader interested in the response of contemporary reviewers to O'Neill's plays (and there are some excellent, perceptive pieces, from Alexander Woollcott and Stark Young to Douglas Watt, Richard Watts, Brooks Atkinson, and Walter Kerr) may find some of those reviews reprinted most conveniently in the *New York Theatre Critics' Reviews* (New York: Critics' Theatre Reviews, gathered yearly). As for scholarly work, to begin at the beginning: Charles Fish, "Beginnings: O'Neill's 'The Web,' " *Princeton Univ. Library Chronicle*, 27, No. 1 (Autumn 1965), 3–20, concerns what O'Neill said was the first play he ever wrote (actually "A Wife for a Life" may have been written earlier). Fish recounts the play's action, describes the revisions in the manuscript, indicates themes that would be recurrent, points possible early Strindberg influence, includes facsimiles of two manuscript pages, and considers briefly other of the earliest plays. Although it treats aspects of *Mourning* and *Iceman*, the central concern of Ivan H. Walton, "Eugene O'Neill and the Folklore and Folkways of the Sea," *Western Folklore*, 14 (1955), 153–69, is the use of chanties, sailor lore, superstition, and language in the early sea plays, the *Glencairn* cycle, *Anna Christie*, and *The Hairy Ape*. Based only on internal evidence and no demonstration that O'Neill ever read the obscure story, William Goldhurst, "A Literary Source for O'Neill's 'In the Zone,' " *AL*, 35, No. 4 (January 1964), 530–34, tries to make the case that the play may have been influenced by Arthur Conan Doyle's "That Little Square Box." Goldhurst also includes the more probable nonliterary source suggested in Croswell Bowen's biography. R. Dilworth Rust, "The Unity of O'Neill's *S. S. Glencairn*," *AL*, No. 3 (November 1965), 280–90, suggests how O'Neill welds the four one acts into one long cycle play, with Driscoll the major linking character, through characterization, plot line, and iterative image pairs. Alex Scarbrough, "O'Neill's Use of the Displaced Archetype in *The Moon of the Caribbees*," *West Vir-*

ginia Univ. Bulletin Philological Papers, 19 (July 1972), 41–44, suggests that much of the irony of the play results because avatars of happy island, sea, and ship are actually the reverse of traditional literary usage. A suggestive piece of manuscript detective work is Paul D. Voelker, "The Uncertain Origins of Eugene O'Neill's 'Bound East for Cardiff'," *Studies in Bibliography*, 32 (1979), 273–81, which traces the process by which "Children of the Sea" became *Cardiff*.

Emil Roy, "Tragic Tension in *Beyond the Horizon*," *Ball State Univ. Forum*, 8, No. 1 (Winter 1967), 74–79, is an imaginative piece, and while Roy sees the end of the play as burdened with unresolved tensions and irreconcilable impressions, William J. Scheick, "The Ending of O'Neill's *Beyond the Horizon*," *MD*, 20, No. 3 (September 1977), 293–98, suggests the play's ending resolves tensions and follows logically from what has preceded it. David Y. Chen, "Two Chinese Adaptations of Eugene O'Neill's *The Emperor Jones*," *MD*, 9, No. 4 (February 1967), 431–39, discusses the relationship of *Jones* to *The Yama Chao* by Hung Shen (who acknowledged borrowing the play's form) and Wan Chia-Pao's *The Wild*. Emil Roy, "Eugene O'Neill's *The Emperor Jones* and *The Hairy Ape* As Mirror Plays," *Comparative Drama*, 2, No. 1 (Spring 1968), 21–31, sees these two expressionistic works as mirror plays whose aspects parallel or complement one another. Norman Kagan, "The Return of *The Emperor Jones*," *Negro History Bulletin*, 34, No. 7 (November 1971), 160–62, intelligently examines the reactions to, and significance of, the film version starring Paul Robeson. Kagan's essay is as intelligent in its approach to the matter of race as almost anything else written about the play. John Krimsky, "*The Emperor Jones* — Robeson and O'Neill on Film," *Connecticut Review*, 7, No. 2 (April 1974), 94–99, the recollections of the film's producer, includes some of the same prose that appears in Kagan, a little on Robeson, much more about Krimsky, and very little about O'Neill. Peter J. Gillett, "O'Neill and the Racial Myths," *Twentieth Century Literature*, 18, No. 2 (April 1972), 111–20, is a moderate and intelligent essay on O'Neill's achievement from 1914 to 1924 in presenting black characters in the five so called "negro plays" and points to a greater success in *Iceman*. Most of the discussion, however, is devoted to *All God's Chillun* and *Jones*. James Corey, "O'Neill's *The Emperor Jones*," *American Notes & Queries*, 12 (May/June 1974), 156–57, suggests a minor borrowing from Conrad's *Heart of Darkness*. Quite unlike Gillett, John R. Cooley, "*The Emperor Jones* and the Harlem Renaissance," *Studies in the Literary Imagination*, 7, No. 2 (Fall 1974), 73–83, citing O'Neill's "racial ambivalence" and "the play's racial bias," sees both author and play perpetuating perjorative images of blacks and claims an exploitation of stereotypes too blatant to be overlooked.

John J. McAleer, "Christ Symbolism in *Anna Christie*," *MD*, 4, No. 4 (February 1962), 389–96, without external evidence, links *Anna Christie* to the medieval prayer, *Anima Christi*, in a series of line by line parallels. In Winifred L. Frazer, "Chris and Poseidon: Man Versus God in *Anna Chris-*

tie," *MD*, 12, No. 3 (December 1969), 279–85, however, one critic's Christ and the Bible are replaced by another's Poseidon and myth. Bernard Baum, "*Tempest* and *Hairy Ape*: The Literary Incarnation of Mythos," *Modern Language Quarterly*, 14, No. 3 (September 1953), 258–73, is an interesting essay on how Caliban could be metamorphosed into Yank, and Baum demonstrates how each play is a product of the thought of its own time. Ronald G. Rollins, "O'Casey, O'Neill and Expressionism in *The Silver Tassie*," *Bucknell Review*, 10, No. 4 (May 1962), 364–69, suggests the influence of *The Hairy Ape* on O'Casey. While interesting in his conclusion on the females in the plays generally, Robert J. Andreach, "O'Neill's Use of Dante in *The Fountain* and *The Hairy Ape*," *MD*, 10, No. 1 (May 1967), 48–56, concedes there is much conjecture in the main point about Dante and O'Neill. Drawing on Doris Falk's comments on the play but going beyond them and diametrically opposite Krutch's reading, Marden J. Clark, "Tragic Effect in *The Hairy Ape*," *MD*, 10, No. 4 (February 1968), 372–82, provides an interesting alternative view.

Matthew T. Conlin, "The Tragic Effect in *Autumn Fire* and *Desire Under the Elms*," *MD*, 1, No. 4 (February 1959), 228–35, provides a good comparison with the T. C. Murray play which Conlin concludes is a tragedy while *Desire* is not. The position opposite Conlin and others who do not see the play as tragic is taken by Sophus Keith Winther, "*Desire Under the Elms*," *MD*, 3 (December 1960), 326–32, who argues that this play is a watershed for O'Neill and modern tragedy. Seeing Ephraim as tragic hero, Winther's essay argues against the judgment of Engel, Falk, Bentley, and the limits of the traditional Aristotelian framework. Like Winther in viewing the play as a tragedy, but unlike Winther, seeing Abbie, not Ephraim, as the pivotal character, Murray Hartman, "*Desire Under the Elms* In the Light of Strindberg's Influence," *AL*, 33, No. 3 (November 1961), 360–69, points biographical comparisons between O'Neill and Strindberg, then carefully explores Strindberg's influence on this particular play. Edgar F. Racey, "Myth As Tragic Structure in *Desire Under the Elms*," *MD*, 5, No. 1 (May 1962), 42–46, adds *Hippolytus* of Euripides and Racine's *Phaedra* to the underlying Oedipal theme and argues that Abbie and Eben assume the dignity of tragic stature. Jay Ronald Meyers, "O'Neill's Use of the Phèdre Legend in *Desire Under the Elms*," *Revue de Littérature Comparée*, 41, No. 1 (January-March 1967), 121–25, expands the case of the Phèdre legend as the direct source of the play and posits Abbie as attaining tragic nobility. Peter L. Hays, "Biblical Perversions in *Desire Under the Elms*," *MD*, 11, No. 4 (February 1969), 423–28, argues that religious references inform the play and religion both causes the tragedy and comments on it. Hays concludes that the intellectual message of the play is that harsh Puritanical religion cripples love and destroys men. Hollis L. Cate, "Ephraim Cabot: O'Neill's Spontaneous Poet," *Markham Review*, 2, No. 5 (February 1971), 115–17, sees the father as in part an Emersonian man and explores the old man's language (which Cate indicates is important if he is of truly tragic stature) as an integral part of his nature. Mara Lemanis, "*Desire Under the Elms* and Tragic Form: A Study of Misalliance," *South Dakota Review*, 16, No. 3 (Autumn 1978), 46–55, suggests that although the hallmarks of tragedy and the tragic formula are present in the play, a "misalliance" between stature and deed produces a dramtic hybrid.

Deena P. Metzger, "Variations on a Theme: A Study of *Exiles* by James Joyce and *The Great God Brown* by Eugene O'Neill," *MD*, 8, No. 2 (September 1965), 174–84, proposes a relationship between the two works, allowing for the fact that Joyce's approach differed from O'Neill in every way. A facsimile of the autograph draft of O'Neill's foreword to the play and a transcription with all of O'Neill's cancellations and insertions are included in Mardi Valgemae, "Eugene O'Neill's Preface to *The Great God Brown*," *Yale Univ. Library Gazette*, 43 (1969), 24–29. Frank R. Cunningham, "*The Great God Brown* and O'Neill's Romantic Vision," *Ball State Univ. Forum*, 14, No. 3 (Summer 1973), 69–78, examines psychological and philosophical sources and dramatic techniques in a play Cunningham sees as Romantic affirmation rather than the pessimistic negation often reflected in the later plays. Michael Hinden, "*The Birth of Tragedy* and *The Great God Brown*," *MD*, 16, No. 2 (September 1973), 129–40, studies the influence on O'Neill's play of Nietzsche's exegesis on the origin of tragedy. Charmian Green, "Wolfe, O'Neill, and the Mask of Illusion," *Papers on Language and Literature*, 14, No. 1 (Winter 1978), 87–90, points out thematic parallels and similarities between Thomas Wolfe's *Mannerhouse* and *The Great God Brown*.

John H. Stroupe, "O'Neill's *Marco Millions*: A Road to Xanadu," *MD*, 12, No. 4 (February 1970), 377–82, is an interesting examination of O'Neill's direct source and extensive working notes for the play. A well-presented, capably argued essay, Doris M. Alexander, "*Lazarus Laughed* and Buddha," *Modern Language Quarterly*, 17, No. 4 (December 1956), 357–65, adds the image of Gautama the Buddha to the view of Lazarus as part Christ, part Dionysus, part Nietzschean spokesman, and concludes that in the combination of all four Lazarus becomes fully understandable as a composite of saviors. Carl E. W. L. Dahlstrom, "*Dynamo and Lazarus Laughed*: Some Limitations," *MD*, 3, No. 3 (December 1960), 224–30, sees a weakness in O'Neill's inability to give artistic treatment to the twentieth century ferment in religion, science, and existence and uses the two plays to illustrate the reasons. Cyrus Day, "*Amor Fati*: O'Neill's Lazarus as Superman and Savior," *MD*, 3, No. 3 (December 1960), 297–305, reads Lazarus as a Nietzschean superman and the play itself as a failure as viable drama. In Egil Törnqvist, "O'Neill's Lazarus: Dionysus and Christ," *AL*, 41, No. 4 (January 1970), 543–54, one eminent O'Neill scholar quibbles with the reading of another, Doris Alexander's 1956 piece, since he does not see Buddhism as playing any marked role in the play; Törnqvist then goes on to a detailed discussion of Lazarus as a Christ figure and his Dionysiac nature. An early estimation of O'Neill's other 1928 play is Harry Waton, *The Historic Significance of Eugene O'Neill's Strange Interlude* (New York: Worker's Educational Institute, 1928) which Jordan Miller calls "truly an astonishing document," showing the play to reflect what Waton sees as "great, historic changes taking place in the life of mankind." Doris M. Alexander, "*Strange Interlude* and Schopenhauer," *AL*, 25, No. 2 (May 1953), 213–28, proposes that the predominant intellectual pattern of this play expresses not Freudian psychology as Krutch and others suggest but Schopenhauer's philosophy. William R. Brashear, "O'Neill's Schopenhauer Interlude," *Criticism*, 6, No. 3 (Summer 1964), 256–65, fine tunes the last mentioned article and draws attention to aspects of Schopenhauer's philosophy and influence not touched upon by Alexander on this single play.

One of O'Neill's plays to draw the most scholarly attention is *Mourning Becomes Electra*. Walter Prichard Eaton, "O'Neill — 'New Risen Attic Stream'?," *American Scholar*, 6, No. 3 (Summer 1937), 304–12, is a sensible estimation of O'Neill's relation to Greek tragedy that points out that his debt is greater to Strindberg than to Aeschylus or Euripides, even in *Mourning*. Rudolf Stamm, "The Orestes Theme in Three Plays by Eugene O'Neill, T. S. Eliot and Jean-Paul Sartre," *English Studies*, 30 (1949), 244–55, treats separately, in addition to *Mourning*, *The Family Reunion*, and *Les Mouches*. Using O'Neill's working notes, Doris M. Alexander, "Psychological Fate in *Mourning Becomes Electra*, *PMLA*, 68, No. 5 (December 1953), 923–34, explores how O'Neill constructed his "psychological fate" in the synthesis of Puritan conscience and the parent-child relationship. Alexander is most informative in her lengthy examination of the influence on the play of *What is Wrong with Marriage* by G. V. Hamilton and Kenneth Macgowan, both friends of O'Neill. In Norman T. Pratt, Jr., "Aeschylus and O'Neill: Two Worlds," *Classical Journal*, 51, No. 4 (January 1956), 163–67, a classicist begins by using O'Neill to justify the study of the classics and ends, not surprisingly, with a preference for Aeschylus and his world. Eleazer Lecky, "*Ghosts* and *Mourning Becomes Electra*: Two Versions of Fate," *ArQ*, 13, No. 4 (Winter 1957), 320–38, points to resemblances, differences, and conspicuous parallels in the two plays. Roger Asselineau, "*Mourning Becomes Electra* as a Tragedy," *MD*, 1, No. 3 (December 1958), 143–50, sees the play meeting all the requirements formulated for tragedy by Aristotle's *Poetics*, failing only in language, and examines Lavinia as a true tragic hero. Doris M. Alexander, "Captain Brant and Captain Brassbound: The Origin of an O'Neill Character," *Modern Language Notes*, 74, No. 4 (April 1959), 306–10, proposes O'Neill borrowed an almost unaltered duplicate of the Shaw character, but allows that the American was probably totally unaware of "this extraordinarily complete literary theft." While indicating that the play remains very close to the Greek versions except for the change in setting and a corresponding shift of dimensions in determinism, Victor E. Hanzeli, "The Progeny of Atreus," *MD*, 3, No. 1 (May 1960), 75–81, reads *Mourning* as a very modern tragedy. Philip Weissman, "*Mourning Becomes Electra* and *The Prodigal*: Electra and Orestes," *MD*, 3, No. 3 (December 1960), 257–59, describes Jack Richardson's play as representative of the generation of the 1960s as O'Neill's was of its time. As well, John Stafford, "Mourning Becomes America," *Texas Studies in Literature and Language*, 3, No. 4 (Winter 1962), 549–56, sees *Mourning* as an interpretation of American society. Social and historical in approach, Stafford claims the play is a story characteristically American, including "a major theme of American history and society . . . the rise in importance of women . . . the Dominant Female of American society." In an extended look at *Mourning*, Joseph P. O'Neill, "The Tragic Theory of Eugene O'Neill," *Texas Studies in Literature and Language*, 4, No. 4 (Winter 1963), 481–98, indicates that O'Neill's version of the *Oresteia* expresses an entirely different concept of tragedy by adding the element of human responsibility. In covering a number of plays, Warren Ramsey, "The *Oresteia* Since Hofmannsthal: Images and Emphases," *Revue de Littérature Comparée*, 38, No. 3 (July-September 1964), 359–75, devotes two pages to *Mourning*. Horst Frenz and Martin Mueller, "More Shakespeare and Less Aeschylus in Eugene O'Neill's *Mourning Becomes Electra*," *AL*, 38, No. 1 (March 1966), 85–100, speaks of a direct if unacknowledged influence of Shakespeare and suggests that wherever *Mourning* departs from the *Oresteia* it runs parallel with *Hamlet*. An excellent essay is Thomas E. Porter, "Puritan Ego and Freudian Unconscious: *Mourning Becomes Electra*," in Porter's *Myth and Modern American Drama* (Detroit: Wayne State Univ. Press, 1969), pp. 26–52, 259–63. Ronald T. Curran, "Insular Typees: Puritanism and Primitivism in *Mourning Becomes Electra*," *Revue des Langues Vivantes*, 41, No. 4 (1975), 371–77, invokes a trioka of Rousseau, Hawthorne, and Melville in the examination of the play. The ingenious hypothesis of Joyce Deveau Kennedy, "O'Neill's Lavinia Mannon and the Dickinson Legend," *AL*, 49, No. 1 (March 1977), 108–13, is simply that O'Neill's heroine, Lavinia, is a composite of Emily and Lavinia Dickinson, and Kennedy provides some suggestive support. John Chioles, "Aeschylus and O'Neill: A Phenomenological View," *Comparative Drama*, 14 (1980), 159–87, is a deep and lengthy study by a scholar who has translated and directed *The Oresteia Trilogy*.

Evidence of the surprise of many at the premiere of *Ah, Wilderness!* is Montrose J. Moses, "The 'New' Eugene O'Neill," *North American Review*, 236, No. 6 (December 1933), 543–49. Jacob H. Adler, "The Worth of *Ah, Wilderness!*" *MD*, 3, No. 3 (December 1960), 280–88, proposes that it is a fallacious critical approach to measure the play against other O'Neill plays but seen in the light of the genre of nostalgic family comedy demonstrates that it is a distinguished play. At the premiere of *Long Day's Journey*, many New York theatrical critics pointed the contrast with *Ah, Wilderness!* Quite counter to Adler's approach but just as profitable is John T. Shawcross, "The Road To Ruin: The Beginning of O'Neill's Long Day's Journey," *MD*, 3, No. 3 (December 1960), 289–96, an extended examination of the comedy alongside the tragedy. Drawing on the Gelbs for data, Ima Honaker Herron, "O'Neill's 'comedy of recollection': A Nostalgic Dramatization of 'the real America,' " *CEA Critic*, 30, No. 4 (January 1968), 16–18, suggests community characterizations reveal O'Neill's explorations of provincial American experience. William T. Going, "O'Neill's *Ah, Wilderness!*," *Explicator*, 29, No. 3 (November 1970), Item 28, looks at the source and meaning of the play's title. While most critics see the play as nostalgic comedy, Thomas F. Van Laan, "Singing in the Wilderness: The Dark Vision of Eugene O'Neill's Only Mature Comedy," *MD*, 22, No. 1 (March 1979), 9–18, leans on what is seen as its "dark undertones." Ellen Kimbel, "Eugene O'Neill as Social Historian: Manners and Morals in *Ah, Wilderness!*" sums the debate over *Ah, Wilderness!* and sees the play as warm, nostalgic comedy.

Perhaps inspired initially by its being O'Neill's first play after twelve years of silence, but fed by other and greater sources later, *The Iceman Cometh* may be the most written about of O'Neill's plays. John Henry Raleigh, ed., *Twentieth Century Interpretations of The Iceman Cometh* (Englewood Cliffs, N.J.: Prentice-Hall, 1968) reprints many items including Bentley's "Trying to Like O'Neill." See also Winifred Frazer, *Love as Death in the Iceman Cometh* (Gainesville: Univ. of Florida Monographs, 1967), and the same author's *E. G. and E. G. O.: Emma Goldman and The Iceman Cometh* (Gainesville: Univ. of Florida Press, 1974). An interesting piece on *Iceman* by a critic whose later essay would be more celebrated is Eric Bentley, "The Return of Eugene O'Neill," *Atlantic Monthly*, 178, No. 5 (November 1946), 64–66. Here, Bentley concludes his comments by clearly stating that he judges O'Neill by standards far above those set for any other American dramatist. After going over a bit of old ground, Bonamy Dobree, "Mr. O'Neill's Latest Play," *Sewanee Review*, 56, No. 1 (January-March 1948), 118–26, suggests *Iceman* makes a better novel than drama. Another early estimation of *Iceman*, Rudolf Stamm, "A New Play by Eugene O'Neill," *English Studies*, 29 (1948), 138–45, identifies O'Neill's return to one of his earlier modes and sees the play as impeccable. Helen Muchnic, "Circe's Swine: Plays by Gorky and O'Neill," *Comparative Literature*, 3, No. 2 (Spring 1951), 119–28, develops the comparison and contrast between *Iceman* and *The Lower Depths*. Using the character of Hugo Kalmar and his real life model as evidence, Doris M. Alexander, "Hugo of *The Iceman Cometh*: Realism and O'Neill," *American Quarterly*, 5, No. 4 (Winter 1953), 357–66, responds to Bentley's "Trying to Like O'Neill." Cyrus Day, "The Iceman and the Bridegroom," *MD*, 1, No. 1 (May 1958), 3–9, looks into the religious significance and for the "deeper" meaning of the play, finds O'Neill's diagnosis of the century's spiritual malaise more profound than Miller's *Salesman*, and concludes that there is no more nihilistic play in dramatic literature than *Iceman*. Quite the reverse view from Day is taken by Leonard Chabrowe, "Dionysus in *The Iceman Cometh*," *MD*, 4, No. 4 (February 1962), 377–88, which claims the play is essentially a transposition of *Lazarus* into an idiom suitable for the New York stage and one which is no less Dionysian celebrating the fact of life itself; Chabrowe invokes both plays as support, comparing central characters. William R. Brashear, "The

Wisdom of Silenus in O'Neill's *Iceman*," *AL*, 36, No. 2 (May 1964), 180–88, uses this play to explore O'Neill's tragic vision. Focusing on methodology and the creative process rather than interpretation, Robert C. Wright, "O'Neill's Universalizing Technique in *The Iceman Cometh*," *MD*, 8, No. 1 (May 1965), 1–11, identifies those elements that make for universal appeal and permanence and attempts to negate criticism directed at the play. Robert C. Lee, "Evangelism and Anarchy in *The Iceman Cometh*," *MD*, 12, No. 2 (September 1969), 173–86, is an interesting article on the play Lee considers O'Neill's culmination and demise as an artist. Delma Eugene Presley, "O'Neill's Iceman: Another Meaning," *AL*, 42, No. 3 (November 1970), 387–88, proposes another meaning to the term "ice-man" other than the two ordinarily accepted, and Winifred L. Frazer, "O'Neill's Iceman — Not Ice Man," *AL*, 44, No. 4 (January 1973), 677–78, responds to Presley. James P. Quinn, "*The Iceman Cometh*: O'Neill's Long Day's Journey Into Adolescence," *Journal of Popular Culture*, 6, No. 1 (Summer 1972), 171–77, examines O'Neill's "most definitive rejection of middle-class reality." Winifred L. Frazer, "King Lear and Hickey: Bridegroom and Iceman," *MD*, 15, No. 3 (December 1972), 267–78, is an inventive article pointing parallels between the two characters, the two plays, and the two visions. Nancy Reinhardt, "Formal Patterns in *The Iceman Cometh*," *MD*, 16, No. 2 (September 1973), 119–28, describes visual and aural rhythms, symmetries, and orchestrations that give dynamic shape to the play and demonstrate that it is a carefully planned, tightly organized drama. Stephen R. Grecco, "High Hopes: Eugene O'Neill and Alcohol," *Yale French Studies*, 50 (1974), 142–49, relates biography to the play and reminds us that the man who had been through alcoholic traumas wrote distinctly superior plays, including *Iceman*, during the later "dry" period of his life. Using Milton and the Bible as reference points, Dennis M. Welch, "Hickey as Satanic Force in *The Iceman Cometh*," *ArQ*, 34, No. 3 (Autumn 1978), 219–29, sees Hickey as an embodiment of O'Neill's darkest vision of humanity, an anti-Christ. A unique approach to the play is James G. Watson, "The Theater in *The Iceman Cometh*: Some Modernist Implications," *ArQ*, 34, No. 3 (Autumn 1978), 230–38, which sees *Iceman* as a play about plays, a play composed of a play, acted by actors who take the roles of actors acting. Winifred L. Frazer, " 'Revolution' in *The Iceman Cometh*," *MD*, 22, No. 1 (March 1979), 1–8, uses the German poet Ferdinand Freiligrath's "Revolution" to clarify a source and imply a significance. Timothy J. Wiles, "Tammanyite, Progressive, and Anarchist: Political Communities in *The Iceman Cometh*," *CLIO*, 9, No. 2 (1980), 179–96, reads the play in social and political terms and sees O'Neill depicting a large social theme.

While written by one who saw the play's world premiere by *Dramaten* in Stockholm, Stephen Whicher, "O'Neill's Long Journey," *Commonweal*, 63, No. 24 (16 March 1956), 614–15, is no review but weighty reflections by one who started with a prejudice against O'Neill and concludes that *Long*

Day's Journey Into Night is *the* modern tragedy. Another early evaluation is Annette Rubinstein, "The Dark Journey of Eugene O'Neill," *Mainstream*, 10, No. 4 (April 1957), 29–33. Sophus Keith Winther, "O'Neill's Tragic Themes: *Long Day's Journey Into Night*," *ArQ*, 13, No. 4 (Winter 1957), 295–307, is a look at some of the play's dominant themes by an O'Neill watcher for over three decades. John Henry Raleigh, "O'Neill's Long Day's Journey Into Night and New England Irish-Catholicism," *Partisan Review*, 26, No. 4 (Fall 1959), 573–92, makes observations on the historical attributes and cultural, religious, sexual, and personal characteristics of Irish Catholics as a background against which the play might be better understood. Occasioned by the film version of the play, Sidney Finkelstein, "O'Neill's 'Long Day's Journey'," *Mainstream*, 16, No. 6 (June 1963), 47–51, comments on the relation between the forces of society and what happens in the mind, and calls the play "a searching insight into what bourgeois society" does to human beings. A nice essay is Grant H. Redford, "Dramatic Art vs. Autobiography: A Look at *Long Day's Journey Into Night*," *College English*, 25, No. 7 (April 1964), 527–35, which calls the play a triumph of artistic form over the formlessness of personal history and sees it embodying all the themes given expression in each of his plays. Once again a familiar topic is treated in Kenneth Lawrence, "Dionysus and O'Neill," *University Review*, 33, No. 1 (October 1966), 67–70, this time showing how the elements of the rite of Dionysus (agon, pathos, messenger, threnos, theophany, anagnorsis, peripeteia, and epiphany) are found in *Long Day's Journey*. As Robert C. Lee, "Eugene O'Neill's Remembrance: The Past Is The Present," *ArQ*, 23, No. 4 (Winter 1967), 293–305, makes insightful observations on the psychological need and biographical genesis of the final plays, the article is suggestive on the plays themselves — especially *Long Day's Journey*. Sure that psychoanalysis and literary criticism were made for each other, Albert Rothenberg and Eugene D. Shapiro, "The Defense of Psychoanalysis in Literature: *Long Day's Journey Into Night* and *A View From The Bridge*," *Comparative Drama*, 7, No. 1 (Spring 1973), 51–67, provides a lengthy discussion of psychological defenses in the O'Neill play and a very brief consideration of the Miller play for purposes of comparison. Pat M. Ryan, "Stockholm Revives Eugene O'Neill," *Scandinavian Review*, 65, No. 1 (March 1977), 18–23, describes the circumstances by which *Dramaten* came to give the world premiere of *Long Day's Journey*. One of the most revealing and interesting articles is Judith E. Barlow, "*Long Day's Journey Into Night*: From Early Notes to Finished Play," *MD*, 22, No. 1 (March 1979), 19–28, an account of how O'Neill's early notes, drafts, and "gentling" revisions became the completed play. Also of interest is David McDonald, "The Phenomenology of the Glance in *Long Day's Journey Into Night*," *Theatre Journal*, 31, No. 3 (October 1979), 343–56, the premise of which is that the play is a structure of watchers-being-watched; McDonald points out the intricate visual interplay in a drama noted for its verbal density. Albert Wertheim, "Gaspard the Miser in O'Neill's *Long Day's Journey*

Into Night," *American Notes & Queries*, 18 (November 1979), 39–42, explores an allusion that is repeated seven times in the play.

In a basic and straight-forward manner, John J. Fitzgerald, "Guilt and Redemption in O'Neill's Last Play: A Study of *A Moon for the Misbegotten*," *Texas Quarterly*, 9, No. 1 (Spring 1966), 146–58, goes through the play point by point, act by act, recapitulating scenes and pointing significances. In Jordan Y. Miller, "Murky Moon," *Kansas Quarterly*, 7, No. 4 (Fall 1975), 103–05, a scholar who has contributed much keeps trying to like *Misbegotten* but can not because of two basic flaws, the writing itself and ambiguity.

Drew B. Pallette, "O'Neill's *A Touch of the Poet* and His Other Last Plays," *ArQ*, 13, No. 4 (Winter 1957), 308–19, suggests that *Ah, Wilderness!*, seen in retrospect, was an important transitional step, more important in O'Neill's development than previously realized, and sees in *Poet* a synthesis of various elements of the later plays. Doris Alexander, "Eugene O'Neill and Charles Lever," *MD*, 5, No. 4 (February 1963), 415–20, proposes that O'Neill turned to a Lever novel, *Charles O'Malley, The Irish Dragoon* (1894) for the historical background of *Poet* and speculates that he may even have gotten some of the play's language from that source. Murray Hartman, "The Skeletons in O'Neill's *Mansions*," *Drama Survey*, 5, No. 3 (Winter 1966–67), 276–79, sees in *More Stately Mansions* the dying echo of brooding themes O'Neill had voiced throughout his canon: the war against an acquisitive society, the Oedipal conflict, illusion-reality, and the death wish. Jere Real, "The Brothel in O'Neill's *Mansions*," *MD*, 12, No. 4 (February 1970), 383–89, sees in the play the theme of mankind's universal prostitution, that is, man's inevitable self-debasement, the human capacity to bargain away the very qualities that grant individuals humanity. Orley I. Holtan, "Eugene O'Neill and the Death of the 'Covenant'," *Quarterly Journal of Speech*, 56, No. 3 (October 1970), 256–63, is an informative essay that studies *Poet* and *Mansions* in the light of myths and clusters of ideas found not only in American literature but in American history, such as America as the "New Eden" and the American as the "new Adam." Edward Mullaly, "O'Neill and the Perfect Pattern," *Dalhousie Review*, 52 (1972–73), 603–10, traces O'Neill's theme of America's spiritual disintegration in *Mansions*. Doing business at the same old stand, Arthur H. Nethercot, "O'Neill's *More Stately Mansions*," *Educational Theatre Journal*, 27, No. 2 (May 1975), 161–69, sees in *Mansions* O'Neill doing business at *his* same old stand: dreams of the future, ghosts of the past, the old Oedipal relations, the idea of mental unbalance, and madness. Seeking to demonstrate that O'Neill's plays were linked to nineteenth century concepts and literary forms, Lowell A. Fiet, "O'Neill's Modification of Traditional American Themes in *A Touch of the Poet*," *Educational Theatre Journal*, 27, No. 4 (December 1975), 508–15, compares *Poet* with two contrived melodramas, Steele MacKaye's *Hazel Kirke* (1880) and James A. Herne's *Shore Acres* (1892) and what emerges is the way *Poet* is distinguished from other plays somewhat like it. Elinor Fuchs, "O'Neill's *Poet*: Touched by Ibsen," *Educa-*

tional Theatre Journal, 30, No. 4 (December 1978), 513–16, finds thematic links between O'Neill's play and *Hedda Gabler* but more especially to *The Wild Duck*.

Beginning with the assumption of other critics that the drama is unplayable, Rolf Scheibler, "*Hughie*: A One-Act Play for the Imaginary Theatre," *English Studies*, 54 (1973), 231–48, is a lengthy look at the play with careful attention to stage directions and dialogue. Edwin J. Blesch, Jr., "O'Neill's 'Hughie': A Misconceived Experiment?," *Nassau Review*, 2, No. 5 (1974), 1–8, perceives in the one act a familiar O'Neill theme — man's need for illusion, his clinging to inescapable pipe dreams, and a structure like that of many O'Neill plays — that of mask, unmask, remask. Seeing the play as one of O'Neill's most optimistic, Carol Billman, "Language as Theme in Eugene O'Neill's *Hughie*," *Notes on Modern American Literature (NMAL)*, 3 (1979), Item 25, says this is not another play dealing with life illusion but one that depicts man's difficulty in communicating yet affirming the need for communication and the importance of sharing pipe dreams. A fine, brief yet intricate study of the form, movement, and structure of comedy, here as applied to O'Neill's one act play, Robert Mayberry, "Sterile Wedding: The Comic Structure of O'Neill's *Hughie*," *Massachusetts Studies in English*, 7, No. 3 (1980), 10–19, declares the play concludes by celebrating the creation of a new society, a relationship between Erie and the night clerk that replaces the old society of Erie and the dead Hughie; Mayberry describes the "wedding" as sterile: the coupling of Erie with either night clerk is the intersection of the lie one man tells and the lie another wants to believe. Laurin Roland Porter, "*Hughie*: Pipe Dream for Two," [q.v.] deals with the cultural elements of the play, examines it as a biographical document, and explores family and the function of time in *Hughie*, a play that Clive Barnes in 1976 included with *Long Day's Journey*, *Misbegotten*, and *Iceman* as those that made O'Neill's present reputation.

CONCLUSION

If one reads the New York critics' reviews, certain words describing O'Neill's drama become thematic: "repetitious," "lengthy," and "tremendously long," but from 1920 (Woollcott) to 1956 (Watts): ". . . the giant stature of America's greatest dramatist" — almost always the consistent factor in critics' appreciation of O'Neill is how much higher O'Neill stood alone above anyone else. For the critics of four decades O'Neill resided in an exemplary heaven that he *alone* occupied. And some of the disapprobation of a few of his plays must be seen in this way. He was measured by standards that he, and he alone, was to be judged by.

While many American critics had reservations about some of O'Neill's dramatic works, including, for example, *Days Without End*, Irish critics had no such reservations of their own. When that play was presented in April 1934 by the Abbey Theatre in Dublin, David Sears, the Irish *Indepen-*

dent's playwright-critic, said, "The play requires an intelligent audience and the Abbey audience was beyond reproach. They missed no point. . . ." If it is true that *Days Without End* requires an intelligent audience, much the same can be said for O'Neill as a playwright. This may account for the fluctuation in response to many of O'Neill's plays and, not perhaps paradoxically, at the same time may be responsible for the enduring appreciation of O'Neill's gifts. This intelligence and need for an intelligent and informed audience accounts for the fact that his works have been read, are still read, produced, performed, and, finally, understood. It accounts, as well, for the existence of this collection of critical essays.

It is a pleasure to acknowledge the following friends, colleagues, and institutions whose assistance made this volume possible. My gratitude to the staff of the Pattee Library, The Pennsylvania State University; the Research Council of St. Bonaventure University and the staff of the Friedsam Library, St. Bonaventure University, especially Theresa Covley; Lars Gyllensten, Permanent Secretary of the Swedish Academy; and to David Schoonover and Ralph Franklin of the Beinecke Library, Yale University. My thanks also to Elizabeth Murray who complied a preliminary bibliography and Alyce Sands Miller for her special contribution; Leo E. Keenan for his many considerations; Boyd Litzinger for creating the ambiance that makes scholarship possible; S. John Guson for providing necessary equipment; Lawrence Day Ford for twice-weekly conferences crucial to this work; Andrea Martine for assistance in indexing; once again, and deeply felt, thanks to Jim and Gwen. Finally, most obviously, special appreciation to the writers and scholars whose work constitutes this book, particularly Jack Bryer, Ellen Kimbel, Mike Manheim, and Susan Tuck. All the essays in this volume are published here for the first time by permission of the authors.

JAMES J. MARTINE

St. Bonaventure University

"Peace Is an Exhausted Reaction to Normal":O'Neill's Letters to Dudley Nichols

Jackson R. Bryer

When *Strange Interlude* opened on January 30, 1928, at the John Golden Theatre on Broadway, one of the most enthusiastic — and lengthy — reviews to appear the next morning was written by Dudley Nichols of the *New York World*. Nichols had been a last-minute replacement for Alexander Woollcott, the *World*'s regular reviewer, under circumstances described in detail by both the Gelbs and Louis Scheaffer in their O'Neill biographies.[1] Sheaffer and the Gelbs also draw on Nichols' memories of his friendship with O'Neill which developed in the late 1930s on the West Coast when the O'Neills were living at Tao House, east of San Francisco. Nichols had by then established himself as one of Hollywood's leading screenwriters and was collaborating with director John Ford on *The Long Voyage Home*, a film adaptation of O'Neill's four one-act "S. S. Glencairn" plays.[2]

Neither the Gelbs nor Sheaffer seem to have made much use of O'Neill's letters and telegrams to Nichols that the latter gave to Yale University, along with a fascinating three-page memoir entitled "Concerning Enclosed Eugene O'Neill Letters" and dated November 5, 1959 (Nichols died on January 5, 1960, after what the *New York Times* called in its obituary "a long illness"; so he may well have known he was dying when he wrote the memoir). The memoir gives background details on what Nichols calls "the most important friendship of my life."[3]

He begins by briefly summarizing the story of how he came to review *Strange Interlude* and by reporting that "Gene told me in later years how grateful he was for my review . . . the newspaper for which I wrote, the *World*, was extremely influential at that time and Gene felt my review contributed much to the overwhelming success of that production." Later, in 1928, Nichols contributed a long and appreciative introduction to a Modern Library edition of *The Emperor Jones* and *The Straw*. The introduction and the review are both gratefully recalled in O'Neill's first letter to Nichols, dated April 20, 1932. In that first letter O'Neill also says, "There's nothing I would like better than to have the pleasure of meeting you." But Nichols' memoir notes that he had actually met O'Neill "on an occasion in 1927, but there were other people present and we had not enough personal contact for

33

him to remember it, nor did I remind him until many years later." Nichols' description of that first meeting is well worth quoting in its entirety:

> This meeting was in the apartment in New York of Nemirovitch-Dan-chenko of the Moscow Art Theatre on the day when Gene delivered to Danchenko the script of his new play *Lazarus Laughed*.[4] Danchenko, whom I knew well, was eager, as was Stanislavski, to give this play, ignored in America, its premiere in Moscow. I remember Danchenko telling O'Neill with glowing eyes and deep sincerity, "*You* are one of us, *you* are a Russian", which was about the highest praise this old Russian could think of.

Nichols adds two "postscripts" to this story. One tells of visiting anarchist and Russian expatriate Alexander Berkman near Paris a few months later and seeing on his desk the same script of *Lazarus Laughed* that O'Neill had given to Danchenko which Berkman was now translating into Russian for the Moscow Art Theatre. But there never was a production of *Lazarus Laughed* at the Moscow Art Theatre or anyplace else in Russia and, in 1936, when Nichols and his wife visited Danchenko and Stanislavski in Russia, he asked Danchenko why.

> He looked slightly embarrassed, cleared his throat, and said, without directly referring to the regime, that "It had been found too mystical." I could see that the old man secretly felt badly about this, but there were other Russians present and I did not pursue the matter further, for such discussions could be dangerous to men even in the high position of Stanislavski and Danchenko. Naturally I understood that a regime based on "dialectic materialism" would have no truck with such a play as *Lazarus*, no matter how beautiful the drama. Gene had always seen that great actor, Kachalov,[5] as the only actor who could play Lazarus and I'm sure he was right. Kachalov was still full of vigor and a member of the Moscow Art Theatre company, and he loved the play, but the repertory of the theatre was greatly restricted at that time. . . .

After the two 1932 letters, which were apparently responses to letters from Nichols praising O'Neill's recent work, most particularly *Mourning Becomes Electra* and *Dynamo*, there was no further correspondence between them until 1940. By then, Nichols who had first gone to Hollywood in 1929, had become a major screenwriter. In 1935, he had won the Academy Award for his screenplay of *The Informer*;[6] in 1939, he had done the screenplay for *Stagecoach*. In both these films he had worked with director John Ford (Nichols was associated with Ford on fourteen films); and, in 1940, Nichols who, he says in his memoir, "always . . . was trying to induce the studios to film O'Neill plays," persuaded Ford to use his influence with producer Walter Wanger to back an adaptation of the "S. S. Glencairn" plays. Ford and Nichols visited the O'Neills at Tao House early in 1940 and, according to Sheaffer, O'Neill "warmed quickly to the film-making pair, especially to Ford, a big hearty Irishman with a fund of irreverent stories about Hollywood."[7]

It was from this visit, according to Nichols, "that my real friendship commenced. He was pleased with the film we made of his plays and subsequently I became a frequent visitor at Tao House." The developing friendship is documented in the correspondence by the use of first names in the salutations and closings. *The Long Voyage Home* is the subject of several letters and telegrams; the Gelbs called it "the most successful of all the movie adaptations of O'Neill's plays";[8] and Sheaffer saw it as "the finest movie ever made from O'Neill's writings."[9] Sheaffer also notes that Nichols was one of the handful of people O'Neill allowed to read *Long Day's Journey Into Night*;[10] and the Gelbs record that O'Neill discussed *The Iceman Cometh* "intimately" with Nichols "during the time he was writing it."[11] During this period also, Nichols, who apparently wanted to abandon screenwriting and write for the stage, gave O'Neill a copy of his play "House in the Sky" to read and comment on—which O'Neill did, with admirable tact, in his letter of July 7, 1940. Nichols continued to try to convince producers to film O'Neill's plays, but the only occasion on which he succeeded in doing so was when, in 1947, he formed his own independent production company and produced, directed, and adapted a film version of *Mourning Becomes Electra*.

By 1949, when the correspondence ends, O'Neill's tremor had worsened considerably and his December 4th, 1948, letter may well have been, as Nichols indicates in his memoir, "one of the very last which he accomplished with his own hand. It evidently took him two days to write this, for even to sign his name had become a task." Nichols also laments that O'Neill never finished the play he had been working on during his last years in California. First titled "The Thirteenth Apostle" and later called "The Last Conquest,"[12] it was a work which, Nichols reveals, he "offered, at the last, to write . . . out for him as he had told it to me and then keep rewriting successive drafts until it would be very near to what he imagined, but of course this was impossible. He could no more do this than he could dictate his work. His handwriting was a part of his mind, almost a part of his imagination, which is what makes his MSS so fascinating. His hand stopped, his work was stopped, and he knew it." And, indeed, in his last letter to Nichols on March 20, 1949, there is the prophetic and poignant sentence, "No play is being written—and no play will be produced."

At the end of his memoir, Nichols expresses the wish that O'Neill's letters and telegrams to him "be kept together as a unit and preserved as a memento of a friendship, and that they . . . be made available, for whatever slight use they may prove to have in the future, to accredited biographers and worthy scholars who are interested in the study of Eugene O'Neill's life and work." It is thus entirely in keeping with Nichols' intention that the correspondence appears here together, uncut, for the first time. No deletions have been made within letters; but two brief cards written in 1941 and 1942, the latter a Christmas greeting, and a three-line letter of February 3, 1948, which does little more than acknowledge receipt of a telegram from Nichols and report that "My arm is still very painful," have been omitted.

The nineteen letters and telegrams that remain should have considerably more than the "slight use" which Nichols modestly hoped for them. O'Neill obviously felt a closeness to and a kinship with Nichols from the outset, probably because of Nichols' sympathy for and understanding of his plays — as expressed in the long and highly positive review of *Strange Interlude* and the introduction to the Modern Library volume. O'Neill's letters are intimate and self-revelatory virtually from the start. They also tell us much about his opinions of the two film adaptations of his plays on which Nichols worked. His December 16, 1942, letter is particularly valuable as a prime expression and explanation of the wartime malaise which consumed O'Neill and prevented him from allowing any of his plays to be produced until after 1945. His December 4, 1948, letter similarly epitomizes his pessimism near the end of his life when he could no longer write and when his animosity towards the medical profession sounds remarkably similar to that of James Tyrone, Sr. But, throughout, there are phrases and paragraphs that allow us to hear O'Neill in his own words on a variety of subjects and, as such, they are a valuable supplement to the biographies. Presented as a unit, their intimacy and highly personal tone imply just how important this friendship was to O'Neill.

In transcribing the letters, the following abbreviations have been used to describe physical form: ALS, autograph letter signed by author; TLS, typed letter signed by author; WIRE, telegram. The numbers enumerating the total pages of the letters most usually refer to individual leaves; occasionally they indicate one side of one leaf of stationery. Most often in this correspondence, O'Neill wrote on stationery with his address embossed at the top; but all such headings have been standardized into upper- and lower-case type and have been placed flush right, regardless of their position in the actual letter. Similarly, while O'Neill customarily placed the date at the bottom of the letter, here it has been placed flush right under the heading at the top of the letter; the date, however, has been rendered as O'Neill wrote it. In the one instance where a date has been supplied for a letter, it has been listed in brackets with a footnote indicating the reason for the supplied date. O'Neill's occasional spelling and punctuation errors and misspellings of personal names have been retained. Obviously inadvertent misspellings and typographical errors have been silently corrected. Paragraph indentation has been standardized, as have the positions of closings and signatures. The length of dashes has been standardized to one em, although both in typing and in his handwriting, O'Neill used one hyphen for a dash.

1. ALS 1 p.

1095 Park Avenue
April 20th 1932

Dear Mr. Nichols:

I found your letter here today on my return to town for a couple of days. I was immensely pleased to get it! It was especially gratifying, coming just after "Electra" had closed, when one gets the feeling that in people's minds the play is now finished and forgotten. So, much gratitude to you! It was damned kind of you to write — and I can only hope that in a time to come of true perspective and estimation the trilogy will in some measure justify your high opinion of it.

I remember with deep appreciation your fine review of "Strange Interlude" — also your preface to the Modern Library edition of "Emperor Jones"!

There's nothing I would like better than to have the pleasure of meeting you. Unfortunately, I am only here for a few days now and all my time is tied up. But next fall I will probably be in town for quite a time and we can fix it up then to get together. Or perhaps you may get down Georgia way sometime in our neighborhood. If so, there is welcome on the mat for you — so be sure to come and see me.

All good wishes to you — and again, thanks!

Yours most sincerely,
Eugene O'Neill
[Sea Island Beach,
St. Simon Island,
Georgia]

2. ALS 3 pp.

Sea Island Beach
Georgia
May 29th 1932

Dear Mr. Nichols:

I'm damned glad you didn't throw that letter away permanently! Because reading it gave me a deep satisfaction and pleasure that I would not like to have foregone. A fair number of letters come my way about this or that in connection with my work, but most of them are silly stuff, as you may guess, and it is almost never I receive one from anyone whose judgment I give a damn about. Such letters as yours, which convince me by their sincerity that my plays have left an enduring mark on people of imaginative perception and spiritual insight, are about the finest reward I could wish! Better even than reward, encouragement! And this latter is often sorely needed. For despite acceptance by the notoriety that is modern fame — (and because of it, even though one remains uninfected!) — it is sometimes difficult to "pull up one's socks" and go on. One gets weary and bewildered, among the broken rythyms of this time one misses one's beat and line of continuity, one gets the feeling of talking through a disconnected phone, foolishly, to oneself.

So, you see, much gratitude for your letter is in order — and most certainly is felt by me! Not that I can preen my vanity up to the point where I may unblushingly second your high opinion of what I have accomplished. But it's a heartening challenge to keep on trying to justify such an opinion. And it's the dream that I may sometime say what must be said as it must be said that keeps me going — Showshop or no Showshop!

Funny, your writing me at this particular time about affirmation. I am changing inside me, as I suppose one always does, or ought to do if there is growth, when one has passed forty, and even the most positive affirmative Nay! of my past work no longer satisfies me. So I am groping after a real, true Yea! in the play I'm now starting[13] — a very old Yea, it is true, in essence, but so completely forgotten in all its inner truth that it might pass for brand new. Whether I will be able to carry the writing of it up to Yea! remains to be seen.

This play is, incidentally — and most confidentially! — a development from my old idea for the second play of the "Dynamo" trilogy. So what you say about "Dynamo" came at a timely time!

Also, some days before your letter arrived, I was making first notes on an idea that had suddenly come to me — a really tremendous affirmative conception for an opus magnus! But it must wait until I feel grown up enough to write it — if ever. I'm certainly not fool enough to think I'm capable of it yet — but I'll keep hoping![14]

All of which rambling on about my aims and ambitions I hope you'll feel your letter brought on your head — and not attribute to monomania!

Yes, Revolution seems beside the real mark to me, too. So many Revolutions there have been since the Greeks, and Man's soul has grown dumber and dumber. If he even had more to eat that might be something — but he still seems to be giving starvation a battle. As for Russia, wait until they have to stand the ordeal of success. Just now, on the way up to some somewhere, it's all so excellently easy for them.

I can't imagine what happened to Electra No 2.[15] I saw the last rehearsal before they opened their road season and they really gave an excellent performance. Reed was no Nazimova, of course, but she wasn't poor by any means. Abel was certainly no Earle Larrimore (whom I think has done the finest work of them all) but he was anything but bad. And Judith Anderson I thought extremely good and better than Brady in many places. The grind of the road, I suppose, got them.

All good wishes to you. I'll hope to see you in N.Y. when next I go up. It will all depend on work as to just when that will be. I told you Fall in my last letter, but I may stick on my job here longer at a stretch than that. But remember that what I said about if you get down this way at any time always holds good.

I know the New Milford neighborhood.[16] Its beautiful country. You will get a lot out of being there, I think.

Write again when you're in the mood. And don't stick me on no Messiah pedestal! I'd never dare meet you then and be a witness to your devastating disillusion!

Eugene O'Neill

3. TLS 2 pp.

Tao House
Danville
Contra Costa County
California
April the 22nd 1940.

Dear Dudley Nichols,

We were delighted to get your two long letters and it is good to learn of the progress being made on the Glencairn picture. I was beginning to think, what with the interminable bicker of lawyers and agents, it would never get started until everyone concerned was fed up with the mere thought of it.

As for my interest in this film, I assure you I am most sincerely interested and I will be extremely grateful if you keep me informed on how it is taking shape. And I'd like a lot to read your final script, if you can spare a copy. You see, I have a sure hunch you have made a damned fine job of it. I ignore your misgivings because I always suffer from the same doubts about anything of mine. There isn't a damned thing I've ever done that I didn't feel at times was insufferably lousy because it fell so short of what I had hoped to do. So don't be diffident about your script. You know me well enough, I hope, to realize I'm no petty carper, that I do understand a different medium is a different medium and appreciate the difficulties of transforming one into the other — and furthermore that I by no means consider myself God's Immaculate Gift to the Art of Drama, nor rate my stuff as inviolate as the Sacred Books. So send your script without trepidation lest I foam at the mouth and destroy my dental work rending it apart!

The cast for the picture, as you surmise, doesn't mean much to me. I know only the work of Mitchell, Fitzgerald, and Kerrigan[17] — but I do know they are fine actors.

I'm eager to see how you get around the problem of bringing the story into the present time. That puzzled me a bit when you and Ford were here, and later on I thought of further details that didn't fit. But, of course, I realized you hadn't started work on that angle yet, and that it could be worked out.

Don't talk about flu. I've been having my dose — not as bad as yours but a week in bed and I'm still bogged down by the after effects. It seems to be a particularly vile brand of the pest that is current on the Coast this year. It caught me when I had been feeling punk in general, anyway — low blood pressure and such. I haven't been able to do much work since soon after you were here. Maybe the unexpectedness of a sale of film rights sort of wore me down, or something. The producer lads down your way sure are frightened to touch my stuff. Maybe the Glencairn film will break the spell. I hope so, because in a few years I'm afraid money won't buy much any more and it will be too late. I once received nine million marks royalty from a brief repertoire run of "Anna Christie" in Berlin. It meant about fifteen dollars, as I remember — and that was before the worst of their inflation.

Speaking of royalties reminds me of the "Desire Under the Elms" production which has just closed in London — and a request I want you to make for me to Mr. Ford. "Desire" ran in London almost three months, and is now touring the provinces — a wartime miracle I rate as second only to the Angel of the Marne.[18] Not that it played to anything, but it managed to get by. Well, where Ford comes in is, I am encountering delay in prying royalties out of Albion's clutches, and I suspect the delay is not caused by German submarines but is part of an ancient plot to keep the O'Neills impoverished and sober. So I want him to write out a brief Gaelic curse I can add to my evening prayers. Nothing drastic, you understand. After all, they are at war and I like them a little better than Hitler. Besides, the royalties (less $37\frac{1}{2}\%$ income tax) are too frugal to justify really strong language. Just something mild like "May every Limey son of a bitch of a misbegotten Tory bastard in the British Government fall down seven flights of stairs and rupture his accursed rectum in three places". I'm sure it can be done in a couple of words of Gaelic.

Why don't you try and pay us a flying visit before you go East? It's beautiful in our valley now, and it was no polite chatter when we told you and Ford we would be delighted to have you both or either of you here again any time you could make it.

Give Ford our best — and here's wishing all the luck there is to the picture!

Cordially,
Eugene O'Neill

4. TLS 2 pp.

Tao House
Danville
Contra Costa County
California
April the 27th 1940.

Dear Dudley Nichols,

I've just finished reading the 'script and I most sincerely congratulate you on the fine job you have done. You have preserved the flavor and spirit of the original plays wonderfully well. As for the things you mention in your letter — like the tarpaulin and anchor touches — I am all for them. I believe a picture of a play should concentrate on doing those things which the stage cannot do. Then a balance can be struck in which the picture medium brings fresh drama to the play to take the place of the stuff which belongs to the stage and cannot be done as well in pictures. So the more of such enhancing additions, the merrier, as far as I am concerned. And believe me, although I see as few pictures as I see stage productions, I can appreciate and feel the purely visual drama of your 'script, and think of "The Long Voyage Home" solely as a new unified picture drama, forgetting the four one-act plays written for the stage.

There are a few things which bother me. They relate to facts. Undoubtedly you and Ford have checked on them and I must be wrong. But here goes. One extremely important one, because if it isn't fact, you will have everyone on your necks. You have the ship loading shells and high explosive from the U.S. Now isn't it true our Neutrality Act doesn't permit us to sell arms or munitions, the only exceptions allowed being planes and plane parts, etc.?

The other things have to do with ship stuff. You have a mess room steward doing a steward's job and bunking in the forecastle. And you haven't any bo'sun on your tramp. It's true no bo'sun appears in my plays but he is mentioned. In the plays there is no situation where there might not be a reason for his never being in the scene, but in the picture he would *have* to be around directing the men at times. Query No. 3: Twenty-five percent bonus for crew? Is that what they get in this war?

These are picayune queries, I admit, prompted by what I once knew of tramp steamer conditions, etc. Well, here's a suggestion that may give you a few extra shots. As I remember, "In the Zone", it conveys no suggestion of a double lookout (at least), which a ship would probably have at such a time. One man on the forecastle head, one in the crow's nest. It gives you a chance to add crow's nest stuff, particularly dramatic in a storm when you get a tremendous effect of the roll up there. And here's a memory. When due for a crow's nest watch in a storm, the man about to relieve would wait in the door to the forecastle alleyway while a wave dashed over the forecastle head. Then as the wave receded down the deck, timing it just right, he would sprint for the ladder up the mainmast to the crow's nest — the idea being to get there and start climbing before the next sea came over and caught him. The same thing, in reverse, then happened with the man he relieved who came down and then sprinted for the forecastle door.

But never mind this query and suggestion stuff! The important thing I want to say in this letter is how much I like your adaptation and how grateful I am to you and Ford. I can see the grand picture it will be. In fact, I now visualize some of your effects a good deal more clearly than I remember the details of the plays on the stage!

But I wish you two weren't so goddamned non-commercial. Because I have a new love interest angle which would bring box office queues ten miles long. You remember the Yank-anchor scene? Well, have him go over the side down to the anchor. And what do you think he finds caught on one of the flukes? A blonde! And by her panties! It seems she has fallen off a yacht — or something. Well, you have to admit this is a new way of getting the gal on the boat. And then — But hell, what's the use of talking to a coupla guys like you what ain't got no practical theatre sense. Go on and make a fine picture, if you're that nuts!

On this elevated spiritual plane I close. Mrs O'Neill joins me in all best to you and Sean O'Fearna[19] — and again, much gratitude to you both.

Cordially,

Eugene O'Neill

P.S.I.

May I keep the 'script or do you need it on the job?

P.S. II.

By all means, fly up for a visit if you get a chance, but don't feel you ought to because your 'script needs explaining or because I want to wish any suggestions on you.

5. TLS 1 p.

Tao House

Danville

Contra Costa County

California

May the ninth 1940

Dear Dudley Nichols,

I quote from a letter just rec'd from Bennett Cerf of Random House: "Walter Wanger is very anxious for us to bring out, in book form, Dudley Nichols' movie script based on your four plays of the sea. Such a publication might emphasize the importance of the picture and, furthermore, might prove a profitable venture. Before I think any future about the scheme, however, I want to be sure that you have no objection to the publication of this script. Of course there will be a statement in the book that the scenario was based on your four plays. Have we your permission to go ahead with this scheme if we want to? I will deeply appreciate a line from you be return mail".

Now I want to leave this up to you. Frankly, I don't see anything in it, either from your angle or mine. If you were going to keep on writing for pictures, it might be a boost — *provided* the picture proved to be a smash artistic and commercial success. But that's a big gamble, and if the picture doesn't go over exceptionally well, the publication of the script would count for nothing. On the other hand, if you are now setting yourself free from Hollywood to do the writing you really want to do, it would be a bad mistake, in my opinion, to have the first book you publish a screen adaption. It would only serve to link you up in critics' minds with pictures — would get you off to a bad start. You know what I mean. It doesn't matter how good your script is. It's a question of having a tag hung on you — being pigeon-holed as something you're trying to get away from.

I've been attempting to think of this objectively from your angle. I may be all wrong. Let me know how you feel about it. I've written Cerf I was writing you and if you thought it could help you in any way, I would gladly give my consent. Let me know at once, will you, because Cerf wants a decision as soon as he can get it.

Haven't read your play[20] yet but I will as soon as I feel better. At present, hobbling around on a walking stick with my hip still protesting bitterly, I'm in a mood where Hamlet would seem like a piece of tripe.

All best from us!
Eugene O'Neill

6. TLS 1 p.

Tao House
Danville
Contra Costa County
California
May the 22nd 1940.

Dear Dudley:

Just a belated line to thank you for your long letter. I apologize for not writing sooner but the war news has had me glued to the radio, sunk in enraged despondency. I haven't been able to think of anything else — and am not now.

All I want to tell you is, I wrote Cerf to go ahead with the publication of your script, provided you were given a chance to bring it up to date, so to speak, so it would be in every detail the picture as finally released, and also revise it as you wish to make it less a technical script and easier for the layman reader to follow. I felt, from your letter, this would be what you would insist on if the script was your property.

I also mentioned that it was a strange sort of publication when neither the writer of the script nor the writer of the plays was to be paid anything! Not the sort of arrangement the Authors League would approve. It sets a damn bad precedent. I honestly don't believe there's a nickel for anyone in this proposed publication, but as a matter of principle you and I should be on legal record as entitled to our bit.

Well, I haven't heard anything from Cerf since. I guess he hasn't seen Wanger yet. I'll let you know as soon as I do hear.

Carlotta joins me in all best to you.

Very sincerely,
Eugene O'Neill

7. WIRE 1 p.

DANVILLE CALIF
JULY 6 [1940]

DUDLEY NICHOLS =

I SAW THE LONG VOYAGE HOME LAST NIGHT AND CARLOTTA AND I ARE
ENTHUSIASTIC. IT IS A GRAND PICTURE AND FORD SHOULD BE PROUD OF IT. SO
SHOULD YOU. MUCH GRATITUDE FOR ALL YOU DID TO PRESERVE THE SPIRIT.
EXPECT A LETTER FROM ME SOON ABOUT YOUR PLAY. I MEANT TO WRITE LONG
AGO BUT EVENTS HAVE HAD ME TOO DOWN TO DO ANYTHING. ALL BEST FROM
US =

GENE

8. TLS 2 pp.

Tao House
Danville
Contra Costa County
California
July the 7th 1940.

Dear Dudley,

Ford sent the picture up and we saw it in a projection room in San Francisco Friday night. I wired you my reaction yesterday. It's a grand job. I hope it may make some money for them. I am sure it will be a great artistic success, unless the critics have all gone blind and deaf.

But I want to tell you about your play now and apologize for my neglect in not having written you long ago. That is the sort of lousy trick which is not really like me. The fact is, I read it and stuck it in a drawer of my desk, telling myself I would write you in the next day or so. Then I simply forgot all about it! An unpardonable business, which never could have happened under normal circumstances, but ever since the May debacle started in Europe I have been in a thoroughly demoralized state of the bitterest pessimism. Unable to think of anything else, or do any work until this last week when I began to get hold of myself again. My health wasn't too good, either, and that didn't help matters. It wasn't until the night before last, after seeing the film, that my memory suddenly clicked and thought Christ Almighty, I've never written Dudley about his play! Put it down to war amnesia, will you?

I reread "House In The Sky" last night. It is damned good dramatic writing — up to a certain point. I liked the first act and half of the second. I was held by it up to that point. Then it began to falter and loose its line and bite as drama and wander about, the characters fading from life and becoming mouthpieces for viewpoints. It becomes writing in dialogue instead of dramatic writing. And when at the end it picked up drama again via Lazarus, I wasn't moved because it seemed like a disconnected episode which had lost its significance as an essential part of your theme.

In short, a lot of rewriting is indicated before your play will do the stuff you're driving at. It muffs it now. It talks itself out of it. In the first part, I felt the people were worth writing a play about. But at the end, I didn't.

I know you want frank criticism and I'm giving it. But don't think I'm doing so in a complacently superior spirit. I've made the same mistakes many times, and probably will again. The thing you must remember about the play is that it has damned good stuff in it which should encourage you to keep the old nose on the legit grindstone.

I had a letter from Cerf a few days ago about the publication of your "Long Voyage Home" script. To his astonishment, he had just received a wire from Wanger calling the deal off. Cerf thought it was all settled to go ahead. So did I — although when I heard some weeks ago that Wanger was thinking of having reproductions of paintings included, I began to have my doubts. What happened, do you know? Cerf evidently doesn't.

Carlotta joins me in all good wishes to you. Again, much gratitude for your screen script of the four one-actors. On the screen, as on paper, it keeps the spirit of them in spite of the change in medium.

Very sincerely yours,
Gene

9. TLS 1 p.

Tao House
Danville
Contra Costa County
California
October the 13th 1940.

Dear Dudley,

It was fine to get your letter. I was beginning to be afraid you might have felt I was a bit too free and unfair in my criticism of your play. I didn't really believe that, but still experience has taught me that authors don't love adverse criticism. I couldn't swear in any court that I exactly dote on it. In fact, it usually makes me sore as hell.

I've seen the New York reviews of "The Long Voyage Home" and, as I've just written Ford, I'm delighted with them. For his sake and yours mainly. You both deserve the praise the picture received for the work you did. And didn't the boys praise it! I've never seen better reviews. Let's hope your prophecies about country wide financial results prove to be too pessimistic. The big hope is, I think, that people all over the country have been a bit knocked out of their groove by the world crisis and are more apt than before to appreciate something with real guts that is outside the usual pattern. Well, we'll see.

I've been working hard since I got over the worst of my war jitters last Spring. Am just completing another play outside the Cycle. "The Iceman Cometh" which was finished a month or so before you and Ford were here, was the first one. This play is called "Long Day's Journey Into Night." I like these two a lot. But am not going to produce either for a long time. The future for a free writer seems to grow shorter each day and I want to stick at writing and get all I can finished while I can. That's why the Cycle[21] has been on the shelf. These two outside plays I've done have been on my mind for years. Now they are written. Not that it can be of any consequence in the world we will soon have to face, but it's at least a personal satisfaction. Just what I'll do next I haven't decided yet. Perhaps take up the Cycle again. Perhaps do another of the many outside ideas I have notes for. All I know is, unless my health trips me up again, I'll sure stick constantly on the writing job. Work is the only anodyne that enables me to keep any sort of mental balance. Archimedes isn't in good repute these days when so many other answers are necessary, but all the same there is a lot to be said for his answer.[22]

Here's hoping you and Mrs Nichols can pay us a visit. Carlotta, I know, has written you about this.

All best to you!

> Very sincerely,
> Gene

10. TLS 3 pp.

> Tao House
> Danville
> Contra Costa County
> California
> December the 16th 1942.

Dear Dudley:

Coincidence: The day before your letter arrived we mailed you a Christmas card (Connecticut address) on which I wrote "Why don't we hear from you?" So your letter was warmly welcomed. We had guessed that you must be passing through a trying period of readjustment to the war — like all the rest of us — and had heard from Bob Sisk[23] about the Hemingway movie job[24] and also heard or read of your working with Renoir.[25] But all that was some time ago. We didn't know if you were still in Hollywood.

I am delighted to learn how satisfied you are in the collaboration with Renoir, and that R.K.O. really kept hands off the film you've just made, and gave you authority and freedom. That is practically a miracle, isn't it? Here's hoping they don't suffer a change of mind and revert to type. Film making can be something fine. Only a fool would deny that. But, as in the theatre, it can only happen when imaginative creative minds have a chance to use the medium without interference.

But enough of that. I'm merely agreeing with what you know. And all I really want to say is that I think you were wise to make a final decision and concentrate on what you know you want to do.

Regarding "Desire Under The Elms", I hope you may finally be in a position to do that. I needn't tell you it would be a great joy to leave it in your hands. There is only one hitch. If I get a decent offer for it (financially speaking) in the near future, I would have to accept for purely financial reasons. Things are none too good with me in that respect. It will be a tough battle to survive this war and have anything left. However, there is no offer for "Desire" and probably won't be, so what the hell am I talking about.

Russel Crouse[26] has just written me from New York he saw in one of the dramatic columns that Boris Karloff was being considered for a film version of "The Hairy Ape". Have you heard any talk of this in Hollywood? I know nothing about it, but then I might not be approached until whoever is interested had everything else lined up. Of course, I don't pay any attention to theatrical column rumors, but sometimes they are true. And this one has a certain plausibility as a shrewd showmanship notion. Karloff, so Crouse, who ought to know, assures me, is really a fine actor, when not swamped in junk pictures, and an intelligent man.[27]

No, "The Iceman Cometh" would be wrong now. A New York audience could neither see nor hear its meaning. The pity and tragedy of defensive pipe dreams would be deemed downright unpatriotic, and uninspired by the Atlantic Charter, even if the audience did catch that meaning. But after the war is over, I am afraid from present indications that American audiences will understand a lot of "The Iceman Cometh" only too well.

If this indicates that I am an optimist about a United Nations victory, but a pessimist about any intelligent, greedless peace, that's it, exactly. The so-garrulous liberal intelligentsia of this world always naively forget that a peace is made by and of men, and if men have changed at all spiritually since the last war, it is for the worse. Also, war uses up all the self-sacrifice human nature can spare. Peace is an exhausted reaction to normal. As Marco tells the Khan in "Marco Millions": "I've never read much in any history about heroes who waged peace". If there are any noble-minded statesmen or diplomats in the world to-day who can be relied on to make an unselfish peace and then keep on waging it, I don't see them. They all seem to believe any end justifies any means — and the end to that is total ruin for man's spirit. Whether there is social revolution or not, it won't matter a damn. What have you left when you turn over a manure pile — but manure?

Well, that's not so cheery, I better stop. Your description of your household retainers is damned amusing. You certainly don't lack the proper religious environment!

My health has been rotten for over a year and Carlotta has had her troubles, too, with arthritis and a bad back. But she is a wonder — manages to do a hell of a lot of housework and still remains cheerful, although she loathes it. We have only a cook now — and lucky to have her. Freeman[28] is in the Marines and we have no one outside but the farmer. I can't drive a car any more and Carlotta never could. So we are more or less marooned — even before gas rationing. We get the hardware man from Danville to drive us to Oakland when I have to go in for treatments every two weeks. All of which sounds tougher than it is. Now we're used to it, we manage all right and it's no great hardship.

As for work, Pearl Harbor caught me enthusiastically writing a new non-cycle play, "A Moon For The Misbegotten". After that, I couldn't concentrate. Managed to finish the first draft but the heart was out of it. Haven't looked at it since. There is a fine unusual tragic comedy in "A Moon For The Misbegotten" but it will have to wait until I can rewrite the lifeless post-Pearl Harbor part of it. All I've been able to do in the past ten months is rewrite one of the Cycle plays, "A Touch Of The Poet", and do a little work on "The Last Conquest" (the World-Dictator fantasy of a possible future, and the attempted last campaign of Evil to stamp out even the unconscious memory of Good in Man's spirit — you will remember I sketched the idea to you the last time you were at Tao House). But again in this play, I soon feel my creative impulse blocked by the hopeless certainty that it could not be understood now, or its possibilities admitted — more than that, a feeling in myself that, until this war, which must be won, is won, people should concentrate on the grim surface and not admit the still grimmer, soul-disturbing depths. I censor myself, so to speak, and with this shackle added to recurring spells of illness and mental depression — In short, "The Last Conquest" remains for the most part in scenario, although it constantly haunts me.

Of course, this is no way for the free creative spirit to act. It's answer to war should be that of Archimedes: "Get out of my light. Your shadow is disturbing my problem". Should be, in theory. But this total war is different. It is, unfortunately, really *total* and no answer can evade it.

Carlotta joins me in all best. We would like to see you, but I guess there is no possibility of that. Even if you had to come to San Francisco, I don't see how you could get out here. Thirty miles each way and we are on A gas ration — and thumbing a ride has become practically impossible, so I'm told!

Let me hear from you whenever you're in the mood.

As ever,

Gene

11. WIRE 1 p.

NEW YORK NY
APR 9 1946

DUDLEY NICHOLS = RKO RADIO PICTURES

YOUR REQUEST ABOUT MOURNING BECOMES ELECTRA REACHED ME THROUGH LYONS OFFICE TODAY. I HAVE ALREADY BEEN DISCUSSING POSSIBILITY INDEPENDENT PRODUCTION DEAL WITH THEATRE GUILD AND VERY IMPORTANT FEMALE STAR. THEATRE GUILD OWNS 50 PERCENT OF THE RIGHTS. MY RIGHTS ARE NOW LEASED ON 7 YEAR BASIS AND IF WE WERE TO MAKE ARRANGEMENTS OTHER THAN THOSE WE HAVE BEEN DISCUSSING FOR AN INDE-

PENDENT PRODUCTION WE WOULD WANT PARTICIPATION RATHER THAN OUTRIGHT SALES. BEFORE MAKING ANY DECISION ABOUT THIS OR EVEN AN OPTION WOULD LIKE TO KNOW WHAT YOUR VIEWS ARE ABOUT THE TRANSACTION. YOU KNOW HOW MUCH I WOULD LIKE TO HAVE YOU DO THIS AND GUILD FEELS SAME WAY. THANKS FOR THE BOOST YOU GAVE TO THE ICE MAN COMETH. PLEASE COMMUNICATE WITH ME DIRECTLY. THE BARCLAY 111 EAST 48 STREET NEW YORK. AS EVER ALL GOOD WISHES =

= EUGENE O'NEILL

12. WIRE 1 p.

NEW YORK NY
APR 12 1946

DUDLEY NICHOLS = RKO STUDIOS =

DEAR DUDLEY DO NOT WORRY ABOUT YOUR NOT PRODUCING PICTURE LANGNER[29] AGREES YOU SHOULD HAVE FULL AUTHORITY AND ANY SALE MADE WOULD STIPULATE THAT STOP I WOULD NOT ALLOW ELECTRA TO BE PRODUCED UNLESS, AS YOU SAY, ANY STUPID OR INCOMPETENT INTERFERENCE WAS PRECLUDED STOP ALL BEST =

GENE.

13. TLS 1 p.

[New York, N.Y.]
22 August 1946.

Dear Dudley:

About the shanty records,[30] Carlotta has just finished telephoning to the Gramophone Shop, and has found out about a place where records can be re-pressed with small harm to the originals — or with luck, with no harm at all. So we will see about doing this and let you know. I hate to trust some one from RKO's New York office with these records, which are now so terribly hard to get.

As far as his picture goes, Glenn Ford looks all right, but I can't tell much from that. I take your word that he has all the stuff to do Orin.[31]

Also I hope we'll get Mason[32] for either Brandt or the General.

Certainly I would be willing to let you compete with any bids that might be offered in the future for film leases, with your proposed independent set-up. No, there will never be any question of my wanting my own productions. You overestimate my wealth, and I never invest money in the theater. This explains why I have some money rather than none at all. You don't want to see me out in front of St. Patrick's with my dark glasses and my little fox terrier and my large tin cup, do you? Or do you think that would make a good picture?

I remember your telling me over the phone some time ago that there might be humorous touches connected with Katina's[33] pictures. These went down great with me, but were taken seriously by another member of the family, so I am in the doghouse, and so are you, and so is Mrs. M.

All good wishes. I am still speaking to you.

Gene

14. WIRE 1 p.

NEW YORK NY
1947 APR 4

DUDLEY NICHOLS
= 504 SOUTH PLYMOUTH BLVD
LOS A =
MANY THANKS FOR SENDING ME THE PHOTOGRAPH THINK COSTUMES ARE GRAND AND THE MEMBERS OF THE CAST LOOK EXACTLY RIGHT AFFECTIONATE BEST TO YOU AND ESTA[34] =

= GENE =

15. WIRE 1 p.

NEW YORK NY
1947 JUN 12

DUDLEY NICHOLS =
504 SOUTH PLYMOUTH BLVD =
FROM ALL THE SERIES OF PICTURES YOU HAVE SENT I BEGIN NOW TO HAVE A FEELING OF THE PICTURE AS A WHOLE AND ITS KINSHIP IN MOOD AND INNER QUALITY WITH THE PLAY. BEST EXAMPLE OF THIS IS THE WAY MISS RUSSELL[35] CONTINUES TO GROW AND GROW AS LAVANIA. REDGRAVE IS IDEAL ORIN. EVERYTHING LOOKS FINE TO ME ABOVE ALL I OWE YOU A DEBT OF GRATITUDE FOR THE WAY YOU HAVE KEPT THE SPIRIT OF THE PLAY ALWAYS IN THE FILM AND I APPRECIATE THE TERRIBLE STRAIN OF WORK AGAINST CONSTANTLY UNFORESEEN OBSTACLES BUT THE RESULT WILL BE THE BEST FILM EVER TO COME OUT OF HOLLYWOOD I KNOW. CARLOTTA JOINS ME IN ALL BEST YOU AND ESTA =

GENE.

16. TLS 1 p.

Penthouse
35 East 84th Street
New York — 28 — New York
August 27th 1947

Dear Dudley:

Thank you for your letter of August 25th.

In regard to the Preliminary Billing Sheet 7-21-47 I want you to know that I approve of eliminating cards 5 and 6 and of putting my name on a separate card before the card that bears the title of the play.

Again, let me tell you how immensely gratified I am by the magnificent job you have done in bringing "Electra" to life on the screen.

As ever,
Gene
(Eugene O'Neill)

17. TLS 1 p.

Penthouse
35 East 84th Street
New York 28
[May 5, 1947][36]
Monday

Dear Dudley:

I have just finished looking over the photographs that arrived this morning. There were three envelopes. Those of Hazel and Peter are fine. Above all, the ones of Katina seem greatly improved from those you sent before. There is so much more of New England simplicity in her dress and head dress. And so much less of the Clytemnestra (if you know what I mean). Genn gets over an excellent, true to the line quality in all the photographs. Miss Russell strikes me as infinitely more Lavinia in looks than I had hoped for, — although I wish Hollywood make-up men would let mouths retain their character instead of following a pattern used for everybody. The town's-folk are wonderful types, every one of them. I liked the scene where Ezra is laid out beneath his father's portrait. It is simple and dignified. In short, I agree with what you said in your letter that everything is going fine now.[37]

Please give my grateful thanks to all concerned.

Love to you and Esta —

As ever,
Gene

18. ALS 2 pp.

Point O'Rocks Lane
Marblehead Neck,
Massachusetts
Dec. 4th 1948

Dear Dudley:

Your letter of Nov. 26*th* arrived here two days ago. This is our home — our last since we can never afford to have another, or stand the strain of another moving — the terrible sheer physical strain of it. It is a grand *little* place perched on a point of rocks with the old Western Ocean beating on those rocks right below my study window as I write you. There is peace here for me, and for Carlotta, too — after all the five years of cities, apartments, hotels — fifty years in jail they seem, as I look back on them. The interior of our rebuilt home is as charming as only Carlotta can make one. And now at last, with everything to the last book in place (or nearly so) we can sit back and rest a while, and I can hope to start writing plays again.

This letter is not a fair sample of my handwriting. It is too good, (aided by medicine), but I *can* write again fairly legibly without aid for more than a few lines — a thing I haven't been able to do for years. The damned tremor, as a whole, is worse all over — legs are bad, etc. but I seem to have regained some control over my hands. You can't know how much that means to me! But I better knock wood! The damned thing has nothing predictable. One good thing is, there is a lot of research into tremors going on in Boston now. They are waking up to the fact that there may be a lot of tremors contained in the old word Parkinson — or that is what I get from their talk.

The above was written yesterday p.m. Now it's the following morning and I am writing without any more sedative to steady my hand. Not so bad, what? But it's slow work with a lot of concentration required.

The things you say about Hollywood decay are equally true in the "legit", from the little I hear. There is nothing one can do about it. It is simply one symptom of a world-wide passing into an existence without culture — the world of mob-destiny. Kismet! And to hell with it!

I haven't seen the cut version of "M.B.E." and never will. And I ducked seeing the beautiful musical mess derived from "Ah, Wilderness".[38] I hear and hope it is a financial flop of the worst sort.

We are so sorry to learn of Esta's "allergy", but it's fine news to know she is well now. Judging from Carlotta's experience, "allergy" is just the name for another quack's racket. Your father sure said the last word on how best to conserve one's health!

I hope you are able to make the film you speak of all on your own without any interference whatever.

Last but not least, I want to tell you how much your *poem* moved me. Congratulations! It is fine work!

My hand is petering out on control, so I'll put a stop on this strain on your eyesight. Love from us to you both. Carlotta will write Esta soon. At present she is in bed recovering from a terrific cold. Yes, *cold*! Not virus Z, nor one, or two, or three, or four, or five-day Flu, or any of the pet names the Docs cook up to make things sound dangerous and mysterious and worth ten bucks now per visit. I confidently predict that in a few years some eminent research shark is going to discover, with the aid of a ten ton mycroscope, a new and violent virus with fourteen legs and four balls causing a totally new disease called "Pain-In-The-Arse Piles". Merciful Allah, will all us suckers go for that one! We will all be telling each other: "Now I know what has ruined my life!"

(I better exit on that)

As ever
Gene

19. TLS 1 p.

Point O'Rocks Lane
Marblehead Neck,
Massachusetts
March 20th 1949

Dear Dudley:

I am dictating this to Carlotta because I feel you should know the truth of my physical condition. After writing you my cheery letter I got worse and have continued to be so. Some well meaning gentleman in New York put a report in his column that I had conquered my tremor and was at work on a new play. This has caused us no end of trouble. Poor sufferers of Parkinson's saw this, believed it, and wrote to me. Their letters are very sad and very bad for my morale and Carlotta's. As she has the job of answering them. Some of the letters came from England!

Well – I am not better – I am worse. No play is being written – and no play will be produced.

Love to you and Esta –

As ever,
Gene

Notes

1. Arthur and Barbara Gelb, *O'Neill* (New York: Harper, 1962), pp. 658–60; Louis Sheaffer, *O'Neill: Son and Artist* (Boston: Little, Brown, 1973), pp. 285–88. See also Alexander Woollcott, "Giving O'Neill Till It Hurts – Being Some Highly Unofficial Program Notes for the Most Punishing of His Plays," *Vanity Fair*, 29 (February 1928), 48, 114; Dudley Nichols, "The New Play," *New York World*, January 31, 1928, pp. 11, 12; Alexander Woollcott, "Second Thoughts on First Nights," *New York World*, February 5, 1928, Metropolitan Section, p. 3M.

2. O'Neill's four plays are "Bound East for Cardiff," "The Long Voyage Home," "In the Zone," and "The Moon of the Caribbees."

3. For permission to publish O'Neill's letters to Nichols and to quote from Nichols' memoir, I wish to thank David Schoonover and Ralph Franklin of the Beinecke Rare Book and Manuscript Library, Yale University, and Edward Tripp and John Ryden of the Yale University Press.

4. Vladimir Nemirovich-Danchenko was a Russian director and co-founder with Stanislavski of the Moscow Art Theatre.

5. Vassily Kachalov was a leading actor of the Moscow Art Theatre.

6. In 1933, Nichols was one of the founders of the Screen Writers Guild that, along with the Screen Actors Guild, came into being because of the 50 per cent pay cut that was forced on film employees by producers who refused to reduce their own salaries. As these two Guilds grew in membership, the size of the Academy of Motion Picture Arts and Sciences decreased due to wholesale resignations; and the producers tried desperately to keep the academy alive. When Nichols was announced as an Oscar nominee, he declared "that he would consider the choice of a handful of writers no honor at all" and should he win, he would renounce the award, which he did. See "Stormy Advices From Hollywood," *New York Times*, December 29, 1935, Sec. 9, p. 5; "Nichols Declines Award," *New York Times*, March 10, 1936, p. 26.

7. Sheaffer, pp. 504–05.

8. Gelb, p. 831.

9. Sheaffer, p. 505.

10. Sheaffer, p. 517.

11. Gelb, pp. 831–32.

12. For information about this play, see Sheaffer, pp. 523, 535–36; in his memoir, Nichols mistakenly refers to the second title of the play as "The Last Dictator."

13. *Days Without End.*

14. "Testament for Tomorrow." See Virginia Floyd, ed. *Eugene O'Neill at Work: Newly Released Ideas for Plays* (New York: Frederick Ungar, 1981), pp. 234–35.

15. A road company of *Mourning Becomes Electra*, with Judith Anderson as Lavinia, Florence Reed as Christine, and Walter Abel as Orin, in the roles played in the original production by Alice Brady, Alla Nazimova, and Earl Larrimore, respectively; after its tour, the play reopened on Broadway on May 9, 1932, but lasted for only 16 performances (the original production had played 150 performances).

16. Nichols had recently purchased a home in New Milford, Connecticut.

17. Thomas Mitchell who played Driscoll in the film; Barry Fitzgerald who played Cocky; and J. M. Kerrigan who played Limehouse Crimp.

18. A vision seen by solders during the night after the First Battle of the Marne (September 5–9, 1914). Called the Angel of Mons, she was described as a figure wearing the dress of the Virgin, carrying God's flaming sword, and riding a big white horse; and supposedly rode down from Heaven, faced the retreated German armies, and prevented them from readvancing.

19. John Ford, whose real name was Sean Alysius O'Feeney, but whose family name in Ireland had been O'Fearna, which Ford's parents had changed when they emigrated to America before Ford was born.

20. "House in the Sky." See Letter #8.

21. "A Tale of Possessors Self-Dispossessed," which O'Neill originally envisioned as five plays but which grew to seven, eight, nine, and, finally, to eleven. Only the first two, *A Touch of the Poet* and *More Stately Mansions*, have been published and performed professionally.

22. See Letter #10.

23. Former head publicity man of the Theatre Guild and now a movie executive; he was one of the O'Neill's most trusted friends.

24. Nichols had done the screenplay for the movie version of *For Whom the Bell Tolls.*

25. Nichols wrote the screenplays for two films directed by Jean Renoir, *Swamp Water* (1941) and *This Land is Mine* (1943). He was also co-producer of the latter.

26. Head publicity man of the Theatre Guild and co-author, with Howard Lindsay, of *Life With Father* (1939) and several other plays and musicals.

27. *The Hairy Ape* did not become a movie until 1944 when United Artists produced it with William Bendix as Yank.

28. Herbert Freeman, who was the O'Neills' chauffeur and utility man for more than ten years.

29. Lawrence Langner, one of the managing directors of the Theatre Guild.

30. O'Neill had apparently offered to provide Nichols with some samples of the music he felt would be appropriate for the film version of *Mourning Becomes Electra*.

31. Michael Redgrave played Orin in the film.

32. Probably James Mason who was not in the film; Leo Genn played Adam Brant and Raymond Massey played "the General," Ezra Mannon.

33. Katina Paxinou, who played Christine in the film; see Sheaffer, pp. 571–72, 590–91.

34. Mrs. Dudley Nichols.

35. Rosalind Russell, who played Lavinia in the film.

36. The letter is postmarked May 5, 1947, and in 1947, May 5th was a Monday. [It has been inadvertently placed out of sequence — Ed. Note.]

37. *Mourning Becomes Electra* was not nearly the critical success *The Long Voyage Home* had been. Most reviewers expressed deep respect for O'Neill's play and for Nichols' faithful adherence to it; but many felt that in that fidelity lay some of the film's weaknesses. Bosley Crowther in the *New York Times* (November 20, 1947, p. 38) found it "a static and tiresome show" and "a millstone upon the screen." Philip T. Hartung of *The Commonweal* (November 28, 1947, p. 175) praised the acting but saw the production as "uncinematic" and "static and talky." John McCarten, writing for the *New Yorker* (November 22, 1947, pp. 119–20), echoed both Crowther and Hartung in faulting the movie for being "a literal photographic reproduction of the stage play."

38. "Summer Holiday," a film musical version of *Ah, Wilderness!*, starring Walter Huston, which had opened in 1948. The "cut version of 'M. B. E.' " may refer to a shortened version of the film, cut by RKO from almost three hours to about ninety minutes in response to critics' complaints about its length.

The Long Voyage Home: Illusion and the Tragic Pattern of Fate in O'Neill's S.S. *Glencairn* Cycle

Steven E. Colburn

Though there are no direct links provided between the four plays commonly grouped together as the S.S. *Glencairn* cycle, many readers have commented upon the strong, underlying unity of these plays.[1] The few details that they share consist primarily of the character-names that reappear in the plays[2] (though the characters attached to them are not necessarily the same from one play to another), and the setting of the ship itself (though only two of the plays actually take place on the *Glencairn*, and, of these two, one is set in the forecastle, while the other takes place on the deck). Thus, in terms of character and setting, one finds surprisingly little continuity between the plays. Nor is there any direct continuity in exposition of plot-details, for the plays do not share a common background of antecedent action. Yet still the impression of unity exists, so that one must move to a deeper level of the texts, to their underlying thematic and symbolic structure, in order to explain the persistence of this impression. As a group, the *Glencairn* plays are unified by their variation upon a single theme, human illusion, and a common structural pattern, the tragic design, which communicate with the audience at a level of the text where similarities and differences of surface detail become unimportant.

On the thematic level, the plays are unified by the theme of illusion, which is represented by the central conflict between the forces of illusion and actuality in each play. At the center of this conflict is a protagonist who struggles during the course of the play to maintain the illusion he harbors.

In two of the plays, *Bound East for Cardiff* and *The Long Voyage Home*, the protagonist's fellow seamen assist him in sustaining his illusion, while in the other two, *The Moon of the Caribees* and *In the Zone*, they work actively to destroy it.

It is in this movement of O'Neill's protagonist from illusion to truth that the structural unity of the *Glencairn* plays is revealed, for the fortunes of these illusion-ridden heroes describe a recurrent pattern of circumstances and events. The subject of these plays, like all tragedy, is the unsuccessful struggle of Man against the tragic mechanism of his fate. Yet the fate O'Neill's characters struggle against is no longer that of magical or supernatural forces, or the moral dictates of an omniscient God (as in traditional tragedies), but that of the material forces of a naturalistically-conceived world: the powerful psychological forces within their own personalities, the social milieu in which they have formed their characters, and the physical laws of the universe in which they live.

In *The Moon of the Caribbees*, we see a very characteristic treatment of the theme of illusion by O'Neill. As Edwin A. Engel has pointed out in his study of the recurrent character-types in O'Neill's work, the characters we see in this play reappear again and again in the plays which follow:

> There is a resemblance between the seamen's forecastle of the S.S. *Glencairn* and the interior of Harry Hope's saloon, an affinity between the homeless sailors of the early sea plays and the human derelicts of *The Iceman Cometh*, an identity between the implied philosophy of the first and the expressed philosophy of the last play. . . . Men of diverse nationalities, both the seafarers and the bums are held together not by bonds of brotherhood but by an animal-like gregariousness. They are, on the whole, doltish, quarrelsome, even treacherous. Their sensibilities, already dull, are further blunted by liquor. Their antics, like the ape's, provoke laughter rather than pity. A member of the group but contrasted with his fellows, both in the *Glencairn* pieces and in *The Iceman Cometh*, is the man of feeling, a pensive figure with an acute consciousness, lonely and life-weary.[3]

This description is particularly useful in pointing out the underlying thematic unity of the *Glencairn* plays, and in *The Moon of the Caribbees* we see how O'Neill has used this configuration of opposed forces, represented by groups of characters in the play, to focus the reader's attention upon the sufferings of one such pensive man, Smitty, whose laments for his lost love bring him into conflict with the social group of which he is a part.

The tropical island off which the ship lies anchored is a magical place of transformation, where the liberating influences of moonlight, music, women, and rum combine to release the social inhibitions of the crewmen, turning their dull, monotonous lives for a time into a joyous, Bacchic celebration. Yet into this licentious atmosphere of Dionysian revel intrudes the melancholy, suffering figure of Smitty, a modern-day Pentheus, whose sobering presence gradually destroys the spell the island has cast over the crew, and reveals to the men the illusory nature of their moon-madness. Their celebration, like that of the Bacchae, turns to an unrestrained frenzy of physical violence, and is revealed, once the spell is dissipated, as a nightmarish unleashing of the powerful aggressive, anti-social impulses which lie hidden in the deepest recesses of human nature.

The thematic correspondence of *The Moon of the Caribbees* with the *Bacchae* is not so surprising when one considers the fact that O'Neill was an early admirer of the radical philosophy of Friedrich Nietzsche. In *The Birth of Tragedy*, for example, Nietzsche outlines his materialistic conception of the birth of the tragic form in literature — which is, in essence, that tragedy is born out of the need to dramatize or express the fundamental human conflict between the irrational, impulsive claims of the individual in his struggle toward freedom from restraint, and the rational, regulative claims of society which require the suppression of these drives.[4] Nietzsche finds the clearest dramatic expression of tragedy's origin in Euripides' *Bacchae*, where he names the two competing forces (the Apollinian and Dionysian) after the gods around which the opposed forces are marshalled in the play.

Though Nietzsche may well have been the source of O'Neill's conception of the tragic view of life, he is by no means without company in propounding a materialistic view of the relation of the individual to his society. One finds similar ideas in the philosophy of Nietzsche's contemporaries, Karl Marx and Frederick Engels, who focused on the economic (rather than the social) relations between the individual and his society in such works as the *Communist Manifesto*.[5] Nor has materialistic philosophy died out in our own century, where one finds echoes of these ideas in works such as *Civilization and Its Discontents*, where Sigmund Freud, emphasizing the psychological relation of the individual to the state, focuses on the "primary mutual hostility" between human beings and civilized society which perpetually threatens it with disintegration,[6] as well as in the works of social philosophers such as Erich Fromm — who, in *Escape From Freedom*, portrays the development of nationalism as the historical working-out of this fundamental conflict between society and the individual.[7]

The Nietzschean cast of O'Neill's tragic philosophy is clearly expressed in the subject-matter of the *Glencairn* plays, as Frederick I. Carpenter's comments upon the contributions of these early plays to O'Neill's later development make clear:

> Dream, Drunkenness and Death have been described as the subject matter of O'Neill's dramaturgy, and as the key to all his plays. Drunkenness was the theme of *The Moon*; Dream and Death are central in *Bound East for Cardiff*, the first and perhaps the best of the early plays. And these themes were repeated again in *Long Day's Journey Into Night*, the last and the best. Is O'Neill's spirit and life-attitude morbid, pessimistic, and depressing, in these plays — as has often been argued? The question is cru-

cial. . . . in O'Neill's best plays, it is the unconscious evil and the weakness of human nature that cause tragedy.[8]

In *The Moon of the Caribbees*, as we have said, the theme of illusion centers around the magical transformation of the crew of the *Glencairn* into Bacchic revellers, who celebrate the temporary suspension of the behavioral restraints their disciplined life imposes upon them. Opposed to this large, spectacular action is the smaller drama of Smitty, whose melancholy over a lost love prevents him from joining in the revelry, and eventually leads to the breaking of the spell the island has cast over the men. The thematic structure of the play is built up from an alternating movement of episodes which juxtapose, in parallel series, segments of these two actions. As Chester Long has pointed out in his careful study of the structure of the play, the two actions are closely interrelated:

> Smitty's continual isolation and helpless melancholy seems to stem from his inability to relate to others — some internal flaw in him, some flaw in his will; yet the mood depends on the contrast of Smitty's maudlin isolation, the crew's pointless activity, and the women's ruined savage innocence, as all three factors are significant when considered in the light of the omnipresent moon, sea, and land. The ultimate punishment of these creatures seems to be their contributing to their own insignificance, frustration, and deprivation by their fruitless interest in money (Bella and the girls), escape pleasures (the crew), and solipsism (Smitty). . . . Smitty does not see that the reason he is isolated first from the woman he is remembering, then from the crew, and finally from the woman Pearl exists in his selfish bids for sympathy, which he characteristically follows by blunt, sudden, tactless, cruel, and senseless rejection of the familiarity he establishes through his maudlin appeals.[9]

The interrelation of parallel actions in the play is also reinforced on the symbolic level, where the character of the Donkeyman, Old Tom, provides a link between the two actions. In fact, the Donkeyman — whose name suggests a Bottom-like figure (a man with the head of an ass) — is the only person in the play able to understand and communicate with the introspective Smitty, and the dialogue between them serves to counterpoint the celebrations of the other crewmen in the background. Though the Donkeyman seems able to understand and sympathize with the melancholy Smitty, he also carries the external signs of his allegiance to the revellers, for his name suggests his allegiance to the unreflective beastiality of the others. In this play, the Donkeyman serves as mediator between two forces which are irreconcilable; the beautiful spell the island has cast over the men will be broken in the end, and the celebration will culminate in an outbreak of violence, just as Smitty's nostalgic self-pity will be revealed as an illusion. At the end of the play, the claims of the individual and the group reappear untransformed and unreconciled, and the sum of human experience is revealed to be the tragic history of an illusion whose future, as Freud predicted, is long and painful, yet fortunately not infinite.[10]

In *Bound East for Cardiff*, O'Neill shows us the persistence of human illusion in the face of a cruel, yet uncaring, natural world. If the environment of the sailors is subject to the magical, transforming powers of nature, as we have seen in *The Moon of the Caribbees*, it is equally subject to its randomness. In *Bound East for Cardiff*, we see the ironic consequences of one character's illusions in the face of a naturalistically-conceived universe. Though the play has a conventional interior setting, with all the action taking place within the forecastle of the ship, O'Neill still manages to make the reader intensely aware of the powerful forces that control the larger, natural drama taking place offstage. In fact, the structure of this play is organized around two concurrent actions: the difficult transatlantic passage of the *Glencairn* through the stormy, fog-bound seas, and the slow, agonizing death of the injured sailor. As in *The Moon of the Caribbees*, the focus of attention alternates between these two actions as the characters come and go from the stage. At the center of both actions is the dying sailor, Yank, whose dialogue with Driscoll, the friend that tries to comfort him, forms the foreground of the action in the play, which is intercut by scenes in which other characters enter and report on the progress of the voyage (which forms the offstage, background action of the play). Just as they do in *The Moon of the Caribbees*, the two parallel actions assume an ironic counterpoint at the end of the play, when the fog outside lifts at the moment of Yank's death. The force of this ironic ending is increased by the fact that the fog serves as a central, unifying symbol throughout the play, and has accrued a number of symbolic values.[11] In this play, the conception of the teleological justice of the retributive fate of the gods seems to have been replaced by the cosmic irony of the amoral operation of natural laws in the universe. After all, Yank's injury is the result of an accidental fall into the hold during a routine errand — not the supernatural intervention of a vengeful god. The voyage of the ship, headed blindly through the fog toward Cardiff, is a drama that is described but never enacted on the stage. It takes place primarily in the imagination, and perhaps because of this, it is easy to understand the voyage of the *Glencairn* as a symbolic projection of the fate of the individual in a naturalistic universe. In this sense, the lifting of the fog at the end of the play is a bitterly ironic comment upon the helplessness of the individual in such a universe.

Perhaps it is important to realize that *Bound East for Cardiff* was the first of the *Glencairn* plays to be written, and as such contains elements one would expect to find repeated in the other plays of the cycle if one is to argue for their unity as a group. F. I. Carpenter, in his brief study of the cycle, provides three pieces of evidence in support of this position:

> Second of the *Glencairn* plays, but first to be written, and the first of all to be produced, is *Bound East for Cardiff*. Later, O'Neill commented on it to a critic: "Very important from my point of view. In it can be seen, or felt, the germ of the spirit, life-attitude, etc., of all my more important future work." This play resembles *The Moon* in that its action is unimpor-

tant. But it introduces what are to be the central themes and symbols of all
the later plays: death, religion, and the eternal "fog" which blinds men in
their quest for truth.[12]

Though this judgment is sound in an overall sense, and is persuasive in
showing the importance of *Bound East for Cardiff* to the other plays of the
Glencairn cycle as well as to O'Neill's later plays, it contains a single flaw
which threatens the credibility of the entire argument: "This play resembles
The Moon in that its action is unimportant." This statement is patently un-
true, for, as I have attempted to show in my discussion of the play, *Bound
East for Cardiff* is a play that is profoundly concerned in a thematic sense
with the role of accident in human life, and, as such, the particular set of
circumstances that drive the action are of great importance in the ironically
counterpointed structure of the play. In the profoundly materialistic drama
of O'Neill, the role of accident, as well as that of instinct, plays an important part in the depiction of human fortune.

Throughout his career, O'Neill seems to have been fascinated by the
behavior of men in groups, as his early dramatizations of the group dynamics of the crew of the *Glencairn* — together with those of the treasure-
hunters in *Where the Cross Is Made*, the superstitious natives in *The
Emperor Jones*, the Wobblies in *The Hairy Ape*, and the derelicts of Harry
Hope's saloon in *The Iceman Cometh* — clearly suggest. Yet though O'Neill
repeatedly explores the processes by which groups form, operate, and disin-
tegrate, his interest lies not only in the actions of the group as such, but also
in their effect upon the individual consciousness. This double focus of attention is reflected in the structure of *In the Zone*, where the opposition of the
claims of the group, represented by the seamen of the S.S. *Glencairn*, with
the personal claims of the protagonist, Smitty, bring about the tragic sequence of events in the play.

With *In the Zone*, O'Neill turns to the subject of group aggression in an
even more explicit fashion than its treatment in *The Moon of the Caribbees*.
As in other plays of the cycle, there is a dual purpose represented in the
structure of the play: to demonstrate the tragic pattern of fate that controls
human experience in an uncaring, naturalistic universe, and to trace the
destructive consequences of personal illusions that interfere with the participation of individuals in the society to which they "belong." The two parallel
actions of *In the Zone* are expressed in the counterpoint of the larger war
background of the play, and its effects on the behavior of the crewmen, with
the personal tragedy of Smitty's lost love, which separates him from the concerns of the crew. As in *The Moon of the Caribbees*, the conflict between the
interests of the group and those of the protagonist is precipitated by a sudden change in external conditions. As the ammunition-laden *Glencairn*
passes into the war zone, the anxieties of the crew surface in their increasing
suspicion of Smitty's introspective, secretive behavior, which they gradually
come to see as anti-social and snobbish. Eventually, their suspicion leads
them to action, and they reveal by force the secret love-sorrow of this "dan-

gerous" ou⁺sider — whom they have made, in their imaginations, into a German spy.

In dramatizing the process by which the outsider, Smitty, is turned into a scapegoat or ideal object of release for the war-induced anxieties of the crew, O'Neill has anticipated much of the recent speculation about the fundamental processes of human aggression. In Konrad Lorenz' study of the biological bases of human aggression, *On Aggression*, for example, Lorenz' description of the conditions which lead to the release of the aggressive impulse are remarkably similar to the sequence of events dramatizing the conflict between Smitty and the crew of the *Glencairn* in *In the Zone*:

> The first prerequisite for rational control of an instinctive behavior pattern is the knowledge of the stimulus situation which releases it. Militant enthusiasm can be elicited with the predictability of a reflex when the following environmental situations arise. First of all, a social unit with which the subject identifies himself must appear to be threatened by some danger from outside.
>
> A second key stimulus which contributes enormously to the releasing of militant enthusiasm is the presence of a hated enemy from whom the threat to the above "values" emanates. This enemy, too, can be of a concrete or of an abstract nature.
>
> A third factor contributing to the environmental situation eliciting the response is an inspiring leader figure.
>
> A fourth, and perhaps the most important, prerequisite for the full eliciting of militant enthusiasm is the presence of many other individuals, all agitated by the same emotion.[13]

In the feeling of camaraderie, trust and cooperation that unifies the inhabitants of the forecastle, the commonly-held fear of German aggression in the war zone, the instigation and leadership of Driscoll, and the restricted size of the men's environment, one finds the ideal conditions for the outbreak of aggression against Smitty that is dramatized in the play.

Though the end of the play brings the shattering of the nostalgic illusions of Smitty, the protagonist in the conflict, the closing image of the play reveals the inescapable presence of the forces which have controlled the behavior of the crewmen from the beginning — and which, no doubt, will continue to shape the course of human conflicts in the future:

> DRISCOLL — [*Stalks back to the others — there is a moment of silence, in which each man is in agony with the hopelessness of finding a word he can say — then* DRISCOLL *explodes:*] God stiffen us, are we never goin' to turn in fur a wink av sleep? [*They all start as if awakening from a bad dream and gratefully crawl into their bunks, shoes and all, turning their faces to the wall, and pulling their blankets up over their shoulders.*
>
> (*LVH* p. 114)

In the final play of the cycle, *The Long Voyage Home*, O'Neill explores the tragic operation of fate upon the ambitious desires of the individual will. Olson, the simple protagonist of this play, is much like Yank, the protagonist of *The Hairy Ape*, for which he may have served as a model. At the center of each play is a protagonist who struggles to maintain the illusory ideal of freedom and escape that he harbors. The plays are also similar in plot structure, as both focus on the operation of fate in foiling the attempt of the hero to break away from the life to which he is adapted. Unlike the wartime atmosphere of *In the Zone*, where the hostile actions of the group form a counterpoint to the fortune of the hero, the subject of *The Long Voyage Home* is not *intragroup* aggression, but *intergroup* aggression — the preying of members of one group upon those of another — and, unlike the action of *In the Zone*, the sailors here are not aggressors, but victims. The operation of fate upon the individual in *The Long Voyage Home* is represented by the attempt of one of the seamen of the *Glencairn*, Olson, to escape the repetitive cycle of economic enslavement to which the sailors are subject. Unlike his counterpart, the Yank of *The Hairy Ape*, his goal is simply escape, not reform. Yet even this simple project is foiled, as is Yank's, by the opportunistic basis of the social milieu in which he must work and live. This play reminds one of nothing more than the tragedies of character and environment one finds in the works of naturalists such as Stephen Crane, Frank Norris, Jack London, Theodore Dreiser, and Robinson Jeffers — a literary tradition to which the *Glencairn* cycle is clearly indebted. *The Long Voyage Home* is, to use a well-known example, O'Neill's *Maggie*, for in this play, more than in any of his others (with the possible exceptions of *The Hairy Ape* and *All God's Chillun Got Wings*), O'Neill uses the destruction of the illusion-ridden hero and the tragic operation of fate in human life to demonstrate the tremendous power of the forces of character and environment upon the career of the individual. In *The Long Voyage Home*, we see the ironic outcome of these forces upon Olson, who attempts to break out of the destructive patterns of social interaction which keep him in economic enslavement to the owners of the ships he works on.

Yet if *The Long Voyage Home* were simply a naturalistic tragedy, O'Neill would not be so great a writer, for in addition to this familiar thematic structure, he has provided us with a symbolic stratum in the play which invites us to compare *The Long Voyage Home* with Homer's *Odyssey*, and to see the play as a modern reworking of the archetypal voyage of the mythic culture-hero. Like the account of Odysseus' *nostoi* (returns) given by Homer in the *Odyssey*, Olson's voyage aboard the *Glencairn* is an asymptotic approach toward his goal. Like the frustrated hero of the *Odyssey*, when the action opens Olson has been away from home for ten years,[14] and the action of the play dramatizes his retrogressive movement between Stockholm and "Bewnezerry." And like Odysseus (who voyages from Troy to Ithaca), Olson is on the final leg of his return home when he puts ashore in London (as is Odysseus when he puts ashore at Circe's island), where his encounter with the impressment gang of "a low dive on the London water front" leads to his being shanghaied into yet another voyage.

When John Ford adapted the S.S. *Glencairn* plays for the screen in 1941, the plays were treated as interrelated episodes of a single story, which was called *The Long Voyage Home*. This was the first public presentation to explicitly emphasize the cycle's thematic unity. In this practice, Ford departed both from the arrangement of the plays by the publisher, who presented them to the reader under a general subject-heading as *The Moon of the Caribbees and Six Other Plays of the Sea* (Boni and Liveright, 1919) along with three esentially unrelated plays, as well as from the practice in theatrical productions (their first production as a group was at Provincetown in November, 1924), where the plays were billed according to their common setting under the title *S.S. Glencairn*. In rethinking the overall structural organization of the cycle and the thematic interrelationships between the plays, Ford went against both these traditions, and reversed the positions of the third and fourth plays, placing *In the Zone* before *The Long Voyage Home*, putting the latter play into the terminal position of emphasis for the first time. This reordering of the latter half of the cycle was, I think, a fortuitous action, given the nature of Ford's project. Considering the topicality of the wartime setting of *In the Zone* in 1941, when the United States was once again at war with Germany, as well as its traditional position as the terminal episode, one might well have expected him to put it last. That he did not choose to do so is to his credit as an interpreter of the plays, for by placing *The Long Voyage Home* last he deliberately prevented such a topical response to the cycle — forcing the audience to see *In the Zone* in its proper thematic relation to the other plays of the cycle, and allowing the psychological emphasis to fall on *The Long Voyage Home*, which presents the central themes and unifying symbols of the *Glencairn* cycle in the most archetypal and schematic form.[15]

Though there are no direct links provided among the four plays commonly grouped together as the S.S. *Glencairn* cycle, many readers have commented upon the strong, underlying unity of these plays. As we have seen, this diffuse impression is built upon the deep, underlying unity of theme and symbolic structure that is displayed in the cycle, and points to the major concerns of O'Neill's later work. In *The Moon of the Caribbees*, O'Neill dramatizes the tragic mechanism of fate, and the fortune of the illusion-ridden hero, by exploring the alienation of the individual from his proper position in the society to which he "belongs," and the mysterious welling-up of the irrational, Dionysian forces to which human nature is subject. In *Bound East for Cardiff*, he contrasts the hard life of the sailor with the idealistic aspirations of the dying hero to show us the ironic persistence of human illusion in the face of a cruel, yet uncaring natural world. With *In the Zone*, O'Neill dramatizes the tragic fate of the outsider in his confrontation with the behavioral mechanisms of group aggression brought on by the war hysteria of WWI. In *The Long Voyage Home*, O'Neill uses the failure of the hero, in a modern, ironic reworking of the Odysseus myth, to express most clearly his naturalistic view of human life, in which the forces of character and environment triumph over the idealistic, rebellious will of the individual.

Notes

1. Important studies of the plays include: Edwin A. Engel, *The Haunted Heroes of Eugene O'Neill* (Cambridge: Harvard Univ. Press, 1953), pp. 10–15; Doris V. Falk, *Eugene O'Neill and the Tragic Tension* (New Brunswick, N.J.: Rutgers Univ. Press, 1958), pp. 20–22; Clifford Leech, *Eugene O'Neill* (New York: Grove Press, 1963), pp. 9–16; D.V.K. Raghavacharyulu, *Eugene O'Neill* (Bombay: Popular Prakashan, 1965), pp. 21–22; Barrett H. Clark, *Eugene O'Neill* (New York: Dover, 1967), pp. 56–65; Chester Clayton Long, *The Role of Nemesis in the Structure of Selected Plays of Eugene O'Neill* (The Hague: Mouton, 1968), pp. 59–74; Timo Tiusanen, *O'Neill's Scenic Images* (Princeton: Princeton Univ. Press, 1968), pp. 43–56; Travis Bogard, *Contour in Time* (New York: Oxford Univ. Press, 1972), pp. 80–91; and Frederick I. Carpenter, *Eugene O'Neill*, rev. ed. (Boston: Twayne, 1979), pp. 80–84; in the absence of a standard text for the plays, I have followed the practice of many O'Neill critics in using *The Long Voyage Home: Seven Plays of the Sea* (New York: Modern Library, 1940) for the texts of *The Moon of the Caribbees, Bound East for Cardiff, In the Zone,* and *The Long Voyage Home*; all subsequent page references will be to this edition, and will be cited in the text.

2. Only three names — Driscoll, Cocky, and Ivan — appear in all four plays, while five names — Olson, Davis, Smitty, Paul, and Scotty — appear in three of the plays, and one name, Yank, appears in two.

3. Engel, p. 10.

4. Friedrich Nietzsche, *The Birth of Tragedy*, in *Basic Writings of Nietzsche*, ed. Walter Kaufmann (New York: Modern Library, 1968), pp. 1–144.

5. Karl Marx and Frederick Engels, *Manifesto of the Communist Party (Communist Manifesto*, 1848), in *Collected Works*, 6 (New York: International Publications, 1975), pp. 477–519.

6. Sigmund Freud, *Civilization and Its Discontents*, trans. James E. Strachey (New York: W. W. Norton, 1962).

7. Erich Fromm, *Escape From Freedom* (New York: Holt, Rinehart and Winston, 1941).

8. Carpenter, pp. 82–84.

9. Long, p. 63, 67.

10. Sigmund Freud, *The Future of an Illusion*, trans. James E. Strachey (New York: W. W. Norton, 1961).

11. This ironic parallel of onstage and offstage action, as well as the symbolic use of fog, are almost certainly borrowed wholesale from Henrik Ibsen's *Ghosts* (1881), which O'Neill is likely to have known in translation and perhaps may have seen produced in New York.

12. Carpenter, p. 82.

13. Konrad Lorenz, *On Aggression*, trans. Marjorie Kerr Wilson (New York: Harcourt, Brace and World, 1966), pp. 271–73; this view of the biological bases of human behavior finds confirmation in the work of social anthropologists such as Lionel Tiger, *Men in Groups* (New York: Random House, 1969), sociologists such as Eric Hoffer, *The True Believer* (New York: Harper and Bros., 1951), and social psychologists such as Sigmund Freud, *Civilization and Its Discontents*, trans. James E. Strachey (New York: W. W. Norton, 1962); for a useful collection of modern viewpoints on this subject, see: Philip Appleman, ed. *Darwin*, 2nd ed. (New York: W. W. Norton, 1979), pp. 387–471.

14. Mentioned on pp. 76–77.

15. For the facts in this passage, I have drawn upon the discussion of the film version of

the plays in Leech, p. 15, as well as my own viewing of the film; the argument advanced here is based on my own analysis of the plays, the film, and the relation between them, and differs considerably from that of Leech, who dismisses the film's interpretive value.

Romantic Elements
in Early O'Neill
Frank R. Cunningham

All his life Eugene O'Neill envisioned a theatre "returned to its highest function as a temple where the religion of a poetical . . . and symbolic cele-bration of life is communicated to human beings, starved in spirit by their soul-stifling daily struggle to exist as masks among the masks of living."[1] O'Neill succeeded, at least in his early plays, in creating such a theatre, one of Romantic affirmation rather than the tortured and pessimistic negation of life's values so often reflected in the later plays. In *Beyond the Horizon* (1918), *Anna Christie* (1920), *The Emperor Jones* (1920), *The Hairy Ape* (1921), *Desire Under the Elms* (1924), and in his dramatic adaptation of Coleridge's poem, *The Ancient Mariner* (1923–24), O'Neill worked out his themes and conflicts in terms of the great Romantic motifs and mythic pat-terns: dynamic organicism, the creative imagination as the basic process of Romantic affirmation of the organic universe, man's archetypal journey from stasis to the recognition of the existence of such a universe, the concept of timelessness or Edenic time, and the cyclical nature of existence.[2] O'Neill's early Romantic period was one of exploration into the meanings of mystical affirmation, and it resolved itself not in conclusions of stark natu-ralism but in a joyous acceptance of the very recurrence of life.

Significantly affirmative in theme and resolution, *Beyond the Horizon* transcends the naturalistic stereotype to which most critics have consigned it. Alan Downer said of the play, "O'Neill seems to visualize the process of living as a stream of consciousness in which the life line is always becoming fouled."[3] Yet, if indeed the spiritual lifelines of the Mayos are fouled, it is also true that Robert and Andrew, at some time during their development, share a desire to transcend actuality and go far off beyond their horizons for the realization of their dreams. In so doing they represent O'Neill's aware-ness of a possible solution to the problem of man's ever-snarled lifelines, as their search for value embodies a perspective of the mythic quest. Robert Mayo abandons his Romantic nature, choosing instead to stay on the farm, while his brother, Andrew, unfit for a nomadic existence, undertakes a sea voyage — a quest for which Robert is much better suited. At the end of the play, Andrew returns to the farm a broken man — he has perverted the true meaning of the mythic journey by becoming merely a money-grubbing speculator. He finds Robert, too, a failure: his wife, Ruth, having married the wrong brother, is prematurely aged, and Robert's dreams have all but vanished. But not quite: Robert finally realizes that he has betrayed his real

Romantic nature, and as he dies he climbs the hill near the farmhouse for a view of the rising sun. With his last breath, he welcomes his reabsorbtion into the universe, into the continuum of life:

> You mustn't feel sorry for me. Don't you see I'm happy at last — free — free — freed from the farm — free to wander on and on — eternally! Look! Isn't it beautiful beyond the hills? I can hear the old voices calling me to come — And this time I'm going! It isn't the end. It's a free beginning — the start of my voyage! I've won my trip — the right of release — beyond the horizon.[4]

Robert Mayo dies with his dreams restored, freed from the fetters of Ego to commune with the Other. Having accepted his previous mistake of denying his true nature, he has cast off that false identity and assumed an identity that is at one with the Everlasting Now.

O'Neill's great objective in *Beyond the Horizon* was to show man as capable of organic growth in a dynamic universe. In his next great realistic play, *Anna Christie*, he refined his vital, Romantic themes further. The young prostitute hopes to find regeneration as she returns to her father's coal barge docked in the harbor. But her revelation of her past threatens to separate her forever from her father and from Mat Burke, her lover. Finally, however, Burke returns, understanding at last that Anna's love for him is sincere, and the lovers plan to marry, realizing that tomorrow they will return "to that old Devil sea." O'Neill's resolution is a Romantic triumph as Anna, Chris, and Burke reestablish a symbolic connection with life by their return to the sea. F. I. Carpenter is correct in noting that "the three central characters are all children of the sea, and each grows to understand and to accept his destiny."[5] Anna rises above her meretricious past to an altruistic love. Burke transcends his Puritanical prejudices against "bad" women and establishes a connection to life through his love for Anna. And Chris learns the most important Romantic lesson: that man cannot shut out life. In sending Anna to Minnesota to grow up, he had hoped to shield her from the reality of sin in the world. He learns that all men must finally return symbolically to the sea, to objective reality, so that they can undertake their journey to self-knowledge and exploration of the non-self. Each character, then, not only becomes regenerated by the sea, but learns to accept his own past, so that he can truly belong again to the source of all life.

O'Neill's use of Romantic elements was not limited to the realistic plays. His great expressionistic dramas *The Emperor Jones* and *The Hairy Ape* also embody affirmative philosophical themes in plays more famous for their theatrical structure and somber tone. Brutus Jones quests into his deepest unconscious, but the quest is a journey to nowhere; for Jones does not reach the culmination of the Emersonian circle, but rather ends where he began, confirming only the original Center of Indifference. His physical death via the chief's silver bullet is like the emotional death of Ahab: as he runs in the same circles over and over again, he assumes mythic proportions, a powerful man whose reason leads him ultimately to disaster. He becomes a man finally so obsessed by a search for self that he loses all possibility for salvation because he forgets the only source of that salvation — the loss of self in the Other. The jungle as a source of natural life is ignored by Jones in his mad flight, just as the sea as a life-source is ignored by Ahab. In his pathetic attempt to reach the sea, Jones stands as an ironic commentary by O'Neill: man will continue to run in fruitless circles so long as he remains essentially within himself. Brutus Jones ends as a terrifying example of O'Neill's failed Romantic man.

In *The Hairy Ape*, Yank the stoker strives, unfortunately without success, to break the bonds of mechanism and stasis which the inhumane demands of his trade impose upon him. At the beginning of the play, he exults in his natural strength and in his function of providing power for the ship. At this point, he is at least a pale reflection of the Romantic man in that he propels the ship forward by his brute labor, his energizing force. He believes he belongs, albeit his belief deludes him. He feels, he says, that he has some meaning:

> I'm de end! I'm de start! I start somep'n and de woild moves! It — dat's me![6]

Of course, Yank has not sufficient understanding to realize the falseness of his belief. He is not free; he actually has no part at all in an organic process. The old Irishman, Paddy, tries to tell him this by his exalted reminiscences of the old sailing days, his warnings to Yank that the stokehole is really a mechanistic prison. Paddy stands as O'Neill's true Romantic in the play, a man whose day has sadly passed by in the age of the machine. If it is true that the thrust of the play's meaning is that Yank can find no place or value to which to "belong," it is also noteworthy that Paddy stands as the last vestige of what was worth belonging *to*:

> We belong to this, you're saying? We make the ship go, you're saying? Yerra then, that Almighty God have pity on us! Oh, to be back in the fine days of my youth, ochone! Oh, there was fine beautiful ships them days — clippers wid tall masts touching the sky — fine strong men in them — men that was sons of the sea as if 'twas the mother that bore them . . . we was free men — (with a sort of religious exaltation). Oh, to be scudding south again wid the power of the Trade Wind driving her on through the nights and the days! Full sail on her! . . . Then you'd see her driving through the gray night, her sails stretching aloft all silver and white, not a sound on the deck, the lot of us dreaming dreams . . . 'Twas them days men belonged to ships, not now. 'Twas them days a ship was part of the sea, and a man was part of a ship, and the sea joined all together and made it one.[7]

Paddy is close to the sea as a source of life; he alone among the stokers realizes the debasement inherent in the mechanistic way of life. He belongs because he is at one with the external world of nature. His lament for the passing of the old ways catalyzes Yank; the younger stoker begins to realize that his power is being wasted in the service of mechanism, that his labor is

little more than slave labor. Thus O'Neill suggests a major thematic preoccupation in the play: Yank's developing awareness that he does not belong
anywhere in a mechanistic society. Although the play's conclusion is pessimistic, as Yank finally gains "communion" only by uniting with a gorilla
in the clasp of death, his quest for value and for a higher level of existence is
in the Romantic tradition. Yank fails to find meaningful connection because the universe in which he lives will not allow it. O'Neill's final irony is
that meaningful life is impossible without the Romantic view of an organic
universe. Whereas Paddy could gain a sense of unity and community in the
natural, creative process of sailing, Yank ends only in death inside a cage —
symbolic of the wasteland society has always provided him. Whereas for
Paddy death is a freeing of self into the Romantic Everlasting Now, for Yank
death comes only as a static cessation of movement.

O'Neill's little-known adaptation, *The Ancient Mariner*, is a striking
example of how deeply involved was the dramatist in Romantic thought in
his early career. Published only in 1960 in the *Yale University Library Gazette* in an uncritical edition by Donald Gallup,[8] the play has received no
previous critical comment. Throughout his stage directions — which com-
prise O'Neill's total contribution to the Coleridge poem save for a few
words — O'Neill makes great use of the mask to delineate and emphasize the
Mariner's change in character from a death-bringer to an organicist. It is
instructive to examine the stage directions for the physical production of the
play, so that we may see how O'Neill structured and shaped Coleridge's seminal Romantic poem so as to reinforce his own Romantic concerns. The adaptation opens with the Mariner in front of a large screen to indicate a
house, on which the shadows of the wedding guests are to be seen. The Mariner is depicted as "a prophet out of the Bible with the body and dress of a
sailor" (p. 63); his hands are raised up to the sky and his lips move in prayer.
True to the opening lines of the poem, the Mariner is dramatized as rejecting the first two wedding guests, who have "mask-like faces of smug, complacent dullness, and walk like marionettes" (p. 63). Instead he grabs the
Third Wedding Guest by the shoulders, for the young man is described as
"naturally alive — a human being" (p. 63). Thus even in the opening action,
O'Neill reveals a thorough grasp of the direction of Coleridge's poem as he
directs the Mariner to scorn the mechanistic man and cleave to the organic
humanist. Significantly, the Mariner stands upon the top step of the porch
as he begins to tell his tale, for O'Neill realizes that the old man has come to
the glorious ending of his quest for the meaningful life.

As the Mariner begins to speak, the Chorus appears from stage left: six
sailors who all wear the masks of drowned men. At the first appearance of
the albatross, the sailors "sing a hymn to a sort of chanty rhythm" (p. 66).
The albatross itself is described by O'Neill in mystical terms:

> The albatross appears above the mast. It is like a huge dove of the Holy
> Ghost. A mystic halo surrounds it with light. The sailors fall on their

> knees. Sunlight floods down seeming to come from the Albatross. The ice
> disappears. The sailors take bread from their pockets and offer it to the
> Albatross. The bread is in wafers like Communion wafers. (p. 66)

O'Neill emphasizes the importance of the albatross as a symbol of affirmation and peace in the next sequence when the Mariner confesses to the Wedding Guest that he shot the albatross. "The Mariner sinks to his knees,
bowing his head. The chorus fall on their faces. Fog hiding the sun. The
corpse of the Albatross is laid out on a bier by the mast, a mystic light pro-
ceeding from it" (p. 67). Here O'Neill shows his accurate grasp of the significance Coleridge attaches to the killing of the albatross: that the act
effectively excommunicates the Mariner from the organic universe and renders him subject only to misery and suffering because he is now out of touch
with the natural processes of the vital, dynamic world of nature.

After the ship becomes becalmed, O'Neill describes the sun as "copper,"
blazing down mechanically and mercilessly upon the Mariner's guilt. The
chorus stare accusingly at the old man, and upon a screen backstage O'Neill
directs "death-fires" to dance "on sky and sea" (p. 69). An apparition rises
beside the ship, and O'Neill underscores the guilt of the life-killer in the
following direction:

> The Spirit points accusingly at the Albatross, then to the Mariner — then
> makes a gesture of command. The Chorus rise as one and hang the A. [*sic*]
> about his neck. Its wings are at right angles making a white cross. (p. 70)

Following the death of the six sailors, the moon "floods them with a
ghastly light" (p. 72). Just as O'Neill uses the death-mask to show the nadir
of Romantic hope, however, he also utilizes the mask to show the Mariner's
exaltation when he finally realizes that his only possible route back to the
organic life is to recommune with the water-snakes — the ugliest aspect of
that life. As the old man recounts how he "bless'd them unaware!" O'Neill
describes his mask and his action: "He is suddenly exalted and weeps. He
rises and makes the motion with his hands of blessing them" (p. 75). Now,
the sails of the ship are to become like "the wings of the Albatross — faintly
luminous." O'Neill directs the light crew to shine a "strange beautiful light"
on the bodies of the dead chorus. "Their masks are changed. They now have
those of holy spirits with halos about their heads" (p. 76).

Throughout the regeneration of the Mariner, O'Neill significantly keeps
us aware of the participation of the Wedding Guest in the experience by
having him on stage during much of the action. As the "Spirit" pronounces
that the Mariner "hath penance done, / And penance more will do," the
Guest, like the Mariner, "is discovered lying insensible." Thus O'Neill shows
us that he realizes the importance of the Guest to the Romantic Theme of
Coleridge's poem: *all* men share in the process of self-creation; the burden
for the frequent mechanization of the world is not simply to fall upon one
man. The final two series of stage directions strongly emphasize the community of man inherent in the Mariner's rediscovery of himself. O'Neill de-

picts him as a "prophet proclaiming truth" (p. 85) as he turns to the audience and intones the closing lines of the poem, "He prayeth best, who loveth best/All things both great and small. . . ." As he does so, O'Neill ends the adaptation with perhaps the most Romantic direction of the play:

> He bows humbly, prays for a moment, blesses the W. G. [sic] and the audience, crosses himself and walks slowly off left. The W. G. stares after him dazedly like one awakening from a dream, then he bolts into the house as if running from the dark. A blare of music and a chorused shout of welcome as he opens the door. He shuts it and locks it. His shadow appears on the blind dancing with his bride. (p. 86)

The Wedding Guest has learned the Mariner's lesson as he rushes back into life, into human communion. As the Mariner has recreated himself, by his blessing he recreates the Guest and the audience who watch his final prayer. The prayer and the blessing reunite the family of man once again into a oneness, a community. O'Neill the Romantic momentarily forestalls death by the simple act of celebrating life, and it is important that the final lines concern the dance of life.

In O'Neill's most mature play of his early career, *Desire Under the Elms*, Romantic myth and motif are raised to the pinnacle of dramatic expression and psychological power. Though Ephraim, Eben, and Abbie are driven people during much of their existence, and the play ends sadly with the lovers about to enter prison for their crime of infanticide, the resolution of the play finds them having accepted their fate, having escaped the prison of self. Eben's growth toward selflessness and altruism through his relationship with Abbie represents the Romantic tenet of a boy's mythic initiation into manhood. At first, Eben merely uses Abbie to avenge himself against his father, Ephraim; but gradually, as the hovering spirit of his dead mother loses its control over him, possessiveness turns to love, and Eben loses self by engagement with another human being. For her part, Abbie grows beyond her exploitation of Eben to gain control over the farm and a feeling of security to a realization that she must love him as another human being. "Therefore at the end the two lovers stand united — even exalted by the recognition of their true love."[9] But, as Carpenter rightly states, neither Eben nor Abbie is the hero of *Desire Under the Elms*; the final hero is Nature, the ultimate Romantic value. Nature ends all desire, after all. Against the vastness of the farm and sky, the efforts of the three main characters to possess the farm and each other become finally, less significant than the organic life that remains after the waste of Ephraim's cruelty to his family and Abbie's murder of her infant son. There is, then, a double irony in the sherriff's lines that end the play, as he says to his cronies, "It's a jim-dandy farm, no denyin': Wished I owned it!"[10] If it is true that Eben and Abbie transcend their entrapments in self and time to attain a transfiguration, it is also true that Nature transcends their acts by virtue of its timeless dynamic organicism.

In the Romantic plays O'Neill, like the great American Romantics before him, became myth-maker; as Carl Strauch has said of Robinson, O'Neill, too, "delineated human destiny in the large, abstract, and typifying manner of all myth, rendering each particular life with an awareness of timeless significance."[11] Why, then, the critic-teacher may ask (or may be asked) did O'Neill rise to his later heights by creating myths of a non-Romantic nature? Why do the characters of *The Iceman Cometh* and *Long Day's Journey Into Night* seemingly fail to find their solace in the affirmations of O'Neill's earlier heroes? Hard-and-fast answers to such questions are nearly impossible without dangerous proximity to intentional fallacies; however, the critic can offer some biographical parallels during the period from 1918 to 1924 which may at least illumine the phenomena of the Romantic plays and may perhaps suggest why O'Neill wrote more affirmatively during this period than he ever would again. Doris Alexander has established that O'Neill's Romanticism was tempered by his close association with Terry Carlin and William Laurence who, respectively, introduced him to the mystical contents of *Light on the Path*, a book of Oriental wisdom, and to the affirmative philosophy of Nietzsche.[12] Throughout his life O'Neill reread passages that he had copied from *Light on the Path* and *Thus Spake Zarathustra*. Perhaps the Romanticism of the early plays also stemmed from O'Neill's life-long devotion to the sea, as indicated by his frequent residence near the sea at homes ranging from Provincetown to Bermuda. Louis Sheaffer, O'Neill's most recent biographer, has said that O'Neill was "haunted by the sea," and that it filled him with "religious ecstasy, a sense of being in communion with the secret heart of things."[13] These diverse influences perhaps temper the pessimism of even the darkest tragedy, *Long Day's Journey*, as at least young Edmund finds, in the sea, communion with something beyond his own psychic obsessions as he rhapsodizes to his father of his youthful sea journey:

> I lay on the bowsprit, facing astern, with the water foaming into spume under me, the masts with every sail white in the moonlight, towering high above me. I became drunk with the beauty and singing rhythm of it, and for a moment I lost myself — actually lost my life. I was set free! I dissolved in the sea, became white sails and flying spray, became beauty and rhythm . . . I belonged, without past or future, within peace and unity and a wild joy, within something greater than my own life, of the life of Man, to Life itself![14]

O'Neill once said that tragedy was "an urge toward life and ever more life . . . exaltation; and intensified feeling of the significant worth of man's being and becoming."[15] Certainly in the early works O'Neill reached the symbolical celebration of his hoped-for theatre of the future, and in doing so evolved a tragic form congruent with inherently Romantic ideals. He hoped also that the new theatre, dealing with myths of affirmation and hope, would so treat them that the audience would become a kind of congregation, "actively participating in what is being said, seen, and done."[16]

He envisioned the people actually joining in the choral responses to the chanting of his Mariner, so that they might participate more vitally and fully. Through his own rendering of man's tireless myths of the quest for value and for self-understanding, and man's attempt to create a more organic universe filled with the purposiveness of his dreams, O'Neill's Romantic plays stand as a mythically cohesive force against the corrosiveness of the spirit that besets us all as inhabitants of the modern world.

Notes

1. Barbara and Arthur Gelb, *O'Neill* (New York: Harper's, 1962), p. 62.

2. In using these terms I am following the practice of Professor Peckham in his seminal article on Romanticism: see Morse Peckham, "Toward a Theory of Romanticism," *PMLA* (March, 1951), 5–23.

3. Alan Downer, *Fifty Years of American Drama* (Chicago: Regnery, 1951), p. 65.

4. *The Plays of Eugene O'Neill* (New York: Random House, 1951), III, 167–8.

5. F. I. Carpenter, *O'Neill* (New York: Twayne, 1964), p. 96.

6. *Plays*, III, p. 216.

7. *Plays*, III, pp. 213–14.

8. Donald Gallup, ed. *"The Ancient Mariner,"* *Yale University Library Gazette* (October, 1960), p. 61. All quotations are from this edition, with pagination indicated in the text.

9. Carpenter, p. 107.

10. *Plays*, I, p. 269.

11. Carl F. Strauch, "Introduction to Robinson," in *American Literary Masters*, Vol. 2. (New York: Holt, Rinehart and Winston, 1965), p. 512.

12. Doris Alexander, *The Tempering of Eugene O'Neill* (New York: Harcourt, Brace and World, 1962), p. 230.

13. Louis Scheaffer, *O'Neill: Son and Playwright* (Boston: Little, Brown, 1968), p. 163.

14. Eugene O'Neill, *Long Day's Journey Into Night* (New Haven: Yale Univ. Press, 1956), p. 153.

15. Gelb, p. 486.

16. Gelb, p. 602.

Blueprint for the Future:
The Emperor Jones   Lisa M. Schwerdt

By examining the episodic structure of Eugene O'Neill's *The Emperor Jones* (1920) and noting how the various scenes relate to one another, one can discover the precursors of themes and patterns that O'Neill will explore more fully in later plays. In this early work, O'Neill seems to be using a technique known as "writing as knowing" — writing not to communicate but to discover what is known. In such later works as *Strange Interlude* (1928) and *The Iceman Cometh* (1946) O'Neill will adapt this practice and shift his emphasis, writing more in an attempt to exorcise personal devils, which have been previously identified. This is particularly evident in perhaps his best play, *Long Day's Journey Into Night* (1956), but the element of guilt seen in this later play is present as early as *The Emperor Jones*. Here, O'Neill presents those areas or relationships that man must come to grips with at some point in life. These problems are merely presented, however; there is no attempt to deal with these aspects in depth, nor to suggest solutions.

Since O'Neill is concerned with the individual coming to terms with his place and responsibility in the world, *The Emperor Jones* touches upon all aspects of man's human and spiritual relationships. It is a finely structured play in which the scenes, although complete in themselves, are tied to each other in a hierarchical development. Scenes i and viii stand alone, serving as frames for the play. Scene ii exists independently in looking at the area of man's relationship with himself, but works in tandem with Scene iii in exposing the individual as primarily responsible for the vision that haunts him. Scenes iii and iv represent the area in which man interacts with other men. Scene iv leads into v insofar as the element of social institutions as responsible for action is brought into play and they present the social level on which man interacts. Scenes v and vi function together in presenting a class or group and man's relationship with that element of society, and the interaction occurs on a less personal level. But again there is a slight difference between the two scenes: Scene v shows man in a social role, relating to society as part of a group while Scene vi presents him relating to a group, but in an impersonal sort of belonging which is then extended in Scene vii to its extreme—man's relationship to humanity. Scene vii exists in the same way as Scene ii: each is a representation of an area in which man acts, and each is representative of an extreme. Thus, the play moves from a personal to an impersonal level of interaction and ranges from the most immediate sort of concern—man's relationship with self, to the most far-reaching—man's relationship to humankind. The play's structure can be clearly seen in the following diagram:

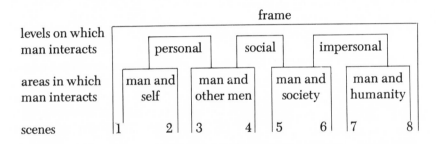

Again and again O'Neill will turn to an examination of these areas as he attempts to define the quality of life man should strive for, and the appropriate methods for achieving it.

The personal level is depicted first since the Little Formless Fears that Jones sees are figments of imagination, shapeless and undefined because they have significance only to the individual; Emperor Jones, alone, knows what they are. Of course, the individual and his motives are important in all plays, but it is not until later in *Strange Interlude* and *Long Day's Journey* that this attempt at externalizing an inner frame of mind becomes refined. O'Neill there takes advantage of these inner attitudes and, instead of leaving them open to personal interpretation as with the Little Formless Fears, has them expressed, and thus defined, by the characters until these personal beliefs carry as much weight as their public statements. Indeed, in *Strange Interlude* there is nearly as much "inner" dialogue as "outer," and in *Long Day's Journey* there are numerous monologues that detail inner visions.

Among the three plays there is also a growing sophistication in the presentation of the personal vision as well as a more specific use of it. *The Emperor Jones* was a first attempt at externalizing an inner belief, but it provided only the information that man had inner fears important to himself. In *Strange Interlude* the characters verbalize their fears and attitudes, but this is primarily helpful to the audience in allowing them to understand what had motivated certain actions. Finally, in *Long Day's Journey*, O'Neill uses the externalization of personal attitudes as a step along the character's path to self-knowledge. Since these long, expository monologues occur under the guise of drunkenness, they are more realistic than the asides delivered as characters "freeze" in *Strange Interlude*, and appear spontaneous rather than planned by the playwright. This "making the personal, public" also comes to serve more of a dramatic purpose. O'Neill moves from dramatizing Jones' beginning loss of control over self, to a justification of a position in *Strange Interlude*, until the verbalization of inner visions in *Long Day's Journey* not only dramatizes a beginning awareness of self and justifies actions, but also documents the struggle in achieving self-knowledge.

O'Neill also had to come to terms with himself and his concerns in other areas. He was interested not only in how man regarded himself, but in how he lived in relationship to others. Jones not only has a vision of the Negro porter he has slain for cheating at dice — a one-to-one relationship — (scene iii), but also of the guard who whips him as a member of the chain gang (scene iv). This is also a one-to-one encounter, but it occurs under the aegis of social strictures. O'Neill will, of course, expand on the relationship of man to other individuals in many plays. Usually this relationship takes on the tone of a personal relationship, (as in scene iii); there are few instances of a personal interaction affected by social institutions. Again, there is movement in the plays from confusion over the responsibility one has towards others, to an awareness of, and acceptance of, that responsibility.

Jones is upset at "seeing" the two men he had attacked, but he suffers no remorse over what he has done or even questions that it could, or should, have been otherwise. In *Desire Under the Elms* (1924) there is conflict between responsibility to others and responsibility to self, but this is most clearly seen among the characters rather than in one character. Peter and Simeon decide they owe something to themselves while Abbie and Eben consider their responsibility toward each other, toward themselves, and toward Ephraim. There is some interference from the social convention of marriage, but it is of less importance than the fact that Abbie "belongs" to Ephraim. Had they lived together outside marriage the problems would still be the same. In *Strange Interlude* there is again conflict, but it is centered within the characters. The personal asides communicate the thought struggles the characters undergo as they decide whether to please themselves or to allow someone else to be happy. This movement is seen most clearly in Nina as her perception changes from seeing others as they can help her, to seeing how she can be helpful to someone else, but Nina does not seem to be aware of this change or, really, of her responsibility.

In *Mourning Becomes Electra* (1931), Lavinia does seem to become aware of her responsibility for others. Her refusal to taint Peter is evidence of her growth from mere consideration of what will suit her needs. She also accepts a family responsibility by deciding to punish herself and, in a sense, sacrifice herself to rid the world of the Mannon curse. In this case, as in *Strange Interlude*, there is the notion of responsibility dealt with under a social aegis—that of the family; but again it is not as important as the personal responsibility Lavinia feels toward Peter. This awareness of responsibility becomes more important in *Long Day's Journey*, where the characters come to realize that they are not individuals put upon by others, but that they too have made demands and are, in varying degrees, responsible for what has happened to other members of the family. This recognition of responsibility for others enables the characters to achieve greater awareness of themselves, as well as a better integration of the multiple sides of their personalities.

Man must also go outside his immediate surroundings and interact with groups he has contact with—his society. In scene v of *The Emperor Jones*, Jones is auctioned off as a member of an identifiable group or class of society. In scene vi he joins a group and participates in their chanting and wailing. Although both of these scenes deal with man and society, there are subtle differences between them. In scene v Jones is involved in a situation that exists as a result of a society; in scene vi he is involved in an impersonal situation. He joins a social group, but has no acquaintance with the members and participates in a more universal activity—singing, a function that transcends class lines or social groups.

O'Neill does not seem so interested in exploring man's role in society as in looking at man in other relationships. Perhaps this is because it is too "large" a concern for a man trying to come to terms with a familial guilt, and too "small" a concern for a man attempting to hammer out his relationship to God and the universe. He does confront the question of man's place in society in *The Hairy Ape* (1921), however. Yank is seen as a member of a class that is all brawn and no brain. When Mildred descends from her upper-class stratum, she is terrified of him, seeing nothing but the animal-like qualities in him. Yank, in turn, becomes disturbed that she does not see him as a fellow human being and sets off in search of his place in society. He is no longer content to be what he is, believing that the justification for his existence will only come through society's acceptance.

Society's role becomes more impersonal in *The Iceman Cometh* (1946). The characters at Harry's are all types, and they respond to each other mainly on the basis of the roles they have played earlier in their lives. Although it appears that the characters demonstrate a concern for each other, this largely stems from personal reasons rather than from altruistic ones. For any one character's pipe dream to be deflated means a negation of all the others as well, so the support of others becomes a support of self. These character exist together at Harry's because they do not fit easily into conventional society. They have either transgressed its rules (like Jimmy going to work drunk) or its ideals (like Wetjoen's retreat from battle). Their problems do not, however, just exist in their society: they are universal weaknesses, and society relates to them impersonally. It is not the man who is condemned, but the act. This universal concern was a major one for O'Neill as he attempted to define his relationship with something larger than man.

In scene vii of *The Emperor Jones*, Jones has seen his demons and is afraid; he joins with the witch doctor in chanting as he did with the Negroes in the previous scene. He has come to realize that he is not important, that he must offer himself as a sacrifice. He may not be important as a man, but his action is; and his responsibility and action are of a very impersonal sort. The crocodile that emerges from the river has no special significance to him; it is more a universal symbol of the uncivilized, pagan, animal that is going to devour man, of universal recognition emerging from the collective unconscious.

Although *Desire Under the Elms* functions on a universal level, it also treats man and his relationship with others. The death of the baby also kills the child in Eben, allowing him to be psychologically reborn. This Jungian rebirth allows Eben to free himself from childish incest wishes. The Oedipal motif raises the subject from a personal vendetta to an impersonal struggle existing throughout humanity, throughout time, joining the characters to something larger than themselves. Much the same thing occurs in *Mourning Becomes Electra*. Although there is an element of man's responsibility to man, the classical structure of the play and its subject of incest tie it to the ages and to all men. There is a sense that these characters are merely pawns acted upon by the impersonal "curse" of the Mannons. *The Iceman Cometh*, too, goes beyond man as he functions in his society to explore man as part of humanity. The many characters in the play are clearly representative of universal types, and the play examines the problem of what gives meaning to life, and how man sustains his will to live.

Although not O'Neill's first work, *The Emperor Jones*, nevertheless, hints at what will follow. In *The Emperor Jones* he set down his concerns without attempting either to delineate or to solve them. The explorations and solutions would come later as he struggled with them, attempting to define his place for himself, and man's place in mankind.

"Belonging" Lost: Alienation and Dramatic Form in Eugene O'Neill's *The Hairy Ape*   Peter Egri

On December 24, 1921, O'Neill wrote to Kenneth Macgowan:

> *The Hairy Ape* — first draft — was finished yesterday. . . . I dont' think the play as a whole can be fitted into any of the current "isms." It seems to run the whole gamut from extreme naturalism to extreme expressionism — with more of the latter than the former. I have tried to dig deep in it to probe in the shadows of the soul of man bewildered by the disharmony of his primitive pride and individualism at war with the mechanistic development of society. And the man in the case is not an Irishman, as I at first intended, but, more fittingly, an American — a New York tough of the toughs, a product of the waterfront turned stoker — a type of mind, if you could call it that, which I know extremely well. . . . Suffice it for me to add, the treatment of all the sets should be expressionistic, I think.[1]

Coming to grips with a Yankee individual's and individualist's — Yank's — predicament[2] at a new stage of the "mechanistic development of society," the play is a puzzle in more ways than one. Its introductory setting both defines and distorts a real scene:

> The firemen's forecastle of a transatlantic liner an hour after sailing from New York for the voyage across. Tiers of narrow, steel bunks, three deep, on all sides. An entrance in rear. Benches on the floor before the bunks. The room is crowded with men, shouting, cursing, laughing, singing — a confused, inchoate uproar swelling into a sort of unity, a meaning — the bewildered, furious, baffled defiance of a beast in a cage. Nearly all the men are drunk. Many bottles are passed from hand to hand. All are dressed in dungaree pants, heavy ugly shoes. Some wear singlets, but the majority are stripped to the waist.
>   The treatment of this scene, or of any other scene in the play, should by no means be naturalistic. The effect sought after is a cramped space in the bowels of a ship, imprisoned by white steel. The lines of bunks, the

uprights supporting them, cross each other like the steel framework of a cage. The ceiling crushes down upon the men's heads. They cannot stand upright. This accentuates the natural stooping posture which shoveling coal and the resultant over-development of back and shoulder muscles have given them. The men themselves should resemble those pictures in which the appearance of Neanderthal Man is guessed at. All are hairy-chested, with long arms of tremendous power, and low, receding brows above their small, fierce, resentful eyes. All the civilized white races are represented, but except for the slight differentiation in color of hair, skin, eyes, all these men are alike.

The curtain rises on a tumult of sound. Yank is seated in the fore-ground. He seems broader, fiercer, more truculent, more powerful, more sure of himself than the rest. They respect his superior strength — the grudging respect of fear. Then, too, he represents to them a self-expression, the very last word in what they are, their most highly developed individ-ual.[3]

The level of stark verisimilitude that O'Neill brands as naturalistic and wishes to transcend can be met with in the stage directions to Act III, scene i of *The Personal Equation* (1915):

A section of the firemen's forecastle in the S.S. San Francisco at dock in Liverpool. . . . Bunks, ranged three deep with a space of two and a half to three feet between them, occupy the rear and left walls. Over the upper tier of bunks in rear, several open portholes. In front of the bunks, low wooden benches. In under the lower tier a glimpse can be had of seachests, suit cases, etc. jammed in indiscriminately. In the middle of right wall, a door. On either side of it, more tiers of bunks. A row of steel stanchions extends down the middle of the room. Everything is steel, painted white, except the board floor.[4]

The factual elements of the sight delineated in *The Hairy Ape* are appar-ently very similar to the ones described in *The Personal Equation*. The di-vergence emerges in the enhancement, dynamics, and interpretation of facts.

The ceiling crushing down upon the men's heads evokes a sense of en-closure or a kind of claustrophobic threat which is also there in some other expressionistic plays by O'Neill. When, for example, the title character of *The Emperor Jones* fires at the ghost-vision of the Guard, "Instantly the walls of the forest close in from both sides, the road and the figures of the convinct gang are blotted out in an enshrouding darkness."[5] In *All God's Chillun Got Wings* (1923) the deterioration of Ella's and Jim's almost Strindbergian marriage and the progressive evolvement of Ella's neurosis are expressed by the oppressive shrinking of the room they live in and the relative growing of the Congo mask Ella hates. Whereas, however, the clos-ing in of walls and the reduction of space in *The Emperor Jones* and in *All God's Chillun Got Wings* are projections of the protagonists' states of mind, the crushing down of the ceiling upon the stokers' heads accentuates the men's usual stooping posture and thus underlines an objective property, a consequence of their toil. The element of enhancement is also manifest in Yank's presentation. While all the stokers possess long arms of tremendous power, Yank is the most powerful of all, he is the "most highly developed individual" of them all, their most robust self-expression. He is, in fact, the expressionistic enlargement of Driscoll in the *Glencairn* plays: *Bound East for Cardiff* (1914), *The Moon of the Caribbees* (1916–17), *The Long Voyage Home* (1916–17) and *In the Zone* (1916–17); of Lyons in the short story *Tomorrow* (1917); and of Mat Burke, himself a sailor of extraordinary strength, in *Anna Christie* (1921); as well as of Yank in *Bound East for Cardiff*, *The Moon of the Caribbees*, and *In the Zone.*[6]

The throbbing, dynamic quality of the stage directions of *The Hairy Ape* as against the stark and grey scene description of *The Personal Equation* makes itself felt in the swelling tumult of sounds, the "shouting, cursing, laughing, singing" uproar of the drunk stokers passing bottles from hand to hand in the cramped space of the crowded room. The arrangement of sounds embodies the auditory equivalent of sense: tentative and dispersed parallels of consonants, vowels, and diphthongs converge in the crescendo of cumulative violence. In the sentence "The room is crowded with men, shouting, cursing, laughing, singing — a confused, inchoate uproar swelling into a unity, a meaning — the bewildered, furious, baffled defiance of a beast in a cage," the inchoate murmur in the [r] of "*r*oom" is increased by the [r] of "c*r*owded," snarls and growls in the onomatopoeic "up*r*oar," and becomes reinforced by the [r]-s of "bewilde*r*ed" and "fu*r*ious." The initial explosion heard in the [k] of "*c*rowded" is repeated and stepped up in "*c*ursing," "*c*onfused," "in*ch*oate," and "*c*age." The diphthong [au] in "cr*ow*ded"is grouchingly reiterated in the [au] of "sh*ou*ting." The level of noise represented by "shouting" is audibly heightened by the sequence of "cursing," "laughing," and "singing," not only because of the meanings of the words but also on account of the similarity of their sound pattern: two syllables, initial stress, -*ing* ending. The hissing [s] in "*c*ursing" is echoed by "*s*inging," swells in "*s*welling," and returns in "furiou*s*," "defian*c*e," and "bea*s*t." The ferocious [f] in "laug*h*ing" reappears in "con*f*used," "*f*urious," "ba*ff*led," and "de*f*iance." Similarly, [ju:] in "con*fu*sed" is soon consolidated in the [ju:] of "*u*nity," just as the [i] sound of "m*ea*ning" characteristically finds its meaning in "b*ea*st," whose initial [b] is the last explosive and explosion in the bursting alliterative chain reaction of "*b*ewildered," "*b*affled," and "*b*east." The power of emotional explosion is further increased by a violently and antithetically pulsating rhythmic stress pattern whose strong beats seem to knock against and storm the bars of a cage in the "b*a*ffled / def*i*ance / of a be*a*st / in a c*a*ge."

The playwright's interpretation of the scene in the two plays is also conspicuously different. In *The Personal Equation* the author's attitude is characterized by quiet demonstration; the indictment mainly lies in the action; the description of the stage simply and almost impersonally enumerates the objects that constitute the objective surroundings of the plot and represent the narrow conditions of the stokers. In *The Hairy Ape* the dramatist's personal participation is fairly obvious; factual representation changes into emotional presentation. Descriptive pictures are substituted by images involving or implying a simile: the shouting stokers are described in terms of furious beasts; they resemble the appearance of Neanderthal Man; the white steel framework of the tiers of narrow bunks gives the impression of a cage and creates the effects of "a cramped space . . . imprisoned by white steel." The final outcome of the stage directions, supported by the title of the play, suggests a dramatic contrast between wild animals trapped, captured, and caged and explosive energy imprisoned, compressed, and contained.

In the compositional pattern of scene i a major and a minor conflict evolve, apparently unexpectedly. The major contrast concerns the opposition of two ways of life, indeed of two historical epochs. They are the periods of the sailing boat and the steamship, a small and a great degree of division of labor, relative unity with nature and absolute isolation from her, calm and speed, pantheism and industrialism. The antithesis is viewed by Paddy, the old Irish sailor, with elegiac yearning:

> Oh, to be back in the fine days of my youth, ochone! Oh, there was fine beautiful ships them days — clippers wid tall masts touching the sky — fine strong men in them — men that was sons of the sea as if 'twas the mother that bore them. . . . Oh, to be scudding south again wid the power of the Trade Wind driving her on steady through the nights and days! Full sail on her! Nights and days! Nights when the foam of the wake would be flaming wid fire, when the sky'd be blazing and winking wid stars. . . . And there was the days, too. A warm sun on the clean decks. Sun warming the blood of you, and wind over the miles of shiny green ocean like strong drink to your lungs.[7]

It is little wonder that Paddy hates the black smoke of the steamship smudging the sea and choking the lung. Yank, however, looks at the contrast with tough acceptance thinking that only work on a steamer makes sense. He is all for steel, fire, energy, movement, and speed; moreover, he, the mover of everything, is all these things:

> I'm de ting in coal dat makes it boin; I'm steam and oil for de engines; I'm de ting in noise dat makes yuh hear it; I'm smoke and express trains and steamers and factory whistles; I'm de ting in gold dat makes it money! And I'm what makes iron into steel! Steel, dat stands for de whole ting! And I'm steel — steel — steel! I'm de muscles in steel, de punch behind it![8]

Paddy extolls the beauties of the past, Yank supposes, because he is a part of the past. He is old, in fact dead, but Yank is young, he is the new that is murdering the old.

Besides this major antagonism between Paddy and Yank, a minor opposition also develops between Long and Yank.[9] Long is a socialist agitator who points out that it is the first cabin passengers, "the damned Capitalist clarss" that should be blamed for dragging the stokers down to be mere wage slaves and for making home hell. His speech, delivered on a bench with a bottle in hand is received by hisses and boos, is branded "Salvation Army-Socialist bull" by Yank, and is rejected by Yank's proud and derogatory differentiation between the idle rich in the first cabin and the working stokers in the stokehole:

> Say! What's dem slobs in de foist cabin got to do wit us? We're better men dan dey are, ain't we? Sure! One of us guys could clean up de whole mob wit one mit. Put one of 'em down here for one watch in de stokehole, what'd happen? Dey'd carry him off on a stretcher. Dem boids don't amount to nothin'. Dey're just baggage. Who makes dis old tub run? Ain't it us guys? Well den, we belong, don't we? We belong and dey don't. Dat's all. . . . As for dis bein' hell — aw, nuts! Yuh lost your noive, dat's what. Dis is a man's job, get me? It belongs.[10]

Delimiting the semantic field of "belong" in the play is evidently not a matter to be decided by consulting an average dictionary. Even where the verb goes with its adverbial government *to*, it is used with a special semantic overtone. When, for example, Paddy flings it in Yank's face that " 'Twas them days men belonged to ships, not now", he means those days when the sailors considered themselves "free men", and looked upon their clippers as their natural homes, places where they "worked under the sky and 'twas work wid skill and daring to it." Quite often, however, the "required" postposition *to* is not required at all; it is in fact, dropped, and "belong" is used in a specific sense. When Yank separates the underdeck stokers from the first cabin passengers saying "We belong and dey don't", he himself gives the explanation: "Dem boids don't amount to nothin.' " He who makes the old tub run, belongs. Working on a steamship, Yank believes, "is a man's job . . . It belongs." It amounts to something, it counts, it is the real thing, it is significant, it makes sense, it requires and objectifies human substantiality, it creates the world and, in doing so, creates man, it represents and brings about human values. It is in these meanings that "belonging" functions as a leitmotif throughout the play.[11]

All this seems to be a far cry from the initial image of cage and prison. All the same, the picture persists and haunts the scene from the background. When Paddy asks Yank ironically and rhetorically whether he wants to be a flesh and blood wheel of the engines, and wishes to belong to the hell of the stokehole, "caged in by steel from a sight of the sky like bloody apes in the Zoo!," he merely seems to give voice to a personal opinion which Yank rejects. When Long curses the hellish lives of wage slaves, sweating, burning up and eating coal dust in the bowels of a steamship, his position may also be considered as a personal view. This, too, is immediately refuted by Yank and the stokers. Nevertheless, after Paddy's painful outburst, his mates are "startled and impressed in spite of themselves," and at the end of Paddy's lament even Yank cannot help "fighting some queer struggle within himself." And when eight bells sounds, "vibrating through the steel walls as if some enormous brazen gong were imbedded in the heart of the ship," all the men, despite their display of strength, autonomy, and independence, "jump up mechanically, file through the door silently close upon each other's heels in what is very like a prisoner's lockstep."[12] Yank may — and does — go on boasting, yet the impersonal power of the gong, the mechanical quality of the stokers' movements, and the prisoner's lockstep of the men suggest and constitute an objective counterpoint to their subjective pronouncements and attitudes. The image of cage and the picture of prison prove to be leitmotifs. They also prove O'Neill's originality which lies, among other things, in what might be termed relative unpredictability. It is very difficult, often impossible, to predict what a scene, an act, or a play by O'Neill will be followed by. When, however, the next scene, act, or play have come, one feels their presence inevitable, their connection with their antecedents necessary, their unfolding organic and retrospectively justified.

Scene ii leads to a conspicuously different world. Two days have passed, and after the stokehole now we are on the promenade deck of the ship where Mildred Douglas, the daughter of the president of Nazareth Steel (chairman of the board of directors of the line) is seen reclining in her deck chair in the company of her aunt. Mildred took up sociology at college, did social service work on New York's East Side, and is now going to visit the poor in London to make her slumming international, as her aunt mockingly refers to her adventurous venture to be safeguarded by hired detectives.

In her protest against her aunt's malicious insinuation, Mildred characterizes her position with a mixture of genuine earnestness, weary bitterness, and mirthless laugh:

> Please do not mock my attempts to discover how the other half lives. Give me credit for some sort of groping sincerity in that at least. I would like to help them. I would like to be some use in the world. Is it my fault I don't know how? I would like to be sincere, to touch life somewhere. . . . But I'm afraid I have neither the vitality nor integrity. All that was burnt out in our stock before I was born. Grandfather's blast furnaces, flaming to the sky, melting steel, making millions — then father keeping those home fires burning, making more millions — and little me at the tail-end of it all. I'm a waste product in the Bessemer process — like the millions. Or rather, I inherit the acquired trait of the by-product, wealth, but none of the energy, none of the strength of the steel that made it. I am sired by gold and damned by it, as they say at the race track — damned in more ways than one.[13]

The contrast of generations described by Mildred with a sociological and historical clarity and precision is a dramatic abbreviation of an international social process represented in full epic detail in generation novels like Thomas Mann's *Buddenbrooks*, Galsworthy's *The Forsyte Saga*, Gorky's *The Artamonov Business*, or Martin du Gard's *The Thibaults*. The dramatic shortcut taken by O'Neill can be viewed as a generic reflection of a

genetic development: the unfolding of industrialization and monopoliza-
tion had an incomparably more dynamic character in the U.S. than it did in
Europe in the last decades of the 19th and the first decades of the 20th century. On the other hand, the thematic, and not only generic, inclusion of
the reduced process in the drama also betrays the dramatist's epic interest.
So do the hardly playable but highly readable reflective parts of the stage
directions introducing Mildred as a fretful, nervous, and discontented
young lady, "bored by her own anemia" and presenting her aunt as a carica-
turistic type with a double chin, lorgnettes, and a pretentious dress worn "as
if afraid her face alone would never indicate her position in life."

Herself a self-conscious embodiment of a self-portraying antagonism,
Mildred, weak as she is, has a special power to antagonize practically everybody in her company and surroundings. She exchanges a few Shavian and
Wildean unpleasantries with her aunt, the elderly lady exhorting her niece
to observe due *amenities* and Mildred deliberately misunderstanding the
word as *inanities*. After Mildred's bitterly self-ironical survey of the degenerative development of the Douglas generations, her aunt observes supercil-
iously: "You seem to be going in for sincerity today. It isn't becoming to you,
really — except as an obvious pose. Be as artificial as you are, I advise.
There's a sort of sincerity in that, you know."[14] At the end of the scene
Mildred slaps her aunt insultingly across the face. She also shocks the Second Engineer who cannot dissuade her from descending into the stokehole
in her white dress; and O'Neill reserves a separate scene to present the effect
of her appearance on Yank.

Although scene ii is thus far removed from scene i both in social sphere
and in atmosphere, it is not unrelated to it. The relationship is one of obvious contrast and — in a more surprising way — one of latent parallel. The
contrast is between strength and weakness; while Yank is identical with
steel, Mildred only possesses steel: the have-nots belong, the haves do not.
The artificiality of the latter is focused by a radiating sunshine:

> The impression to be conveyed by this scene is one of the beautiful,
> vivid life of the sea all about — sunshine on the deck in a great flood, the
> fresh sea wind blowing across it. In the midst of this, these two incongru-
> ous, artificial figures, inert and disharmonious, the elder like a gray lump
> of dough touched up with rouge, the younger looking as if the vitality of
> her stock had been sapped before she was conceived, so that she is the ex-
> pression not of its life energy but merely of the artificialities that energy
> had won for itself in the spending.[15]

Similarities also crop up. The loss of personal autonomy Mildred complains of is parallelled by a comparable reduction in life-style Paddy laments at.[16] Therefore, the leitmotif of cage can appropriately express her
predicament as well. When Mildred's aunt finds it eccentric in her niece
that she of all persons should be interested in finding out how the other half
lives, Mildred apologizes with irony and self-irony: "Pardon me for my out-

burst. When a leopard complains of its spots, it must sound rather gro-tesque. (*In a mocking tone*) Purr, little leopard. Purr, scratch, tear, kill, gorge yourself and be happy — only stay in the jungle where your spots are camouflage. In a cage they make you conspicuous."[17] None the less, Mildred does set out to go down to what Paddy and Long name despairingly and deploringly hell and what she also calls tentatively and exploringly hell: the stokehole.[18] Her descent seems to prompt what her mocking tone suggests anyway: she considers even the habitual framework of her life a cage.

Scene iii is characterized by a masterful construction. The setting of the stokehole possesses the intensity of an expressionistic painting. Lighting is dim, provided by a single hanging bulb piling up masses of shadows in the coal dust-laden murky air. The bulks of the furnaces and boilers are dimly outlined in the background. When the aligned stokers open the furnace doors, "from these fiery round holes in the black a flood of terrific light and heat pours full upon the men who are outlined in silhouette in the crouch-ing, inhuman attitudes of chained gorillas."[19] The picture of the gorillas car-ries on the leitmotif of ape, the imaginary and imaginative image of chains evokes the leitmotif of cage and prison.

The painting is soon animated by the rhythmic emotions of the work-ing stokers who handle their shovels as if they were part of their bodies, swinging as on a pivot from the coal behind them to the furnaces before them. Their movements serve their work, but they also stylize and reshape the stokers' moves[20] in an expressionistic fashion, emphasizing their me-chanical quality and justifying, as it were, Paddy's indictment that work on a steam vessel makes the sailors flesh and blood wheels of the engines.

The expressionistic intensity of color, light, and heat, of rhythm, move-ment, and tempo is coupled with the expressive violence of discordant sounds:

> There is a tumult of noise — the brazen clang of the furnace doors as they are flung open or slammed shut, the grating, teeth-gritting grind of steel against steel, of crunching coal. This clash of sounds stuns one's ears with its rending dissonance. But there is order in it, rhythm, a mechanical regu-lated recurrence, a tempo. And rising above all, making the air hum with the quiver of liberated energy, the roar of leaping flames in the furnaces, the monotonous throbbing beat of the engines.[21]

The passage does not only describe but also evokes a tumult of noise. A num-ber of factors contribute to heightening the effect: the onomatopoeic qual-ity of the one-syllable word "clang"; the auditory parallel between the cross-eyed rhymes of "clang" and "flung," lending even "flung" an onomato-poeic overtone; and the additional cock-eyed rhyme of "grating" and "grit-ting." The clash of sounds is also expressed by the series-connected elemental explosions of alliterated initial explosives in "grating," "gritting," and "grind" distantly echoed by the delayed action blast of [g] in "against"; the grating noise of the [gr] sound combination in "grating," "teeth-gritting," and "*grind*" in which the difficulty and duration of pronouncing a cluster of consonants increases the impression of the teeth-gritting grind of steel against steel; the repeated detonations of the explosive [*t*] in "gra*t*ing," "*t*ee*t*h-gri*tt*ing," and "*s*teel" (used twice); and the alternation and altercation of single and double stress in "grating," "teeth-gritting," and "grind." Expressive noise is further increased by the screeching and creaking effect of the diagonally placed cluster [*st*] in "*st*eel again*st st*eel" and of the long [*i*:] in "t*ee*th" (reinforced by two short [*i*]-s in "gri*tt*ing") and in "*st*eel"; the alliteration in "*c*run*ch*ing *c*oal"; and the roaring [*r*] in "*r*oar" anticipated by the [*r*] in "*r*ising," "libe*r*ated," and "ene*r*gy" and followed, corroborated, and reinforced by the [*r*] in "th*r*obbing." The rising flight and unimpeded leap of liberated energy are sensitively suggested by the liquid consonant [*l*] in "*all*," "*l*iberated," "*l*eaping," and "f*l*ames," by [*r*] in the above listed words, and by a number of spirants such as [*h*] in "*h*um" or [*f*], emphasized by alliteration, in "*f*lames in the *f*urnaces." The fluent pronounceability of liquids and spirants helps to brings home the impression of the unobstructed release of energy, and is opposed to the blocked pronunciation of stop consonants and the affricate [*tʃ*] expressing "the gra*t*ing, *t*ee*t*h-gri*tt*ing grind of steel again*st* steel, of *c*run*ch*ing *c*oal." The "*order*," "*r*hythm," and "*r*egulated *r*ecurrence" in this rending dissonance are repeatedly rendered by the reiteration of the consonant [*r*] in these very words; by the approximate equality of duration and prosodic bars to be heard in the "mon*o*tonous / thr*o*bbing / b*e*at of the / *e*ngines/; as well as by the grammatical parallel between "flung open" and "slammed shut."

Color, light, heat, movement, and noise all combine in conveying the atmosphere and quality of feeding the furnaces. The stoking process is led visibly by Yank, who encourages the men, and invisibly by an engineer, whose whistle irritates the stokers. Yank is able to transmit his enthusiasm to his mates; in his incantatory chanting the rhythm of collective work, of nascent verse, and of sexual gratification pulsate in a unified pattern of exultant joy:

> Dat's de stuff! Let her have it! All togedder now! Sling it into her! Let her ride! Shoot de piece now! Call de toin on her! Drive her into it! Feel her move! Watch her smoke! Speed, dat's her middle name! Give her coal, youse guys! Coal, dat's her booze! Drink it up, baby! Let's see yuh sprint! Dig in and gain a lap! Dere she go-o-es. [22]

Pleasure prevails in the act of creation. Myth is magic. The world is humanized by work. Yank has the last word. The engineer's whistling is of no consequence. "Him and his whistle, dey don't belong. But we belong, see!"[23]

A number of signs, however, seems to contradict Yank's self-assured conviction.

Firstly, the stokers' work is awkwardly mechanical.

Secondly, the engineer's whistle is gaining growing command over them. When it is first blown, Yank curses without resentment. When it sounds again, it elicits cursing rage from the stokers. When it is heard for the third time, it drives Yank into a red-hot cursing fury. A continuation of the enormous gong sounding eight bells at the end of scene i, the whistle has become a leitmotif of the anonymous command of an imposed order.

Thirdly, even when Yank is rebelling against the engineer's revolting and anonymous superiority, he is pounding on his chest "gorilla-like. . . . He whirls defensively with a snarling, murderous growl, crouching to spring, his lips drawn back over his teeth, his small eyes gleaming ferociously."[24] He perceives Mildred dressed all in white. As she looks at his gorilla face, she protects her eyes, cries whimperingly, "Take me away! Oh, the filthy beast!," and faints. She descended into the hot hell of the stokehole in the hope that she had inherited immunity to heat from her grandfather, who had started as a paddler, and thus should be able to bear the reality of the nether world. When, however, she comes to be confronted with its naked, abysmal brutality, she is outraged, "her whole personality crushed, beaten in, collapsed." Her attitude and remark provoke an unexpected reaction in Yank as well: enraged and bewildered, "He feels himself insulted in some unknown fashion in the very heart of his pride,"[25] and sends his "God damn yuh!" and shovel after Mildred and the two engineers who take her away from the stokehole, off the stage, and indeed out of the play. From now on, she will never appear in the scene in person; her spiritual death will only make itself felt as a living insult in Yank's soul. Thus the outer confrontation and collision between Mildred and Yank triggers an irreparable inner conflict both in Mildred and Yank.

Fourthly, the above three factors attain a special significance of being linked at the end of the scene. When Yank's shovel, hurled after Mildred, hits the steel bulkhead with a clang and falls clattering on the steel floor, its sound being followed by the long, angry, and insistent urge of the invisible engineer's whistle, then an instrument of human activity mediating and objectifying human aspirations becomes a mechanical, dead object, steel appears as an outer obstacle rather than as an inner drive; the whistle does prove significant and threatening not to be shrugged off; and the leitmotif of the ape is intensified in fearful and fateful proportions.

Scene iv is a pondering pause. Emerging from their watch, the stokers attempt to interpret what happened. There is reason to think; Yank is found in the position of Rodin's "The Thinker," his mates try to find an explanation; and the spectators are also puzzled over the possible reasons for Yank's extraordinary, prolonged, and even retrospectively seething anger, especially if they are familiar with O'Neill's earlier works.

The Hairy Ape is certainly not the first play where a character is called names, or is, in fact, called a hairy ape. In *The Moon of the Caribbees* Cocky tells Paddy "A 'airy ape, I calls yer,"[26] Paddy takes offence but becomes reconciled in a minute, and the whole affair is no more than the usual flare-up of a squabble between the deck-hands and the "black gang" (the firemen of the stokehole). In *Chris Christopherson* (1919) one of the seamen, Mickey, is described as being "monkey-like in the disproportionate length of arms and legs."[27] Chris himself is characterized by the messroom steward, Glass, as having "arms . . . like a hairy gorilla." This, however, is a mere grumble after Chris, infuriated by one of Glass's insinuations, has grabbed him by the shoulders and shaken him thoroughly. In the final version of the play re-titled *Anna Christie* Burke, the stoker, calls himself "a clumsy ape" and names Chris an "old ape," an "old baboon," and again an "old ape."[28] These momentary insults, however, even if on occasion they may provoke angry reactions, do not cut deep, do not break bones and do not offend the addressee in the very heart of his pride. But Yank is hurt that way. It is not easy to understand why.

Does the cause lie in social antagonism? Paddy certainly points out the social distance between a fine lady dressed like a white queen and the poor beasts in the stokehole Mildred went to visit: "And there she was standing behind us, and the Second pointing at us like a man you'd hear in a circus would be saying: In this cage is a queerer kind of baboon than ever you'd find in darkest Africy. We roast them in their own sweat."[29] Long uses an even stronger language:

> Hinsultin' us! Hinsultin' us, the bloody cow! And them bloody engineers! What right 'as they got to be exhibitin' us 's if we was bleedin' monkeys in a menagerie? Did we sign for hinsults to our dignity as 'onest workers? Is that in the ship's articles? You kin bloody well bet it ain't! But I knows why they done it. I arsked a deck steward 'o she was and 'e told me. 'Er old man's a bleedin' millionaire, a bloody Capitalist! 'E's got enuf bloody gold to sink this bleedin' ship! 'E makes arf the bloody steel in the world! 'E owns this bloody boat! And you and me, Comrades, we're 'is slaves! And the skipper and mates and engineers, they're 'is slaves! And she's 'is bloody daughter and we're all 'er slaves, too! And she gives 'er orders as 'ow she wants to see the bloody animals below decks and down they takes 'er! (*There is a roar of rage from all sides.*)[30]

The audiences know that Mildred did not wish to insult the stokers; on the contrary, she paid them a visit out of sympathy, curiosity, and eccentricity, but the firemen, and especially Yank, did consider her attitude and gesture an affront. Or should one look for the explanation in the opposition of sexes? Yank's humiliation is undoubtedly greater for having been caused by a girl. He was stoking the furnace, "feeding the baby" with erotic overtones. His eyes bore into hers with a fixed gaze. Later Yank refers to her as a "skinny tart," and shouts in a frenzy: "She done me doit! . . . I'll git square wit her! I'll get her some way! . . . I'll show her who's a ape!"[31] Or is Yank's extraordinary anger motivated psychologically? Their hostility is unquestionably a confrontation of naked, shameless, brutal force and well-dressed, ashamed, ethereal gentility. In their collision instinct and inhibition clash, as they do very often in the O'Neill canon. Yank is superstitious, and perceiving Mildred's pale face and white dress, he thinks he sees a ghost. Yank's shock is all the greater since their meeting is totally unexpected and takes place at the very moment when he has turned round to knock down the whistling engineer.

Or can one find the reason in the changed relationship between Yank and his mates? Before his sudden encounter with Mildred, the stokers consider him their undisputed leader, and after the confrontation they laugh *at* him rather than *with* him. Paddy pulls his leg asserting he has fallen in love with Mildred; Yank cannot help confessing he was panic-stricken when he saw Mildred, white as an apparition and lit up in the darkness by the light of the furnaces; and even the usual game of the stokers of deriding all intellectual, moral, and legal concepts with a cynical mockery and with the mechanical leitmotif of "a brazen, metallic quality as if their throats were phonograph horns"[32] changes its character. Whereas earlier the game united Yank with his mates, now it separates him from them: when Yank tells them he is trying to think, they burst out in a chorus of hard, barking laughter. Yank springs to his feet and glares at them belligerently: "Yes, tink! Tink, that's what I said! What about it? (They are silent, puzzled by his sudden resentment at what used to be one of his jokes. Yank sits down again in the same attitude of 'The Thinker.' "[33] The climactic end of the scene finds Yank making an attempt to rush out of the room to force Mildred down on her knees and make her take back her word of insult. If she does not, Yank threatens to bust the face off her. The stokers bear Yank down to the floor, and Paddy calls him a great fool. The stokers' attitude is not unfriendly, yet it shows a tipping over of the balance of power and self-control: earlier it was Yank who admonished his mates (and especially Paddy) to behave reasonably, and how it is the stokers who try to keep Yank from doing something dangerously unreasonable.

Or should one seek the clue to Yank's hurt rage in the fact that Mildred's remark hit upon and touched at least part of a hardly bearable truth? It is undeniable that all the stokers, as O'Neill's stage directions repeatedly underline, look like apes; that even Paddy, criticizing the condition of the stokers being caged in by steel in a dirty stokehole like apes in the zoo, has a melancholy monkey-like face "with all the sad, patient pathos of that animal in his small eyes";[34] and that Yank, at the very moment when he is about to "fix" Mildred for having called him a filthy beast, is shaking "one fist upward and beating on his chest with the other."[35]

All these explanations contain a part of the truth. But even if they are taken together—and O'Neill does present them in interaction—they do not offer a totally satisfactory justification for Yank's extraordinary frenzy. Yank seems to be overreacting, and his apparent overreaction suggests either that he has set out to run amok or that he is driven by a larger cause, as yet unspecified, and he is not simply a hurt stoker with an apish face but a seeker of truth on a fate-marked course. The task of scene iv is not to decide the issue but only to foreshadow it.

As a result of Yank's bewilderment, the scope of reference of the symbolic leitmotif of "belonging" is also modified. Earlier, when Yank had an unshaken belief in his unity with industrial civilization, he had no doubt whatsoever about who belonged and who did not: he did, and the first cabin passengers did not, they were just lifeless things, mere baggage. Even now, when his old confident bravado returns, he professes the same view: "I'll show her I'm better'n her, if she on'y knew it. I belong and she don't, see! I move and she's dead! Twenty-five knots a hour, dat's me! Dat carries her but I make dat. She's on'y baggage. Sure!"[36]

But now Yank is not so sure about things and even about himself as he used to be. When Paddy recalls Mildred's and the Second Engineer's visit to the stokehole, and the officer's pointing at the stokers as if they were caged baboons from Africa, some of whom even like it when they are roasted in their own sweat, Yank does not reject the remark which obviously refers to him but only gives "a bewildered uncertain growl." Accordingly, when he observes that Mildred, standing right before him like a white apparition, "didn't belong," he does not mean that she was insignificant but, on the contrary, that she was fearfully significant: "And dere she was wit de light on her! Christ, yuh coulda pushed me over with a finger! I was scared, get me? Sure! I thought she was a ghost, see? She was all in white like dey wrap around stiffs."[37] Earlier she was unimportant for Yank because she was "dead": impotent, inactive, impalpable. Now she is important because she is "dead": mysterious, ghastly, incomprehensible. Modified in meaning rather than merely repeated, "belonging" proves a real leitmotif.

Yank's cocksureness is also undercut — at least in the spectators' eyes — by another leitmotif suggesting the presence of some implacable power and relentless predicament whose mark he wears and even shares with Mildred, but whose nature is unclear for him. In scene iii Mildred finds it grotesque when a leopard complains of its spots. In observing this, she is adopting and adapting the prophet Jeremiah's rhetorical question: "Can the Ethiopian change his skin, or the leopard his spots?" In scene iv the motif is unwittingly echoed by one of the Voices warning Yank, unwilling to wash, that coal dust "makes spots on you — like a leopard."[38] The short-circuited leitmotif may imply more than the protagonists can guess.

After his humiliation at the hands of Mildred, Yank's immediate reaction, in terms of action, was to take personal revenge. He tried to sneak near and seek out the girl in Southampton, but Mildred's charitable visit was guarded by a full ironical chorus of hired detectives, and they prevented Yank from approaching the millionaire's daughter. "Dey spotted me and gimme de bum's rush,"[39] as he tersely sums up the events which are not shown on the stage, took place between the scenes, and are told in a somewhat epic manner.

Scene v is Long's lesson. Three weeks after the affair in the stokehole he has taken Yank to Fifth Avenue, New York City, to demonstrate that Yank's individual experience is part of a general pattern.

> Yer been lookin' at this 'ere 'ole affair wrong. Yer been actin' an' talkin' 's if
> it was all a bleedin' personal matter between yer and that bloody cow. I
> wants to convince yer she was on'y a representative of 'er clarss. I wants to
> awaken yer bloody clarss consciousness. Then yer'll see it's 'er clarss yer've
> got to fight, not 'er alone. There's a 'ole mob of 'em like 'er, Gawd blind
> 'em![40]

Yank far surpasses his master in radicalism; Long is satisfied with impress-
ing the workers' demands through peaceful means, "the votes of the on-
marching proletarians of the bloody world,"[41] Yank bumps into the
gentlemen, accosts a lady, hits a fat, high-hatted, spatted man, and makes
him miss a bus. Long slinks off (to be sure, left), the man calls the police,
and Yank is arrested. The clanging gong of the patrol wagon, a clamoring
echo, as it were, of the enormous brazen gong which caused the firemen to
file through the door of the forecastle in a prisoner's lockstep at the end of
scene i, indicates the end of scene v. It also shows the consistency of O'Neill's
leitmotifs.

Social antagonism is emphasized by expressionistic distortion and contrast. Yank wears his dirty dungarees and fireman's cap, is unshaved, and
has a black smudge of coal dust around his resentful eyes; the elegant people
leaving the church, in which the Sunday morning sermon attacked the
"false" doctrines the radicals preach, are dressed extravagantly. "The
women are rouged, calcimined, dyed, overdressed to the nth degree. The
men are in Prince Alberts, high hats, spats, canes, etc."[42] Yank is challenging impertinence and attacking aggressivity incarnate; the fashionable
crowd forms "a procession of gaudy marionettes, yet with something of the
relentless horror of Frankensteins in their detached, mechanical unawareness."[43] Whenever Yank scorns them, they pretend they have not heard his
insults, and if *he* bumps into *them, they* beg *his* pardon. Yank is "steel and
steam and smoke and the rest of it", and they are only dolls he "winds up to
see 'm spin." "Yuh don't belong, get me! . . . I belong, dat's me," Yank draws
the familiar conclusion, but this time he does so with a generalizing validity.
His violent, subjective affronts are left unanswered by indifferent, reified
masks.

This is true not only figuratively but also literally. Although in his stage
directions O'Neill did not specify his wish that any of his characters should
put on masks, when his costume designer, Blanche Hays came forth with
the suggestion that society people sauntering on Fifth Avenue should wear
masks, the playwright immediately agreed and was delighted.[44] The advantages of the device are plausible. The masks adumbrate the mechanical attitudes of the unapproachable, gaudy marionettes;[45] emphasize the lifeless
and horrifying quality of ladies and gentlemen who do not "belong"; intensify the incognito of people who are only manifested in an overgeneralized,
assumed, abstract function; and enhance the mass-effect of their procession
dressed in a uniform fashion (as they also do in O'Neill's Coleridge-adapta-
tion, *The Rime of the Ancient Mariner*, 1923, in *Marco Millions*, 1923–25

or *Lazarus Laughed*, 1925–26). Moreover, it is noteworthy that having "second thoughts" on the possibility of an extended use of masks in 1932, O'Neill observed:

> In *The Hairy Ape* a much more extensive use of masks would be of the greatest value in emphasizing the theme of the play. From the opening of the fourth scene, where Yank begins to think he enters into a masked world, even the familiar faces of his mates in the forecastle have become strange and alien. They should be masked, and the faces of everyone he encounters thereafter, including the symbolic gorilla's.[46]

The use of the mask in this concept is conditioned by an expressive and expressionistic projection of a state of mind (as is also the case in *All God's Chillun Got Wings*, 1923), a stranger's perception of a strange and alien relationship between himself and the rest of the world, an unintegrated person's sense of the real having no truth any more, and the true having no reality yet (the mask functions in a comparable way in *The Great God Brown*, 1925), and a seeker's view of values being veiled (also in *Days Without End*, 1927–33).[47]

This afterthought, however, is, of course, no more than an extension of a hidden possibility. In scene v of *The Hairy Ape* Yank's clash with the marionettes of Fifth Avenue is a dramatic collision of personal hatred with impersonal indifference, of natural force with artificial power.

The confrontation of natural and unnatural qualities underlies the meaning of a recurring leitmotif. In scene i in Paddy's lament the sun-bathed world and period of the sailing boat are natural and the smoke-contaminated cage and age of the steamboat are unnatural. In scene ii the beautiful, vivid life of the sea, the great flood of sunshine pouring down on the deck and the fresh sea wind blowing powerfully are Nature herself contrasted with the inert artificiality of the millionairess and her aunt. In scene v the background of the jeweller's and furrier's windows illuminated by intermittent artificial light is shown "in tawdry disharmony with the clear light and sunshine on the street itself."[48] The opposition between the genuine and the artificial becomes even sharper when Yank, the hairy ape, perceives monkey fur in the furrier's shopwindow displayed for sale for two thousand dollars and admired by an absorbed chorus of delighted marionettes. Yank's fury is natural as sunshine and the object of his fury is unnatural as artificial light, monkey fur and "magnificence cheapened and made grotesque by commercialism."[49] In the examined context, from scene i to scene v Yank has changed poles.

Poles and places. In scene vi he is in prison on Blackwells Island. The cells extend in a diagonal line from right front to left rear, as it were, endlessly. The dynamic device O'Neill applies in the composition of his setting is a scenic adaptation of the slanting axis, the epoch-making, structural innovation of Baroque painting, Baroque expressivity being further developed by modern Expressionism.[50]

The persistence and metamorphosis of leitmotifs are very conspicuous in scene vi. Beaten up by the police and flung in jail by the judge who gave Yank thirty days to think his position over, the stoker has an additional reason to assume the attitude of Rodin's "The Thinker," which he, in fact, does.

Finding himself in a cell behind bars, Yank is inclined to suppose that he is in a cage in the zoo. The parallel with the ape multiplies and deepens, and the tension between the descending curve of sinking to the level of an animal and the ascending endeavour of thinking in a human way is intensified.

Earlier metaphors relating to prison are transformed into a set of non-metaphorical images (having symbolic connotations).

A crucial change can be observed in the pulsating range of reference of the leitmotif of "belonging" and "not belonging." Up to this point, in Yank's mind both steel and fire have belonged. From now on, steel does not belong any more, only fire does. Imprisoned by steel, Yank denounces steel:

> Sure—her old man—president of de Steel Trust—makes half de steel in de world—steel—where I tought I belonged—drivin' trou—movin'—in dat—to make *her*—and cage me in for her to spit on! Christ! (*He shakes the bars of his cell door till the whole tier trembles. Irritated, protesting exclamations from those awakened or trying to get to sleep*) He made dis—dis cage! Steel! *It* don't belong, dat's what! Cages, cells, locks, bolts, bars—dat's what it means!—holdin' me down wit him at de top! But I'll drive trou! Fire, dat melts it! I'll be fire—under de heap—fire dat never goes out—hot as hell—breakin' out in de night—[51]

Even a practical solution seems to present itself. One of the captives (an expressionistically anonymous Voice) reads out an article from the *Sunday Times*. It is a longwinded speech by a certain Senator Queen against the Wobblies (the members of the organization the Industrial Workers of the World), who, he asserts, plan to demolish liberty, justice, honor, equal opportunity, and the brotherhood of men, and plot to "make our sweet and lovely civilization a shambles, a desolation where man, God's masterpiece, would soon degenerate back to the ape!"[52] The inmates repeat the rhetorical key-words of liberty, justice, honor, opportunity, and brotherhood with the kind of mocking choric rejection with which the stokers in scenes i and iv repeated think ("Drink, don't think!"), love, law, governments, and God. Yank, hearing that the Industrial Workers of the World, or as the senator nicknames them, the Industrial Wreckers of the World "would tear down society, put the lowest scum in the seats of the mighty" and "turn Almighty God's revealed plan for the world topsy-turvy,"[53] becomes intensely interested in the Wobblies and decides to join their organization. At the climactic end of the scene Yank shakes his cell door to a clanging accompaniment (thus providing an explanatory, mordant and discordant counterpoint to his trustful, self-glorifying and unwittingly self-ironical pounding against the steel bunks in scene i), he tries to break out of prison, bends a bar of his cell, and is flooded by a stream of water hitting the steel bars of his cell with a splattering smash.

Scene vii is characterized by intensely incongruous misunderstandings and grimly grotesque tragicomedy. Having served his term in prison, Yank visits a local branch of the Industrial Workers of the World wishing to join them. At first the Secretary accepts him and suggests he should sit down and read pamphlets. (Yank can hardly read and write.) Yank thinks the organization is clandestine, and behaves as if he were in a romantically forbidden, secret territory. To show his good will, to prove his toughness, and to find his own vengeful satisfaction, he undertakes to blow up anything. "Can't youse see I belong? Sure! I'm regular. I'll stick, get me? . . . Yuh wanter blow tings up, don't yuh? Well, dat's me! I belong,"[54] he assures the Secretary. He would find special pleasure, he goes on, to dynamite "steel — all de cages — all de factories, steamers, buildings, jails — de Steel Trust and all dat makes it go."[55] Having carried out his tasks, he would write Mildred Douglas a letter informing her that the perpetrator of the action was the hairy ape. That will square things, he hopes.

The appalled Secretary explains to Yank that the organization is perfectly legal, suspects that he is an agent provocateur, calls him "a brainless ape," and has him thrown out. Hopeless, helpless, and bewildered, Yank turns to the "Man in the Moon" in the attitude of a gibbering ape to find a spiritual and existential explanation and to be told where to "get off at," but he only receives an absurd answer from a policeman: "You'll get off at the station, you boob, if you don't get up out of that and keep movin'. "[56] The line of descent of absurd drama from *The Hairy Ape* is legitimate.

The scene has a multiple message in the pattern of the play. It touches upon a perennial problem of the American labor movement: the split between theory and practice, the separation of "pamphlet reading" and revolutionary action, the divergence of guiding principles and groping endeavors, the opposition of enlightening consciousness and instinctive revolt.[57]

The dramatic clash between Yank and the Secretary of the I. W. W. is all the more revealing since it betrays a change of concept in the elaboration of the plot. In 1917 O'Neill wrote a short story entitled *The Hairy Ape*. Although he apparently destroyed the manuscript, which was not published, we have a critique of it by Carl Hovey, managing editor of the magazine *Metropolitan*. From Hovey's partly appreciative but ultimately rejecting opinion it turns out that the outcome of the story was the chief protagonist's joining the I. W. W.[58] In the play-version the attempt becomes thwarted and thus the meaning is changed.

The direction of the change is suggested by Yank's bitter soliloquy after his ejection from the local with ill-advised but well-directed parting kicks. Sitting in the middle of the narrow cobbled street in front of the local, and attempting to assume the attitude of Rodin's "The Thinker," he tries to assess his situation and formulate his position in the brooding pattern of the interior monologue:

> So dem boids don't tink I belong, neider. Aw, to hell wit 'em! Dey're in de wrong pew — de same old bull — soap-boxes and Salvation Army — no guts! Cut out an hour offen de job a day and make me happy! Gimme a dollar more a day and make me happy! Tree square a day, and cauliflowers in de front yard — ekal rights — a woman and kids — a lousy vote — and I'm all fixed for Jesus, huh? Aw, hell! What does dat get yuh? Dis ting's in your inside, but it ain't your belly. Feedin' your face — sinkers and coffee — dat don't touch it. It's way down — at de bottom. Yuh can't grab it, and yuh can't stop it. It moves, and everything moves. It stops and de whole woild stops. Dat's me now — I don't tick, see? — I'm a busted Ingersoll, dat's what. Steel was me, and I owned de woild. Now I ain't steel, and de woild owns me. Aw, hell! I can't see — it's all dark, get me? It's all wrong!⁵⁹

In composing the dramatic conclusion (scene viii) of his play, O'Neill faced a three-fold alternative. The first one was to lead Yank back to the company of his fellow-stokers, with his initial complacency gone, self-confidence broken, and self-esteem evaporated. In an early version O'Neill, in fact, chose such an ending.⁶⁰ This solution, however, would have been narrowly naturalistic with the preponderance of the determining power of a physical and social milieu; so the dramatist discarded it.

The second alternative was to follow the line of the 1917 short story and to make Yank find himself among the Wobblies. In 1921, however, O'Neill did not consider a consummation of this kind feasible.

Thus only the third alternative remained open to the playwright: to find a solution whose climactic complexity was fitting and so could be fitted to the involved intricacy of the preceding scenes.

Accordingly, in scene viii Yank visits the monkey house at the zoo. He sees a mate in the gorilla, releases him from his cage, holds out his hand to the ape and plans to go with him to Fifth Avenue to knock the rich off the earth. The gorilla hugs Yank, breaks his bones, throws him into the cage, shuts the door, and shuffles off menacingly.

A number of recurring leitmotifs and returning characteristics are brought to their fullness in this grotesquely tragic denouement. The dominant leitmotif of Yank's comparison to a hairy ape comes full circle here: having been named a filthy beast by Mildred, having understood from Paddy's words that she saw him as a hairy ape, and having suffered the second insult of being called a brainless ape by the secretary of an I. W. W. local, Yank's final call at the monkey house strikes the audience as necessary. The necessity of Yank's last and desperate move is visually enhanced by the scenic picture showing how Yank leans over the railing and stares at the gorilla, who stares back at him, silent and motionless. They appear as one another's mirror image doubles. Is the dehumanizing reversal of Darwinian evolution a threatening trend?

The other major leitmotif of steel, prison, and cage persisting from the forecastle and stokehole scenes to the Blackwells Island cells attains the final stage of its development in scene viii where the gorilla imprisons Yank in his steel cage. Is the toiling worker of the Steel Trust, is the dehumanized man of the machine age essentially a prisoner of circumstances?

The uses and transformations of brutish energy, first serving, then fighting the industrial civilization of the privileged class, reach their ultimate phase as a brute's energy annihilating Yank. Is anarchistic rebellion against revolting conditions both inevitable and self-defeating?

The frequent leitmotif of Yank assuming the attitude of Rodin's "The Thinker" is in its last occurrence (at the opening of scene viii) transferred to the position of the gorilla. What is the range of human consciousness?

Yank's misleading illusions and revealing delusions (imagining independence in the state of dependence, considering the gorilla a helpmate, supposing Mildred was a white ghost, seeing the well-to-do in Fifth Avenue as gaudy marionettes, taking prison to be a cage) culminate in scene viii. Once deeming his association with the hairy ape a gross insult, and now falling a victim to the make-believe that the gorilla is his associate, Yank reads his own delusive moods into the stance of the gorilla whose reactions seem to be conditioned by Yank's deceptions. When Yank admires the gorilla's enormous chest, large shoulders, strong arms, and punching fists, the gorilla, "as if he understood, stands upright, swelling out his chest and pounding on it with his fist"[61] (as Yank did in scene iii). Yank assures the ape he understands his intention of challenging the whole world. When Yank pities the gorilla for being exposed to the insultingly inquisitive laughter and bewildered glances of visitors, and pounds on the rail with his fist, the gorilla also "rattles the bars of his cage and snarls." When Yank calls him lucky, the gorilla growls proudly; when Yank refers to his cage, the gorilla roars angrily; and when the stoker asks him whether he also wants to get even with those who keep and humiliate him in a cage, the gorilla "roars an emphatic affirmative." Yank's wish-fulfilment continues even longer; he praises the gorilla as one who is "regular," who "sticks" (Yank failed to convince the I. W. W. Secretary he himself was "regular" and would "stick"), and he holds out his hand to the gorilla to effect the secret grip of the order (i.e. he reverses the humiliating situation at the Wobblies' local where the Secretary scorned him for supposing the organization was clandestine, required a password, an initiation ceremony, and an affirming grip). Is illusion more palpable for the exalted soul than reality?[62]

The emphatically reiterated contrast between natural beauty and artificial mechanization (Paddy's sailing boat and Yank's steam liner in scene i; flooding sunlight and affected artificiality in scene ii devoted to Mildred and her aunt; genuine and artificial light, stokers and marionettes in the Fifth Avenue scene) appears for the last time in a special form in scene viii. Seeking an emotional unity with nature (though sensing its impossibility in the industrialized present), Yank comes the closest to Paddy's position once rejected vigorously. This is what he tells the gorilla:

I s'pose yuh wanter know what I'm doin' here, huh? I been warmin' a bench down to de Battery — ever since last night. Sure. I seen de sun come up. Dat was pretty, too — all red and pink and green. I was lookin' at de sky-scrapers — steel — and all de ships comin' in, sailin' out, all over de oith — and dey was steel, too. De sun was warm, dey wasn't no clouds, and dere was a breeze blowin'. Sure, it was great stuff. I got it aw right — what Paddy said about dat bein' de right dope — on'y I couldn't get *in* it, see? I couldn't belong in dat. It was over my head. And I kept tinkin' — and den I beat it up here to see what youse was like. And I waited till dey was all gone to git yuh alone.[63]

Do Paddy's yearning historical retrospection and Yank's apparent anthropological retrogression stem from a similar social attitude?

Last but not least, the intellectually decisive leitmotif of "belonging" also plays a determining role in the dramatic coda of *The Hairy Ape*. As long as Yank considered himself an integrated and integral part of monopolistic mechanization and machinery, he supposed that he, practically all workers, steel, fire, speed, engines and furnaces, all forms, means and products of modern industrialization "belonged." Exceptions were unimportant: Paddy was a weakling, Long was "yellow." The first cabin passengers, to be sure, did not "belong," but they did not matter either, they were just "baggage." The engineer's whistle, Mildred's insult, Long's demonstration, the rich marionettes, and the steel bars of prison convinced Yank that there was a full procession of people who did not "belong," that the Steel Trust did not "belong" either, and that steel in general did not "belong" any more. But fire did; hence Yank's effort to join the Wobblies. When he is called a brainless ape by the Secretary and is thrown out of the local of the I. W. W., his faith in himself is shaken, he is forced to realize that even the Wobblies do not think he "belongs," and rather than owning the world, he is owned by the world. His last, desperate attempt to find a friend and brother-in-arms in the gorilla is a lonely man's endeavor to prove that he does "belong" after all, that he is a member of the same club as the gorilla, who as an organic part of a natural order — Nature's order — certainly "belongs," and for whom, therefore, "belonging" is natural and easier than it is for Yank.

The stoker tries to rationalize his predicament in the pattern of what may be called a modified dramatic interior monologue. It is not a simple *aside* since its primary function is not to inform the audience but to express a seething state of a turbulent mind. Nor is it a regular dialogue because — although Yank is talking to the gorilla and the ape is giving reactions which Yank considers adequate "answers" — the gorilla does not, of course, really reply to Yank. The gorilla's reactions may be looked upon as ironically reduced modifications of the gestures of such "silent companions" as the husband in O'Neill's *Before Breakfast* (1916–17) or Miss Y in Strindberg's *The Stronger* (1889). In these monodramas the monologue absorbs and implies the dialogue. Nor can we consider the passage a traditional monologue because its manner of association is freer than that of the customary monologue and it approaches the stream of consciousness form of expression. It is closer to a "modified monologue," which Timo Tiusanen defines as an utterance "spoken in spite of another character, out of inner compulsion, not in reaction to a previous speech, nor aside, as an interpolation of the playwright, . . . a 'Personal Epiphany' spoken while there are other characters present. Whether these other characters hear or not, . . . has no bearing; in the focus there is the *speaker* and his obsession,"[64] — with the difference that Yank's words are not spoken *in spite of* the gorilla but — at least partly — *to* the gorilla, with the aim of defining his own position in relation to the ape's, and with the intention of pointing out that the gorilla firmly "belongs," and is luckier than Yank is. Yank's brooding speech is a part of his effort and strategy of winning the gorilla over to his side. Thus the other "character's" hearing and appreciating Yank's words are by no means immaterial factors.

Yank's manifestation is then a modified dramatic interior monologue in the sense that it is characterized by the revelation of a state of mind whose center of gravity lies in the ego revealed (it is a *monologue*); by a tentative tendency to project a free-associational stream of consciousness with a psychological emphasis on the transition and transformation of oscillating ideas and emotions (it is an *interior* monologue); by a direction advancing the over-all action through contrast and tension (it is a *dramatic* monologue); and by being only relatively self-contained, turning to another figure as well, constituting an act not exclusively (if mainly) of self-expression but also one of communication and interaction (it is a *modified* monologue).[65]

This dramatic idiom suits best Yank's dawning awareness of his plight of "belonging." After expressing his sympathy with the gorilla for having to suffer in a cage the insulting glances of "de white-faced, skinny tarts and the boobs what marry 'em"[66] and hearing the ape rattle the bars of his cage, Yank says:

> Sure! Dat's de way it hits me, too. On'y yuh're lucky, see? Yuh don't belong wit 'em and yuh know it. But me, I belong wit 'em — but I don't, see? Dey don't belong wit me, dat's what. Get me? Tinkin' is hard — (*He passes one hand across his forehead with a painful gesture. The gorilla growls impatiently. Yank goes on gropingly*) It's dis way, what I'm drivin' at. Youse can sit and dope dream in de past, green woods, de jungle and de rest of it. Den yuh belong and dey don't. Den yuh kin laugh at 'em, see? Yuh're de champ of de world. But me — I ain't got no past to tink in, nor nothin' dat's comin', on'y what's now — and dat don't belong. Sure, you're best off! You can't tink, can yuh? Yuh can't talk neider. But I kin make a bluff at talkin' and tinkin' — a'most git away wit it — a'most! — and dat's where de joker comes in. (*He laughs.*) I ain't on oith and I ain't in heaven, get me? I'm in de middle tryin' to separate 'em, takin' de woist punches from bot' of 'em. Maybe dat's what dey call hell, huh? But you, yuh're at de bottom. You belong! Sure! Yuh're de on'y one in de woild dat does, yuh lucky stiff! (*The gorilla growls proudly*) And dat's why dey gotter put yuh in a cage, see? (*The gorilla roars angrily*) Sure! Yuh get me. It beats it when you try to tink

it or talk it—it's way down—deep—behind—you 'n' me feel it. Sure! Bot' members of dis club! (*He laughs—then in a savage tone*) What de hell! T' hell wit it! A little action, dat's our meat! Dat belongs![67]

After the released gorilla has crushed Yank's ribs and shut him up in the cage, Yank is compelled to realize that "Even him didn't tink I belonged." The last painfully ironical word of the play, highlighting once more the crucial concept of "belonging," indicates that the ever shrinking sphere of the human validity of "belonging" has been reduced to zero: Yank "slips in a heap on the floor and dies. The monkeys set up a chattering, whimpering wail. And, perhaps, the Hairy Ape at last belongs." If modern man, for all his conceited complacency, frenzy and fury, hangs in a paralyzed state of benumbed hibernation between animal integration and spiritual values, if he cannot move either forward or backward, and is equally barred from the fostering force of Mother Nature and the sustaining power of valid values, what are the true conditions of human "belonging" in the age of the steamship, the Steel Trust, and monopolistic mechanization?

The reason why most of these puzzling, pressing, and searching questions, however passionately they are posed, are not unambiguously answered, or remain ultimately unanswered, why the play is richer in suggestions than solutions lies in the fact that the drama has a double conflict. On the one hand, it presents the tangible confrontation of the haves and the have-nots, the top-dog and the under-dog, the privileged and the toiling classes; on the other hand, it shows the more abstract opposition of civilization and nature. The two kinds of conflict are not independent from one another: while the rich are displayed as civilized and unnatural, the poor are represented as uncivilized and natural. Nevertheless, the two types of conflict only partially overlap. Whereas the first leads to the conclusion that a particular social system, a specific sort of civilization should be changed by another and better one, the second type of opposition offers the implication that society and civilization in general should be demolished. In the first case, the blame is put on the Steel Trust; in the second one, on steel.

The violent enforcement of one type of conflict through the other is responsible for the expressionistic aspect of *The Hairy Ape*. Whether and how far Yank is an abstract expressionistic symbol or a concrete dramatic character, a cipher or a stoker is a perennial problem of O'Neill criticism.[68] O'Neill himself coupled the duality of his play with a dual approach in describing his attitude. In an interview with a staff member of the *New York Herald Tribune*, published on March 26, 1924, he said:

> *The Hairy Ape* . . . was a symbol of man, who has lost his old harmony with nature, the harmony which he used to have as an animal and has not yet acquired in a spiritual way. Thus, not being able to find it on earth nor in heaven, he's in the middle, trying to make peace, taking the "woist punches from bot' of 'em." This idea was expressed in Yank's speech. The public saw just the stoker, not the symbol, and the symbol makes the play

either important or just another play. Yank can't go forward, and so he tries to go back. This is what his shaking hands with the gorilla meant. But he can't go back to "belonging" either. The gorilla kills him. The subject here is the same ancient one that always was and always will be the one subject for drama, and that is man and his struggle with his own fate. The struggle used to be with the gods, but is now with himself, his own past, his attempt to "belong."[69]

The loss of belonging to Mother Nature and the sense of becoming a social outcast (both precipitated by monopolistic industrialization) led to a partial transcendentalization of values and an interest in abstract symbols. The aspect of expressionism in the play is congruent with this concept of the world.

At the same time, and in the same interview, however, O'Neill also marks off his artistic endeavors from those of the expressionists:

the newest thing now in playwriting is the opposite of the character play. It is the expressionistic play. For expressionism denies the value of characterization. As I understand it, expressionism tries to minimize everything on the stage that stands between the author and the audience. . . . I personally do not believe that an idea can be readily put over to an audience except through characters. When it sees "A Man" and "A Woman" — just abstractions, it loses the human contact by which it identifies itself with the protagonist of the play. An example of this sort of expressionism is *Morn Till Midnight*, with character abstractions like "A Bank Clerk." This is the point at which I disagree with the theory. I do not believe that the character gets between the author's idea and the audience. The real contribution of the expressionist has been in the dynamic qualities of his plays. They express something in modern life better than did the old plays. I have something of this method in *The Hairy Ape*. But the character Yank remains a man and everyone recognizes him as such.[70]

Accordingly, already in scene i of *The Hairy Ape* expressionistic (rather than expressionist) effects crop up. Besides those already analyzed, let it suffice here to point to the ear-rending tumult of sound given by "Voices" at the very opening of the play. The violent shouts, angry exclamations and drunken outbursts of these Voices combine in a mass-effect of an expressionistic turmoil. This, however, is the sum-total of particular fragments of human vicissitudes; the Voice, for example, yelling with exasperation "A slut, I'm sayin'! She robbed me aslape"[71] seems to complain about an event described in detail in one of the *Glencairn* one-acters, *The Long Voyage Home*, hinging on Olson's plight. And emerging from the mass of stokers, Yank, Paddy, and Long are certainly clearly characterized individuals: types with personal names and traits rather than stereotypes with common names and features.

The structure of *The Hairy Ape*, like the character-portrayal of the play, is also Janus-faced. On the one hand, it is made up of a sequence of scenes as in expressionist drama. On the other hand, the scenes are specially organized both internally and externally. Practically each of them shows a short-story oriented inner pattern of a scaled down one-acter having a min-iature exposition, plot development and climactic crisis. This is especially clear in scenes iii, v, vi, vii, and viii. At the same time, the scenes do not fall apart into isolated units but constitute an organic whole and can be grouped into larger structural sections of a dramatic exposition (scenes i to iv), plot development culminating in a crisis (scenes v to vii) and a dramatic denouement (scene viii).

Other structural divisions of the play are also possible. One may, for example, consider scenes i and ii as double exposition, scene iii as the first crisis point with a strong collision, scene iv as an epilogue to the first three scenes and a prologue (or a further exposition) to the section of scenes v to vii in which each scene represents an additional crisis point and scenes vi and vii are especially crucial in the dramatic development leading to the final event of the resolution in scene viii. The fact that the play is susceptible of various compositional articulations indicates the impact of the scene se-quence principle of the expressionist method even in the nonexpressionist aspect of the drama: in a more traditional play structural caesuras cannot be shifted. The sheer possibility of grouping the scenes into larger units in its turn shows the operation of a nonexpressionist principle in the expressionist scene arrangement.

The structure of the play then displays a transitional quality that calls for an elucidation from the viewpoint of the poles between which it repre-sents a transition.

The division of any drama is not a mere technical question depending solely on the dramatist's momentary caprice but a problem of form deter-mined — besides personal choice and taste — by the historical age the play-wright lives in, and the world concept he possesses. If the dramatic characters are autonomous people who are able to create situations with their dynamic actions even on a social soil torn by objective discrepancies, and who are ready to take the initiative in the interaction of individual and society, then the dramatic structure supporting the conflict is brought about by the dynamic lines of force of human action which divide the composition in a natural manner into well-defined phases from the exposition, through the strenuous stages of imbroglio, to the critical culmination of bursting tension, peripeteia, and resolution. This pattern had been created in its main lines by Greek Antiquity, was elaborated by Renaissance art and came to be canonized by classicism.

The resolution of the question in what way the structural units mani-fest themselves, and what means and sections the dramatist adopts to artic-ulate his matter belongs to particular periods of human and dramatic history, and does not concern the basic aesthetic problem. Greek drama did not yet introduce act divisions but it allotted the chorus a significant role in breaking up the play into structural units. Roman drama (Plautus, Terence, Seneca) already used acts. Renaissance-humanist drama, following Latin models, not infrequently availed itself of a division into acts; Shakespeare, however, did not follow this practice: his plays were divided into acts by his editors influenced by the taste of French classicism. The Shakespearean basis of building a drama is the characterizing scene brought about by the deeds of self-asserting characters. The scene as a fundamental structural unit preserves its relative independence, but at the same time it is also a compositional link in an actional chain. The links are combined into more comprehensive organic units by the crucial points of action (*Richard III, Romeo and Juliet, Macbeth,* etc.).

If, however, under specific historical circumstances the dramatic protagonists are no longer able to perform autonomous actions (or not as yet); if under vigorously extending or monopolistically extended social conditions of mass alienation the active and creative interaction between the individual and the world becomes lost; if the dramatic character finds himself a prisoner of a milieu, and the authorial angle of vision is also characterized by uncertainty and abstraction, then, with the devaluation or failure of individual activity realizing human values, dramatic composition also becomes transformed. The traditional structural balance between part and whole is still maintained by Ibsen's dramatic pattern: the conception of the dramatic form as a tribunal makes it both possible and necessary even within the framework of this dramatic strategy to develop and strain a social crisis to a moral culmination. The heroes' spheres of action, however, shrink, their worlds are reduced, their dynamism is broken, their aspirations are limited by their environment. In the well-made play the phases of exposition — intrigue — culmination — peripeteia — and solution only follow the superficial ruffles of "good society" rather than the deep currents of a crisis-ridden society (Scribe, Sardou, Pinero, Jones, Belasco, etc.), its act division only follows the ready-made clichés or sentimental formulas of a smoothly functioning mechanism. In the dramatic literature of the naturalist movement structure becomes loose, and in the violent idiom of the expressionist theatre arrangement by acts is usually exploded and replaced by a dramatic chain reaction of scenes. Where human acts are disqualified, dramatic acts are difficult to maintain. Acts disappear like major and minor keys in expressionist music, and scenes tend to assume equal importance in the dramatic sequence as do musical notes in Schoenberg's atonal twelve-note scale.

By underscoring the importance of scenes, the expressionist theatre seems to continue the aesthetic principles of Shakespearean renaissance drama. In reality, however, it does just the contrary: while renaissance drama sweeps forward along the track of an objective line of development, and its scenes are organic parts of larger units,[72] the structure of expressionist drama projects a subjective series of scenes before the spectator, and usually uses a scene not to prepare for but to replace broader dramatic units. This is its means and method of reflecting a state or view of the world in which reality has no truth any longer, and truth has no reality yet, and in which, therefore, truth can only be guessed at in spite of reality, through and by the instinctive, emotive, and expressive distortion, the dreamlike, nightmarish, and visionary transformation of everyday immediacy; it can be divined as an allegorical and symbolic illustration of mythic formulas and patterns. Where there is no path leading to an aim glimmering in and beckoning from the future, there the short units of the dramatic structure cannot join in larger sections; there only the scene is palpable, and the act does not exist. It is not without reason that after some antecedents the breakthrough in the direction of this kind of dramatic structure took place in such searching plays of deep uncertainty as (part three of) Strindberg's *To Damascus* (1898–1901), *A Dreamplay* (1901), or the five chamber plays, *Storm Weather* (1907), *The Burned House* (1907), *The Ghost Sonata* (1907), *The Pelican* (1907), and *The Black Glove* (1909); that the pattern became widespread during the period leading up to the international crisis of World War I; and that this way of composition was sustained by progressive playwrights expressing their messianistic, revolutionary worldview in post-war times.

O'Neill partook in this general development with a special historical and personal background provided by the vigorous expansion of civilization in the United States after the Civil War, the unparalleled speed and spread of industrialization, the dynamic drive of monopolies, and the social and cultural contradictions inherent in the process, which were stepped up by World War I, enhanced by the period of depression, increased by the advance of fascism, and intensified by World War II. O'Neill experienced the course of events with a passionate interest, tragic involvement, tragicomic sharpness, and psychic imbalance. His individual talent, social position, psychological make-up, and search for values combined into an ideal unity to give voice and ingenious expression to the tensions inside himself that proved to be equivalents of outer objective contradictions.

Even if O'Neill's heroes were not renaissance giants and he himself was more in search than in possession of undiminished personal autonomy, his chief concern throughout his dramatic career was to test the validity of human values against the reality of changed and changing conditions.

As a result, he reversed the process of structural disintegration and achieved compositional reintegration through a long series of dramatic experiments. His development was unequal and its stages represented a typological tendency rather than a strict chronology.

The first stage was the natural gesture of a talented tyro: the writing of condensed one-act plays (*A Wife for a Life*, 1913; *Warnings*, 1913; *Fog*, 1914; *Abortion*, 1914; *The Sniper*, 1915; *Before Breakfast*, 1916–17; *Shell-Shock*, 1918–19; *The Rope*, 1918–19; *The Dreamy Kid*, 1918–19; *Where the Cross Is Made*, 1918–19, etc.).

The second stage was constituted by the four *Glencairn* plays (*Bound East for Cardiff*, 1914; *In the Zone*, 1916–17; *The Long Voyage Home*, 1916–17; *The Moon of the Caribbees*, 1916–17), which were conceived as one-acters but were elaborated with a measure of coherence in concept, theme, character, and method, so that in hindsight they may be looked upon as a loose cycle, a tentative tetralogy.

The third stage was characterized by a series of scenes, arranged in a cascade-connection with a mounting tension, and forming groups of larger units (*The Emperor Jones*, 1920; *The Hairy Ape*, 1921). Both plays show significant parallels with Georg Kaiser's expressionist drama, *From Morn to Midnight* published in Germany in 1916, first performed in England (London) in the translation of Ashley Dukes in March, 1920, published in England in May, 1920, and in the United States in the autumn issue, 1920, of the Boston magazine *Poet Lore*.[73]

In showing the way in which the Cashier of a provincial bank in a small German town embezzles a large sum of money (scene i), is rejected by an Italian lady whom he mistook for a courtesan and for whose sake he committed his crime (scene ii), runs amok through a snow-covered field (scene iii), calls at his home only to realize he can no longer fit in with the humdrum, cozy routine rut of his earlier existence (scene iv), offers an enormous sum to the winner at a bicycle race to enjoy the passionate excitement of the public (scene v), revels in a private supper room in a cabaret with masked prostitutes (scene vi), visits a Salvation Army Hall, is urged by a Salvation Lass to repent, publicly confesses his sin, perceives that the Salvation Lass has summoned the police to earn a reward,[74] and commits suicide (scene vii), Kaiser presents fairly independent and effective scenes. Each is like the lash of a whip. They do not call for any specific external organization among themselves, although scene i launches, scenes ii to vi develop and scene vii ends the action. *The Emperor Jones* betrays a comparable arrangement of scenes with the difference that in O'Neill's play the compositional cohesion in the middle section of flight (scenes ii to vii) is somewhat greater. The crystallization of scenes into longer and firmer structural sections in *The Hairy Ape* has already been pointed out.[75]

The fourth stage can be considered the final phase of structural reintegration: multiple-act plays belong here with an organic division into acts, or scenes and acts (e.g. *Anna Christie*, 1921; *Desire Under the Elms*, 1924; *Mourning Becomes Electra*, 1929–31; *The Iceman Cometh*, 1939; *Long Day's Journey Into Night*, 1939–41; *A Moon for the Misbegotten*, 1941–43; *A Touch of the Poet*, 1935–42; *More Stately Mansions*, 1935–41).

The sheer fact that a play is externally divided into acts does not, of course, necessarily indicate a high degree of inner cohesion, an organic achievement of compositional concentration. The three-act *Servitude* (1914), contemporaneous with early one-acters, falls into three divergent one-act plays. *Bread and Butter* (1914), *The Personal Equation* (1915), or *Now I Ask You* (1916) are dramatic five-finger exercises uncharacteristic of O'Neill's mature art (even if *The Personal Equation* shows a measure of thematic, ideological and structural unity). Some of the one-act pieces like *The Long Voyage Home* (1916–17) or *The Moon of the Caribbees* (1916–17) display a greater dramatic density than do these multiple-act dramas. *Beyond the Horizon* (1918) and *The Straw* (1919) are overwritten. The one-act *Where the Cross Is Made* (1918), though far from being a success, is more concise than its four-act version, *Gold* (1920) appears to be. *Diff'rent* (1920) and *The First Man* (1921) are episodic failures.

From *Anna Christie* and especially from *Desire Under the Elms* on, however, O'Neill was able to wield the multiple-act structure as an organically built and firmly composed dramatic pattern, not without some epic intrusions, but essentially carved from one block, palpable, tangible, concrete. He was paving the way for his great late dramatic performance.

It is remarkable that whereas both plays in which the influence of expressionism is the most marked are characterized by a double conflict (*The Emperor Jones* and *The Hairy Ape*), and while in several of O'Neill's subsequent plays a number of expressionistic effects appear together with elements of a double (or multiple) conflict (*All God's Chillun Got Wings*, 1923; *The Great God Brown*, 1925; *Lazarus Laughed*, 1925–26; *Dynamo*, 1924–28; *Days Without End*, 1927–33), other dramas (also written in the twenties) in which the aspect of expressionism is not present (*Anna Christie*) or is not important (*Desire Under the Elms*) hinge on a single conflict.[76]

These considerations suggest that the double conflict, divided authorial approach, dual characterization, and Janus-faced structure of *The Hairy Ape* are indicative of a transitional position in the unfolding of the O'Neill canon and the development of world drama.

Nevertheless, spectators and readers, while they are aware of the polar possibilities embodied in the play, do not have the impression that it falls apart. This prompts one into supposing that there must be a unifying principle operating efficiently in the drama. This principle is the dramatic presentation of alienation, a state of existence and a form of activity deprived of the values of human essence. The apish traits of the stokers express the imposed alienation of the underdog; the effete properties of the family of the president of the Steel Trust and the procession of gaudy marionettes in Fifth Avenue represent the lucrative, if puzzling, alienation of the top dog;[77] and the mechanical features of both epitomize the alienation of the economic pattern, industrial system, and social order of which they are equally, if diagonally, parts. Both aspects of the conflict, characterization, composition and style of the play manifest O'Neill's enormous effort to come to grips with the plight of alienation; Yank's development lies in moving from the illusion of a nonalienated state, through an awareness of alienation, to an (ultimately unsuccessful) attempt to find unalienated values; and the crucial leitmotif of "belonging" and "not belonging" is the expression of an unalienated and an alienated state. *The Hairy Ape* is fundamentally a dramatic statement of "belonging" lost and a powerful plea for "belonging" to be regained. Hence its artistic significance and universal appeal.[78]

Notes

1. Quoted in Bogard, T., *Contour in Time: The Plays of Eugene O'Neill* (New York: Oxford University Press, 1972), pp. 240–41. O'Neill's description of *The Hairy Ape* is in keeping with K. Macgowan's views, advocated in his book *The Theatre of Tomorrow* (1921), of what the new theatre should be like. On the other hand, Macgowan in his second book, *Continental Stagecraft* (1922), written in collaboration with R. E. Jones, praised *The Hairy Ape* as a true expressionist drama. Cf. Bogard, pp. 175–77.

2. The life-model of the figure was Driscoll, an Irish-born, naturalized American, O'Neill's stoker friend and shipmate, whose extraordinary energy overwhelmed and whose suicide stunned the dramatist. See Sheaffer, L., *O'Neill: Son and Playwright* (Boston, Toronto: Little, Brown & Co., 1968), pp. 196–97, 335.

3. O'Neill, E., *The Hairy Ape. The Plays of Eugene O'Neill* (New York: Random House, 1955), III, pp. 207–08.

4. O'Neill, E., *The Personal Equation*, Act III, scene i, p. 1. A photo copy of an original typescript can be found in The Bancroft Library, University of California, Berkeley, call-marked 74/72 z. I am thankful to The Bancroft Library for having made it possible for me to read the play in 1977 during my ACLS Fellowship at the University of California, Berkeley. *The Personal Equation* is not in fact, a slice-of-life naturalistic drama, but an experimenting tyro's realistic endeavor in the thematically reinterpreted idiom of the well-made play. By wishing to avoid a naturalistic treatment of the scenes in *The Hairy Ape*. O'Neill means a rejection of a literal rendering of bare facts.

5. O'Neill, *The Emperor Jones. Plays* III, p. 195.

6. Cf. Sheaffer, p. 196.

7. O'Neill, *The Hairy Ape. Plays* III, pp. 213–14. For the autobiographical aspect of the passage see Mullett, M.B., "The Extraordinary Story of Eugene O'Neill," *The American Magazine*, 94 (November 1922), 118. Sheaffer, pp. 164–65. The experience of that adjustment, "not belonging" was one of O'Neill's deeply-rooted personal, psychological problems. Cf. Sheaffer, p. 389.

8. O'Neill, *The Hairy Ape. Plays* III, p. 216.

9. The dramatic clash between Long and Yank actually precedes the conflict between Paddy and Yank.

10. O'Neill, *The Hairy Ape. Plays* III, p. 212.

11. O'Neill, *The Hairy Ape. Plays* III, pp. 212, 214, 216, 225, 230, 231, 234, 235, 238, 241, 242, 243, 244, 247, 248, 250, 252, 253, 254.

12. O'Neill, *The Hairy Ape. Plays* III, p. 217.

13. O'Neill, *The Hairy Ape. Plays* III, p. 219.

14. O'Neill, *The Hairy Ape. Plays* III, p. 219.

15. O'Neill, *The Hairy Ape. Plays* III, p. 218.

16. Mildred and her aunt "sitting in their deck chairs are as sadly incongruous as Paddy was down in the forecastle. Bitterly ironical contrasts like this are characteristic of this 'comedy of ancient and modern times.' " Tiusanen, T., *O'Neill's Scenic Images* (Princeton: Princeton University Press, 1968), pp. 116–17.

17. O'Neill, *The Hairy Ape. Plays* III, p. 220.

18. O'Neill, when he sailed as an ordinary seaman on the luxury liner, the S.S. *New York* of the American Line, bound for Southampton, especially resented the women passengers "promenading in fine clean clothes, chatting and laughing, while he was on his knees scrubbing the deck." Sheaffer, p. 194. The same contrast is also expressed in Act I, p. 20 of *The Personal Equation*. For possible literary inspirations strengthening the sense of social tension in O'Neill

(Strindberg's *A Dream Play* and Kaiser's *The Coral*) see Blackburn, C., "Continental Influences on Eugene O'Neill's Expressionistic Dramas," *American Literature*, 13, No. 2 (May 1941), 118–20.

19. O'Neill, *The Hairy Ape. Plays* III, p. 223.

20. Törnqvist, E., *A Drama of Souls* (Uppsala: Almqvist och Wiksells, 1968), p. 159, n. 6.

21. O'Neill, *The Hairy Ape. Plays* III, p. 223.

22. O'Neill, *The Hairy Ape. Plays* III, p. 224.

23. O'Neill, *The Hairy Ape. Plays* III, pp. 224–25.

24. O'Neill, *The Hairy Ape. Plays* III, p. 225.

25. O'Neill, *The Hairy Ape. Plays* III, p. 226.

26. O'Neill, *The Moon of the Caribbees, Plays* I, p. 461.

27. O'Neill, *Chris Christophersen.* A photocopy in The Bancroft Library, University of California, Berkeley, of an original typescript, call-marked 74/72 z. Act I, Scene i, p. 13. I am indebted to The Bancroft Library.

28. O'Neill, *Anna Christie. Plays* III, pp. 35, 49, 61, 74.

29. O'Neill, *The Hairy Ape. Plays* III, p. 229.

30. O'Neill, *The Hairy Ape. Plays* III, p. 228.

31. O'Neill, *The Hairy Ape. Plays* III, p. 232.

32. O'Neill, *The Hairy Ape. Plays* III, pp. 210–11, 227–29.

33. O'Neill, *The Hairy Ape. Plays* III, p. 227.

34. O'Neill, *The Hairy Ape. Plays* III, p. 210.

35. O'Neill, *The Hairy Ape. Plays* III, p. 232.

36. O'Neill, *The Hairy Ape. Plays* III, p. 231.

37. O'Neill, *The Hairy Ape. Plays* III, cf. p. 231.

38. O'Neill, *The Hairy Ape. Plays* III, p. 226, cf. p. 220. Cf. Hughes, A. D., "Biblical Allusions in *The Hairy Ape.*" *The Eugene O'Neill Newsletter* I, 3 (January 1978), 9.

39. O'Neill, *The Hairy Ape. Plays* III, p. 235.

40. O'Neill, *The Hairy Ape. Plays* III, For O'Neill's association with various shades of social radicalism as represented by people like John Reed, Louise Bryant, Terry Carlin, or Hippolyte Havel, and for the delineation of their general activities, see Gelb, A. and B. *O'Neill* (New York: Harper and Bros, 1962), pp. 262–63, 283, 302, 306, 308, 310, 313–15, 318–19, 323, 327–31, 356, 442; 301–02, 309–10, 314, 318–19, 329, 334–35, 338, 345, 357, 361, 364–66, 371–72, 442, 801–02; 286–94, 308–10, 319, 324, 332, 350, 368, 420, 459, 476–76, 509–10, 530, 658; 298–99, 311, 359, 361, 459, 831. Sheaffer, pp. 323, 325, 343–60, 363–66, 373–74, 378, 383, 387, 389–91, 413, 418, 437, 452, 462–63; 346–66, 373–79, 383, 387, 390–91, 394, 405, 407, 409, 413–14, 418, 462–63; 335–38, 341, 346–47, 366, 385–86, 389, 404, 410, 433, 459; 327–29, 331, 341, 347, 352, 404.

41. O'Neill, *The Hairy Ape. Plays* III, p. 236.

42. O'Neill, *The Hairy Ape. Plays* III, p. 236.

43. O'Neill, *The Hairy Ape. Plays* III, p. 236.

44. Gelb, p. 495.

45. In *The Emperor Jones*, too, "there is something stiff, rigid, unreal, marionettish" about the movements of young belles and dandies who have come to find diversion at the slave auction. *Plays* III, p. 196. Cf. pp. 191, 194.

46. O'Neill, "Second Thoughts," "Memoranda on Masks" in Cargill, O., Fagin, N. B., and Fisher, W. J., *O'Neill and His Plays: Four Decades of Criticism* (New York: New York University Press, 1970), p. 119.

47. In *Days Without End* the face of John's double, Loving *"is a mask whose features reproduce exactly the features of John's face — the death mask of a John who has died with a sneer of scornful mockery on his lips. And this mocking scorn is repeated in the expression of the eyes which stare bleakly from behind the mask." Plays* III, pp. 493–4. For a comprehensive treatment of O'Neill's mask technique see Waith, E. M., "Eugene O'Neill: an Exercise in Unmasking" in Gassner, J. (ed.), *O'Neill: A Collection of Critical Essays* (Englewood Cliffs, N. J.: Prentice-Hall, 1964), pp. 29–41; and Tiusanen, pp. 16–17, 35, 46, 88, 139–40, 142–44, 152, 168–206, 214, 217, 223, 225–30, 237, 240, 256–57, 265, 269, 279, 285–88, 292, 299, 302–3, 305–7, 311, 314–15, 317–18, 319, 322, 332, 338, 341, 345.

48. O'Neill, *The Hairy Ape. Plays* III, p. 233.

49. O'Neill, *The Hairy Ape. Plays* III, p. 233.

50. T. Tiusanen points out the difference between diagonal settings from left to right rear (as in Act I, scene i of *Beyond the Horizon*) and those running from right front to left rear (as in scene iv of *The Emperor Jones* or scene vi of *The Hairy Ape*). The former follow the natural order of reading and lead the eyes to a distance; the latter counter this order, arrest the eyes, and, we may add, create extra tension. Tiusanen, pp. 76, 104, 233 n. 16.

51. O'Neill, *The Hairy Ape. Plays* III, p. 244.

52. O'Neill, *The Hairy Ape. Plays* III, p. 244.

53. O'Neill, *The Hairy Ape. Plays* III, p. 224.

54. O'Neill, *The Hairy Ape. Plays* III, pp. 247–48.

55. O'Neill, *The Hairy Ape. Plays* III, p. 247–48.

56. O'Neill, *The Hairy Ape. Plays* III, p. 250.

57. O'Neill sympathized with the aims of the Wobblies but he also shared much of Yank's anarchistic impetus. His emotional association with Yank's temper and temperament is obvious in the play. Cf. May, H. F., *The End of American Innocence* (Chicago: Quadrangle Books, 1964), pp. 177, 305, 313, 367, 377. Caughey, J.W, and May, E. R., *A History of the United States* (Chicago: Rand McNally & Co., 1964), pp. 399, 465, 483. Adams, D. K., *America in the 20th Century* (Cambridge: Cambridge University Press, 1967), p. 43. Nevins, A. and Commager, H. S., *A Pocket History of the United States* (New York: Washington Square Press, 1970), p. 286. Crow, H. L. and Turnbull, W. L., *American History: A Problems Approach* II (New York: Holt, Rinehart and Winston, 1972), p. 248. Gelb, p. 156. Sheaffer, pp. 182, 402. Alexander, D. "Eugene O'Neill as Social Critic" in Cargill, et al., pp. 391–92, 395. In his poem "Submarine" written for *The Masses* in 1917, O'Neill identified himself with an attitude not unlike Yank's in scene vii of O'Neill, *The Hairy Ape*:

My soul is a submarine.
My aspirations are torpedoes.
I will hide unseen
Beneath the surface of life
Watching for ships,
Dull, heavy-laden merchant ships
Rust-eaten, grimy galeons of commerce
Wallowing with obese assurance,
Too sluggish to fear or wonder,
Mocked by the laughter of waves
And the spit of disdainful spray.
I will destroy them
Because the sea is beautiful.

That is why I lurk
Menacingly
In green depths.

In Sanburn, R. and Clark, B. H., *A Bibliography of the Works of Eugene O'Neill* (New York: Random House, 1931), p. 120. Whereas, however, in poetry the reference to the beauty of the sea is a sufficient reason for the destruction of the merchant ships, in drama an objective network of motivation is necessary.

58. See Sheaffer, p. 389: "from the denouement of the story — the protagonist's finding himself by joining the Wobblies — it appears that O'Neill was under the influence of Reed, Mary Vorse, and other pro-labor militants."

59. O'Neill, *The Hairy Ape. Plays* III, p. 250.

60. Cf. Gelb, p. 489; Bogard, p. 252.

61. O'Neill, *The Hairy Ape. Plays* III, p. 252.

62. O'Neill is able to transmit the sense of exaltation in scene viii so effectively that in seeing or reading the scene, at certain moments one cannot help asking himself whether Yank, in fact, visited the zoo or only imagined he did. Is the scene real or illusory, actual or symbolic? In a statement of his, O'Neill calls the gorilla symbolic. Cf. "Second Thoughts," Cargill et al., p. 119. The total testimony of the scene, however, seems to suggest that the visit did take place. While Yank imagines that he is coming to better and better terms with the gorilla, he is actually more and more infuriating the animal which ultimately murders him. So the scene can be considered both expressively real and expressionistically symbolic with the former aspect getting the upper hand over the latter.

63. O'Neill, *The Hairy Ape. Plays* III, p. 252.

64. Tiusanen, pp. 46, 47n.

65. For a discrimination between the dramatic monologue and the interior monologue (a term apparently invented by Chernyshevsky), see N. G. Chernyshevsky, "L. N. Tolstoy, Dyetstvo i otrochestvo," *Voyennye rasskazy*," *Izbrannie literaturno-kriticheskie statyi* (Moscow: Gosudarstvennoe Izdatyelstvo, 1953), pp. 291–95. The article was originally published in No. 12, 1856 of the periodical *Sovremennik*.

66. O'Neill, *The Hairy Ape. Plays* III, p. 252.

67. O'Neill, *The Hairy Ape. Plays* III, p. 253.

68. For a summary of positions see Tiusanen, p. 113, n. 4, p. 123, n. 18. Cf. Bogard, pp. 245–48. Koreneva, M., "Eugene O'Neill and the Tradition of American Drama" in Kovalev, Y., et al., *20th Century American Literature: A Soviet View*, trans. from the Russian by R. Vroon (Moscow: Progress Publishers, 1976), pp. 148, 152–55. Floyd, V., "The Search for Self in The Hairy Ape: an Exercise in Futility?," *The Eugene O'Neill Newsletter* I, 3 (January 1978), pp. 4–7. Frenz, H., "Eugene O'Neill and Georg Kaiser," in Floyd, V., ed., *Eugene O'Neill: A World View* (New York: Frederick Ungar Publishing Co., 1979), pp. 172–85.

69. "O'Neill Talks About His Plays" in Cargill et al., pp. 110–11. It should also be borne in mind that O'Neill wrote *The Hairy Ape* in 1921 and gave the interpreting interview in 1924, the year he started work on *Dynamo* (1924–28).

70. Cargill, *O'Neill and his Plays*, p. 111.

71. O'Neill, *The Hairy Ape. Plays* III, p. 208.

72. It is immaterial whether these larger units are marked by the word act or not; Shakespeare's classicistic editors did not invent but only discovered and indicated the presence of more comprehensive dramatic sections which they conveniently and conventionally termed acts.

73. O'Neill began writing *The Emperor Jones* in the middle of September, 1920, and finished his work on October 2, 1920. On the basis of circumstantial probability, chronological evidence, and textual relevance, H. Frenz comes to the conclusion that O'Neill "might have had access to Duke's translation of *From Morn to Midnight* before writing *The Emperor Jones*, and that the playwright "was familiar, at least indirectly, with some aspects of" Kaiser's play, in spite of his personal declaration of independence. See Frenz, H., "Eugene O'Neill and Georg Kaiser," pp. 172, 179. As for the relationship between Kaiser's play and *The Hairy Ape*, O'Neill

himself admitted that he had read Kaiser's work before writing his own, although the idea for his play had been conceived earlier. Cf. Clark, B. H., *Eugene O'Neill: The Man and His Plays* (New York: Dover, 1947), p. 83.

74. Hickey's confession is also listened to by two policemen in *The Iceman Cometh*; they use the confession as damning evidence, but Hickey called the police himself to punish himself.

75. Kaiser drives home the dehumanizing effect of riches in terms of animal imagery. In scene iv the Cashier refers to people swarming to the bank as an endless procession of *sheep* rushing into the slaughterhouse. Learning from the Bank Manager that her husband has misappropriated sixty thousand marks, and realizing that he has left her, the Cashier's Wife calls her daughters *monkeys*. In scene v the Cashier enjoys raging, bellowing, naked mass excitement aroused in the public of a bicycle race by his extraordinary offer of a thousand marks to the winners. He is delighted to see the way in which distinctions of class and differences of civilization melt away in the emotional heat of collective rapture. He finds particular pleasure in a group of people whom he visualizes as a five-headed, five-armed *monster*. When the fire of animal excitement is put out by the appearance of his Royal Highness, the Cashier is no longer willing to throw a single penny under the *snouts* of those *grovelling dogs*. In scene vi the humiliated First Mask addresses the Cashier as *swine*, the Cashier assures the Second and Third Masks that he has no use for their brains, encourages them to gobble caviar, and orders them to be as dumb as the *fish* that *strewed* the *black spawn* upon the Black Sea. They may giggle and *bleat*, but must not speak. They are hired flesh, but when they lift their dominoes, the Cashier calls them *monsters*, horrors. Animal images of this kind may have appealed to the author of *The Hairy Ape* since they apply to the protagonists in both plays partly because of, partly in spite of the economic and social implications of modern civilization. Additional parallels also crop up. In both plays, as L. Sheaffer points out, "the lonely protagonist is jolted out of his rut by encountering a 'lady' and at last finds peace, after a series of bewildering experiences, in death" (Sheaffer, p. 76). H. Frenz calls attention to the coincidence that "Kaiser has written a scene filled with excitement and the noise of a six-day bicycle race and O'Neill, in *The Hairy Ape*, refers in the stage direction to the 'chanting formula of the gallery gods at the six-day bike race' (scene iii)." "Eugene O'Neill and Georg Kaiser," p. 183, n. 4. The reference to the Cashier's box as a cage, to the bank as a prison, to a superior and distant power as the man in the moon, to rich customers as a procession; the use of masks, the scenic effect of similarly dressed elegant gentlemen; the adoption of a dramatic interior monologue, the nightmarish distortion and expressive projection of images; the release of instincts, social tensions, the shedding of civilized habits, the lonely search, through particular stations, for sustaining values, the grotesque, sometimes absurd mingling of the tragic, and the commonplace forge further links between the two plays. Nevertheless, O'Neill had an independent vision. The above parallels do not contradict O'Neill's originality any more than some others do which can be found between Kaiser's *The Coral* (1917) and *Gas I* (1918) on the one hand, and *The Hairy Ape* or *Dynamo* on the other. Cf. Frenz, H., pp. 180–81. The dramatic trilogy of *The Coral*, *Gas I*, and *Gas II* (1920) already consists of acts.

76. In *The Emperor Jones*, in the foreground and focus of the drama, an inner conflict unfolds: the Emperor cheating the natives out of their money — and suffering fear, humiliation, psychological disintegration, and death during his unsuccessful escape. The increasing conflict between Jones's complacent and collapsing selves is rendered by the visionary projections of his personal, historical, and even racial memories evoked in the compulsive spirit of the Jungian myth of the collective unconscious. This inner conflict in the foreground is coupled with an outer conflict in the background between money-grabbing or otherwise mean aspirations and the subjugation, humiliation, and rebellion of the underdog. This latter kind of conflict takes a number of forms: the clash between Jones and his subjects, the opposition between Henry Smithers and Jones, the cockney trader leading the natives to the spot where he knows Jones entered the forest, and causing Jones to be killed; the collision between the Prison Guard and Jones, the former hitting Jones viciously and the latter giving the Guard a mortal blow with a shovel; the antagonism between the visionary auctioneer, the planters bargaining with slaves,

and Jones first being subject to them, then rebelling against them and killing them. The inner conflict is largely the consequence of the outer one, but the dramatic presence of the Jungian myth remains a separate entity. The double conflict in *The Hairy Ape* between the haves and the have-nots on the one hand, and between civilization and nature on the other has already been discussed. It is noteworthy that whereas in *The Emperor Jones*, Jones's regression from the safety of modern civilization to the fear of primitive nature is a continuous process, in *The Hairy Ape* Yank cannot move back, does not belong to Nature's level either, and is murdered by the gorilla. In *All God's Chillun Got Wings*, *The Great God Brown*, *Lazarus Laughed*, *Dynamo*, and *Days Without End* the duality of a secular and a metaphysical conflict touches upon aspects of concept, characterization, and style rather than those of structure: these plays already possess an act division. In *Anna Christie* the basic conflict bursts out between the individual revolt of human substance and the deadwood of social and economic circumstances. The two powerful individuals in the play, Anna Christie and Mat Burke, refuse to accept the predominance of a fatalistic outlook. With Anna this goes together with a recognition of the deceptive nature of the opposition between life on sea and life on land to which her father attributes such a great significance. She tells her father openly in the passionate moment of her revolt that there is no difference between people of the sea and those of the land: the youngest cousin on the farm, Paul, was no less of a violent bully than the sailors coming to the brothel were. She refuses to be given orders either by her father or Mat and clearly shows Chris's responsibility. Nevertheless, it can be felt that O'Neill himself was not easily able to get rid of Chris's obsession (he needed three versions to achieve an approximate success); the dramatist is only taking tentative steps in the direction of creating a single, undivided conflict. Even so, the end of the play is ambiguous. In *Desire Under the Elms* there is already a single, organic, if occasionally melodramatic, conflict between the acquisitive instinct and human values. This is manifested in an open clash between Ephraim Cabot and the love of Eben and Abbie. The same collision appears in the contradictory attitudes of Abbie. At first she uses everything and everybody, even Eben and their son, as means to her end of getting the farm; but later she sacrifices everything: the farm, her son, and herself to unselfish love and sincere truth. The fundamental conflict makes itself felt in the fact, too, that whoever is in the service of the grabbing lust, loses his or her humanity. Ephraim Cabot became hardened and lonely, void of human emotions, indifferent even to his sons and wives. Simeon and Peter, toiling hard at the farm for 30 years, turned into clumsy utensils themselves and developed a greedy selfishness in coveting their father's death and property.

77. By way of a suggestive transference, one of the most alienated figures of *Lazarus Laughed*, Caligula, powerful externally, weak internally, is also characterized by apish qualities. O'Neill, *Plays* I, p. 299.

78. Eleanor Flexner thinks that Yank's dramatic motivation is illogical in *The Hairy Ape*: "What might easily account for his confusion and mental collapse—the terrible conditions of work in the stokehole—bad ventilation, the speed-up, the long hours of back-breaking toil—are to Yank a source of pride. Yank's frenzied beating against his prison bars, in itself a legitimate symbol of class frustration, should lead to some more significant denouement than a lunatic's death in the monkey house." Flexner, E., *American Playwrights 1918–1938* (New York: Simon and Schuster, 1938), p. 151. The play, however, is not about bad ventilation but insufferable alienation. Even if O'Neill cannot offer a solution for the way in which alienation can be put an end to, he makes his audiences aware of the need for unalienated values. Yank's inclination to replace the Steel Trust with steel in general corresponds to a wide-spread intellectual and artistic tendency in the twenties. Looking back in 1967 in the preface of a new edition of *History and Class Consciousness* to the time (1922) when the book was written, George Lukács remarks: ". . . every externalization of an object in practice (and hence, too, in work) is an objectification, . . . every human expression including speech objectifies thoughts and feelings . . . objectification is a neutral phenomenon; the true is as much an objectification as the false, liberation as much as enslavement. Only when the objectified forms in society acquire functions that bring the essence of man into conflict with his existence, only when man's nature is subjugated, deformed, and crippled can we speak of an objective societal condition of aliena-

tion and. a͏͏͏ ͏ ͏   ll the subjective marks of an internal alienation.

Th   y and Class Consciousness." Lukács, G., History

anɑ   e (Cambridge, Mass.: MIT Press, 1975), p. xxiv.

The   state of society in which the essence of man is

brou   ishing to blow up the objects of industrial civili-

zatio   is congruent with the substitution of objectifi-

cation   ɔnism to demolish and deform objects and to

projec   henomenon in art stemming, of course, from a

gesture   ry Ape O'Neill dramatizes both the necessary

rise an   ͏ ͏ ͏ͪᴏ dynamite the whole of industrial civilization,

just as ł   ͏ ͏ ͏ᴜsionistic procedures representing an aspect of his overall method.

Cabot's Conflict: The Stones and Cows in O'Neill's *Desire Under the Elms*

June Schlueter and
Arthur Lewis

In his essay on "The Pressure of Puritanism in Eugene O'Neill's New England Plays," Frederick Wilkins quotes the playwright's comment that "the battle of moral forces in the New England scene" is "what I feel closest to as an artist."[1] Wilkins, as well as others, has discussed this battle in terms of opposing characters in *Desire Under the Elms,* looking at Abbie and Eben, who are able to "free themselves from their sordid surroundings and from the Puritan conception of 'sin,' " in opposition to Ephraim Cabot, who, alone and sterile, remains "unaware to the end of the great guilt that is his."[2] Similarly, Roger Asselineau speaks of the life impulse to which Abbie yields and which is the "reverse of the God worshipped by Ephraim Cabot, which has the hardness and immobility of a stone."[3] Clearly Cabot is the "Bible-quoting, tyrannical father" that John H. Raleigh[4] calls him, a man so dedicated to back-breaking labor that he would appear to have become one of the stones with which he and his farm are identified. Yet Cabot is also attracted to cows, sleeping with them when he feels the need for warmth and setting them free when he plans to burn the farm. The stony Cabot may well serve as one polarity in the battle of moral forces that O'Neill mounts between and among his characters. But Cabot's own mind is also a battlefield for the same conflict, which O'Neill expresses symbolically through the old man's relationship to stones and to cows.

Like many of O'Neill's earlier characters, Cabot is not fully in control of his own behavior. As a young man, in a moment of weakness, Cabot left the stony farm after two years of hard work and headed west, where the soil was "black and rich as gold," and stoneless. Farming was easy there, and the promise of prosperity was inviting. But an internal voice, the voice of Cabot's Old Testament God, commanded Cabot to return: "Git ye back t' hum!"[5] Unable to resist the suffering and labor demanded by the Puritan ethic, which was clearly the mainstay of his moral code, Cabot abandoned his crops and rejoined the rocky New England farm, endorsing his action by characterizing God as "hard, not easy! God's in the stones!" (p. 31).

Once he got back to the rocks, Cabot was compelled to construct walls — "Stones. I picked 'em up an' piled 'em into walls" — and began to identify with the stones: "Ye kin read the years o' my life in them walls, every day a hefted stone, climbin' over the hills up and down, fencin' in the fields that was mine, whar I'd made thin's grow out o' nothing' — like the will o'God, like the servant o' His hand" (p. 31). Cabot continues building his "church on a rock — out o' stones an' I'll be in them! That's what He meant 't Peter" (p. 31).

When Cabot married and his wife bore him two sons, he named them Simeon and Peter, clearly suggestive of Simon Peter, the rock upon whom Christ built his church,[6] and, in the case of Peter, derivative of the Greek word "petra," meaning rock. Now, some fifty years after Cabot's own escape to the West, history relives itself through his two sons, who themselves head west, to California. Here again the stones become the symbolic contrast to the freedom and ease of life in the West and the explicit object of rejection. To Simeon and Peter, the "stones atop o' the ground — stones atop o' stones" (p. 4) represent the repression that pervades the farm and perpetuates itself. The two frustrated men are no longer willing to be "slaves t' stone walls" (p. 15) and it takes only a slug of "likker" for them to garner the courage to break away from the "rock-pile of a farm" (p. 17). As they leave the restrictive, valueless stones of New England for the promising, shining gold of the West, they jubilantly declare: "We harby 'bolishes . . . all gates" (p. 17), celebrating their decision in song.

Cabot's third son, Eben, shares Simeon and Peter's nominal identification with stones: "Ebenezer," the fuller version of "Eben," is the name given by the prophet Samuel to the stone he set up in memory of divine assistance.[7] Similarly, Eben shares his half-brothers' bitterness toward stones, seeing them not only as physical walls of restraint but as internal ones that have hardened his brothers' hearts: "makin' walls till yer heart's a stone ye heft up out o' the way of growth onto a stone wall t' wall in yer heart!" (p. 7). To Eben, who himself rejects the stone philosophy not by leaving, as his brothers do, but by loving, the heart and stones are incompatible.

Indeed, Cabot's life since his return to New England has been a loveless one, in which hard work has been his only value. But in his dotage he has surprised his sons by marrying the youthful, vital Abbie, not for the lechery they see in this action but because the conflict of his youth has once again surfaced. Cabot claims he heard "the voice o' God cryin' in my wilderness, in my lonesomeness — t' go out an' seek an' find!" (p. 32), and, in response, he found and married Abbie. But the voice he follows hardly echoes the voice that recalled him to New England five decades earlier; this voice is the one that had summoned him westward and has continued to lure him to the barn, where "it's wa'm . . . nice smellin' an' warm — with the cows" (p. 27).

Despite Cabot's condemnation of his sons' lust "fur the sinful, easy gold o' Californi-a" (p. 19) and his repeated commitment to the hard life, Cabot himself still feels attracted to the warmth of the barn and the softness of the cows. Interestingly, almost every time Cabot speaks of cows, he either calls them queer or speaks of them with "queer affection." When Abbie is cold to Cabot's advances, he retreats to "whar it's restful — whar it's warm — down t' the barn" (p. 32). With some indignation, he points out to his wife that the cows are more responsive than she is: "I kin talk t' the cows . . . They'll give me peace" (p. 32). The morning after Cabot spends the night in the barn, he announces the success of his self-prescribed therapy: "I rested. I slept good — down with the cows. They know how t' sleep. They're teachin' me" (p. 38).

In marked contrast to the hard, cold stones, the cows offer Cabot softness and warmth, perhaps even the satisfaction of a latent sexuality his Puritan ethic has denied. Indeed, on at least two occasions Cabot calls his son Eben a calf, and in both situations the association with sex is manifest. When Abbie defends Eben against Cabot's rage over his son's sexual advances, the old man concedes, "I oughtn't t' git riled so — at that 'ere fool calf" (p. 29) and, less knowingly, calls him a calf on the morning after the sexual encounter between Eben and Abbie. Similarly, when Abbie suggests the two might have a son, Cabot softens to the point of sentimentality, touchingly revealing his life story to the woman concerned only with what is happening in Eben's bedroom next door. At the end of his monologue, Cabot retreats to the barn to be with the cows.

Some months later, after Abbie has given birth to the child that everyone but Cabot suspects is Eben's, the old man celebrates his sexuality in a display of raw energy that astonishes the neighborhood gossips. Outdancing the fiddler, Cabot becomes seemingly superhuman in vitality. The cold self-denial that characterized Cabot earlier has been transformed into the fecund life force identified not with the stones but with the cows.

In the play's final scene, Cabot identifies himself explicitly with the cows. Having endured the humiliation of discovering the child that Abbie bore and killed was not his, but Eben's, Cabot tells himself, "I got t' be — like a stone — a rock o' jedgment!" (p. 54). But at this point he is unable to restore his commitment and resolves instead to burn the farm, free the cows, and head for California: "T' hell with the farm! I'm leavin' it! I've turned the cows an' other stock loose! I've druv 'em into the woods whar they kin be free! *By freein' 'em, I'm freein'* myself!" (p. 57, emphasis added). In his plan to "set fire t' house an' barn an' watch 'em burn . . ." (p. 57), Cabot is renouncing the ethic of work and self-denial to which he has devoted his life; in freeing the cows he is releasing the suppressed desires of those decades, seemingly resolving the moral conflict that he had not consciously acknowledged until now.

But O'Neill, finally, does not allow Cabot to be set free with the cows. Moments after his jubilant declaration that California is "the land fur me" (p. 57), Cabot learns that Eben's entrepreneuring has left him without the financial means to go west. His reaction is severe: "*He stares — feels* [under the floor board for the money] *— stares again. A pause of dead silence. He slowly turns, slumping into a sitting position on the floor, his eyes like those of a dead fish, his face the sickly green of an attack of nausea. He swallows painfully several times — forces a weak smile at last*" (stage direction, p. 57). And then, sardonically, he reaffirms the philosophy by which he has lived the seventy-plus years of his life: "God's hard, not easy! Mebbe they's easy gold in the West, but it hain't God's gold. It hain't fur me" (p. 57).

Once again, the hard New England God is in control: "I kin hear His voice warnin' me agen t' be hard an' stay on my farm. I kin see his hand usin' Eben t' steal t' keep me from weakness. I kin feel I be in the palm o' His hand, His finger guiden' me" (pp. 57–8). The God who called the young Cabot back from the West has recalled him again, this time to a life without sons, wife, and cows: "It's a -goin' t' be lonesomer now than ever it war afore" (p. 58). At play's end, the old New Englander is alone, surrounded by stone walls that permanently separate him from the cows, his private "battle of moral forces" resolved.

Notes

1. Frederick Wilkins, "The Pressure of Puritanism in Eugene O'Neill's New England Plays," in *Eugene O'Neill: A World View*, ed. Virginia Floyd (New York: Frederick Ungar, 1979), p. 244. O'Neill made the comment in 1946.

2. Wilkins, p. 244.

3. Roger Asselineau, "*Desire under the Elms*: A Phase of O'Neill's Philosophy," in *Eugene O'Neill: A Collection of Criticism*, ed. Ernest G. Griffin (New York: McGraw-Hill, 1976), p. 64.

4. John H. Raleigh, *The Plays of Eugene O'Neill* (Carbondale: Southern Illinois University Press, 1965), p. 31.

5. Eugene O'Neill, *Desire Under the Elms*, in *Three Plays of Eugene O'Neill* (New York: Vintage Books, 1959), p. 31. Subsequent page references from this text will be cited parenthetically.

6. Matthew 16:18. The identification of Simon Peter as the rock reflects the Catholic interpretation of the biblical passage.

7. I Samuel 7:12.

Dion Brown and His Problems   Joseph S. Tedesco

When Cybel walks in on Brown in the last scene of *The Great God Brown* and realizes that he has been wearing Dion's mask, she says: "So

that's why you never came to me again! You are Dion Brown!"[1] The remark
exasperated many critics and led the most sympathetic among them to consider Eugene O'Neill's use of masks a great experiment but the play a total
failure. Of greater significance is that the new name epitomizes not only the
problems of the titular character but those of interpreting the play.

O'Neill felt the play's structure and techniques were basically sound
and said so on several occasions. Writing to Macgowan from Bermuda after
just finishing the play, he says: "I think it's grand stuff, much deeper and
more poetical in a way than anything I've done before, and the masks will
work in fine with it."[2] To Barrett Clark's estimate that the play would last
only two weeks, long enough for the O'Neill fans to look at it, O'Neill responded:

> You may be right, but I somehow feel there's enough in it to get over to
> unsophisticated audiences. In one sense *Brown* is a mystery play, only in-
> stead of dealing with crooks and police it's about the mystery of personal-
> ity and life. I shouldn't be surprised if it interested people who won't
> bother too much over every shade of meaning, but follow it as they follow
> any story. They needn't understand with their minds, they can just watch
> and feel.[3]

However certain he was of the play's artistic excellence, he put himself
"in the dock" with a letter to the press some three weeks after the play
opened that explained among other things the literary onomastics, motiva-
tions of the characters, and symbolism of the play. Some of the major points
in the explanation were: that the name Dion Anthony referred to Dionysus
and St. Anthony (the Anchorite) and alluded to the conflict in modern times
between "the creative pagan acceptance of life" and "the masochistic, life-
denying spirit of Christianity" which results in "mutual exhaustion"; that
Margaret is the modern descendent of the Marguerite of *Faust*—"the eternal girl woman . . . properly oblivious to everything but the means to her
end of maintaining the race"; that "Cybel is an incarnation of Cybele, the
Earth mother, doomed as a pariah in a world of unnatural laws . . ."; and
that "Brown is the visionless demi-god of our new materialistic myth—a
Success—building his life of exterior things, inwardly empty and resource-
less . . . a by-product forced aside into slack waters by the deep main current of life desires."

This unusual gesture from a playwright fixed the range of interpretation so irrevocably that there is hardly a commentary on the play that
doesn't base its remarks on O'Neill's explanation. The Dionysus reference
together with the "masochistic, life-denying spirit of Christianity" phrase
alone virtually polarized all elaborations of O'Neill's remarks around
Nietzsche's works especially *The Birth of Tragedy*. Later, in the same letter,
he expressed his hope for the way audiences would be affected by his play:

> And now for an explanation regarding this explanation. It was far from my
> idea in writing *Brown* that this background pattern of conflicting tides in

the soul of Man should ever overshadow and thus throw out of proportion the living drama of the recognizable human beings, Dion, Brown, Margaret and Cybel. I meant it always to be mystically within and behind them, giving them a significance beyond themselves, forcing itself through them to expression in mysterious words, symbols, actions they do not themselves comprehend. And that is as clearly as I wish an audience to comprehend it.[4]

Still, six years later in "Second Thoughts" about *The Great God Brown*, O'Neill states that he ". . . would make the masks symbolize more definitely the abstract theme of the play instead of, as in the old productions, stressing the more superficial meaning that people wear masks before other people and are mistaken by them for their masks."[5]

What is dubious about using O'Neill's explanation as a foundation for interpretation are some non sequiturs: if Brown is such a nonentity, why spend two acts on him? To show how wrong he is? Or, how he should get his just deserts? The "visionless demi-god" phrase characterizes the conflict between the two men somewhat simplistically: the agonizing artist as hero vs. the Philistine businessman as villain. If the spirit of Christianity is so "masochistic and life-denying" why is the ascetic tendency in Dion shown as triumphant? Here are his dying words: "Forgive me, Billy! Bury me, hide me, forget me for your own happiness! May Margaret love you! May you design the Temple of Man's Soul! Blessed are the meek and poor in spirit!" (350).

The Nietzschean interpretations, while totally dependent upon O'Neill's explanation, do provide varied and illuminating insights into the play's structure. One of the early interpretations of the play is by H. Steinhauer who says the play obviously "depicts the pagan-Christian conflict on the problem of sex. Pure paganism is embodied in Cybel . . . , and her direct antagonist is the successful businessman Billy Brown. . . ."[6] E. A. Engel, a few years later, sees O'Neill as reiterating his faith in the doctrine of Eternal Recurrence, which, according to Nietzsche, is the "highest formula of affirmation that can ever be attained." He also sees the play as expressing the end of hope for the creative life, and O'Neill, having failed to solve the artist's dilemma, as reconciled nevertheless to the tragedy of existence.[7]

A very detailed study, made by E. Törnquist, which begins with O'Neill's "public explanation" and important facts gathered from the original drafts of the play, develops great insight into the Dionysian struggle within the artist. Based on the assumption that the mask is supposed to represent a protective device, Törnquist feels that "despite O'Neill's statement to the contrary, the mask scheme . . . seems not only mystic but confusing . . . [because] there is no unifying principle underlying the scheme. Or, if there is one, no one including the author himself has revealed it."[8] M. Hinden, viewing *Brown* as a "symbolic epic that crowns the early Nietzschean phase of [O'Neill's] career," considers the play a drama of a divided self alluding to "the original Dionysian unity . . . Nietzsche's 'Primordial Oneness' undergoing the throes of individuation and moving once again through pain and suffering."[9] L. Ben-Zvi, drawing parallels with Joyce's *Exiles*, considers O'Neill together with Joyce "to have fashioned one of the most important ideas used by Nietzsche in *Zarathustra*: the notion of eternal recurrence of the same event," and for O'Neill as well as Nietzsche "the fact of suffering and defeat is meliorated by the recognization of the continuation of the life force."[10] The great irony connected with the Nietzschean interpretations and their dependence on O'Neill's "explanation" of the play is that in the original draft, according to Törnquist, "Dion Anthony significantly carries an 'ordinary' name: Stanley Keith."[11]

Even if the Nietzschean approach dominates interpretations of *Brown*, it is odd that Jungian psychology has not been used more often as a theoretical frame of reference for analysis of the play. O. Cargill mentions Jung as a major key to *Brown* but devotes most of his attention to *Lazarus Laughed.*[12] D. Falk does a brief Jungian analysis of the two main characters as symbols of a divided self. Both parts, through the psychological process of individuation, would emerge "combined in an individual in a sort of harmonious compromise when the tension between opposites is not resolved but accepted as the inevitable condition of all growth and change."[13]

O'Neill's preference for Jung is well known since he not only has said as much but also included Jungian concepts in the structure of his plays, particularly *The Emperor Jones* and *The Hairy Ape*. Interestingly enough, there are clear indications that material for *The Great God Brown* may have been drawn from *The Psychology of the Unconscious* and *Psychological Types*, two major works of Jung available to him and widely circulated during the 1920s.[14] The St. Anthony referred to by O'Neill as a source for Dion Anthony is discussed by Jung as an example of the effort made "to stamp out the activity of the individual unconscious among monks."[15] At the end of the fourth act Cybel, after her "Spring again" speech, is asked by the captain what the name of the dead man is. She responds: "Man!" and the captain asks: "How d'yuh spell it?" (375). This sequence has great similarity with a quotation from Nietzsche used by Jung in his discussion of the Apollinian-Dionysian distinction: ". . . alienated Nature, hostile or enslaved, celebrates once more her feast of reconciliation with her prodigal son — Man."[16] Jung's concepts and the extent to which they explain O'Neill's structure of the play are, however, the real test of his use of them.

A Jungian interpretation of *The Great God Brown* must begin with O'Neill's use of masks and their obvious relationship to the fundamental concept of persona (the ancient Greek word for mask) in Jung's psychology and also with the special way O'Neill applies Jung's concept to theatrical practice. What the use of masks does for the stage is to place the drama immediately on a symbolic level and preclude any demand for verisimilitude by a realistic style which often results in photographic superficiality according to O'Neill. The ultimate effect of O'Neill's use of masks is to portray inner action and penetrate the depths of his characters' personalities. This is accomplished by the visible relationship between the mask and the real face behind it. The mask represents not only what the world sees but what the character wants them to see — an attitude towards the world expressed in a mask. The real face expresses the true inner state of the character, which is covered by the mask. Dramatically then, the audience has a visible representation of the psychic life of the character.

This relationship between the real face and the mask is O'Neill's theatrical adaptation of Jung's psychological concepts of anima and persona. The ego, the centre of the field of consciousness, bears a relationship to objects outside of itself and is disposed to them in different ways. The sum total of this relationship, Jung calls the persona. For the relationship between the ego and the unconscious self, Jung uses the term anima:

> We can therefore speak of an inner personality with as much justification as, on the grounds of early experience, we speak of an outer personality. The inner personality is the way one behaves in relation to one's inner psychic processes; it is the inner attitude, the characteristic face, that is turned toward the unconscious. I call the outer attitude, the outward face, the *persona*; the inner attitude, the inward face, I call the *anima*.[17]

By adapting this basic principle of psychological relationships to the stage in this way, O'Neill succeeds in visibly presenting psychological action within the characters.

As the play opens, Dion's mask portrays "a mocking, reckless, defiant, gayly scoffing young Pan." The inner attitude, reflected in the face beneath, is "dark, spiritual, poetic, passionately supersensitive, helplessly unprotected in its childlike, religious faith in life" (310). As his characterization progresses through the play, his mask reflects his increasingly defiant attitude towards a world that rejects him. Especially ironic is Margaret's response: love for his mask but fear and indifference towards his real self. At the same time, Dion's real face mirrors the turbulence of a terrible conflict within himself, apparently between an effusive vivaciousness of spirit and a restraining conformity of attitude.

Dion's problem, according to Jung, would be his tendency to identify more with his unconscious self than the world around him, i.e. his greater attention to his "soul-image."[18] At first it is his mother in whose image "he will create himself so she may feel her life comfortably concluded" (311); then it is Margaret about whom he says: "Now I am born — I — the I! — one and indivisible — I who love Margaret!" (316) and finally to Cybel: "You're strong. You always give. You've given my weakness strength to live" (336). But, to the world that rejects him — Billy Brown (at age 4), Dion's father, and especially Margaret who does not recognize the real Dion — he is defiant, satirical, and recalcitrant. The epitome of what the world means to Dion is personified in William Brown — The Great God Brown. Yet it would be a caricature to see Dion as the great artist persecuted unjustly by an unjust world. His artistic ability is never convincingly demonstrated. The creativity that Brown envies is more Dion's ability to please the public. On the the face of it, Dion's attacks on Brown seem out of proportion to the offense.

According to Jung, Brown's problem would be directly opposite to Dion's. He wears no mask at the beginning of the play because his consciousness identifies more with objects outside himself than those in his inner life. In the Prologue, we see him accept the work-success ethic from his parents quite naturally: he will go to college, he will become an architect, and he will eventually become a great success with his father's firm. He adapts and adjusts to the demands of the world about him so congenially that his natural face needs no mask: his inner attitude doesn't consciously exist because it is identical with his outer one.

Margaret, from the beginning of the play, is as close as Brown comes to a soul-image, and although he protests his love for her, she is at best a desirable object as Cybel the prostitute is. He lacks Dion's "creativity" precisely because it is difficult for him to sense the images and contents of his unconscious self. From the time they were boys, Brown admires the style, the face (the mask) that Dion shows to the world, and he wonders what it is about Dion that attracts women like Margaret and Cybel. People, like inanimate objects, are reducible to a formula. Brown's glibness betrays this attitude.

Margaret and Cybel are symbolic characters and basically supportive of the main characterizations. They undergo no radical change in the play. To different degrees they are soul-images of Billy and Dion, respectively. Margaret's consciousness, like Brown's is directed towards objects, including people, who are inscrutable objects to her. Margaret accommodates herself not so much to the world as it appears but to the world as related to her instinctive understanding of motherhood and offspring. She masks herself in front of Brown, the draftsmen, even her children. To Dion, she is unmasked but sees him as an object to be mothered not as a person to be "seen into." "And I'll be Mrs. Dion — Dion's wife — and he'll be my Dion — my little boy — my baby!" (324).

Cybel's consciousness, like Dion's, looks towards the interior and has the ability to "read into" people more so than Dion. "You were born with ghosts in your eyes, and you were brave enough to go looking into your own dark . . ." (337). Cybel has come to an accommodation with the world by means of her prostitute's mask without compromising her relationship to her inner self. She is a mother in a spiritual and psychological sense who gives birth to souls — a sharp contrast with Margaret's motherhood.

The interplay of these four characters produces profoundly tragic consequences at different symbolic levels. Dion from the outset is confronted with a world that is unaware of his inner nature and responds to his probings insensitively. Consequently, the persona he develops is in effect a thick-skinned attitude. This results in his virtually being cut off from reality and proves to be his undoing. Working for Billy Brown, the epitome of this insensitive world, for the sake of Margaret's domestic demands is what kills Dion, not just drink. Cybel, as a spiritual mother, merely makes the situation temporarily tolerable and postpones the inevitable. At the moment he is about to die, he understands the need to be reconciled with the world and begs Billy's forgiveness with the wish: "May Margaret love you! May you design the Temple of Man's Soul" (350). However bright the reconciliation, Dion dies, defeated.

Brown, from the moment his parents imbue him with "the stuff . . . to win if he'll only work hard enough" (309), turns his gaze outwards and begins to attend to objects and is literally distracted from his unconscious self. He seeks the popularity of Dion as well as the adoring attention of Margaret, but even after he achieves professional success, he still has not attained them. When he finds Dion at Cybel's, he then tries to buy her exclusive attention. Ultimately, his undoing is somewhat similar to Dion's: seeking the love of a woman who is in love with a mask and cannot see the people behind the masks. Wearing Dion's mask, he begins to suffer as Dion did because of Margaret's failure to recognize him. Consequently, he begins to feel the inner life within himself for the first time, so much so, that he needs a mask to cover the real Brown who is now different from the Brown he shows to the world.

As the suffering begins to ravage his inner life, his former attitude towards the world (his persona) disintegrates both in fact and symbolically. All of act IV, scene i shows his mockery of society and the world which dominated his conscious life until now. Speaking of the capitol building he has just finished, he says: "This design will do just as well for a Home for Criminal Imbeciles! . . . Long live Chief of Police Brown . . . Mayor Brown . . . Governor Brown, Senator Brown, President Brown! Oh how many persons in one God make up the good God Brown?" (365). After giving all the credit for the design to Dion in the presence of Margaret and the committee, he tears up the drawings and reappears wearing Dion's mask, leaving behind the "dead" mask of William Brown which is carried out as a corpse at the end of the scene.

In the next scene, after Cybel enters his apartment and realizes that he has been wearing Dion's mask, she calls him Dion Brown and warns him against the mob in front of which he says: "Welcome dumb worshippers! I am your Great God Brown!" (373). They shoot him and as he lies dying before Cybel, he asks her for the prayer she taught him — she whom he now calls mother. Cybel responds: "Our Father Who Art!" Then with a sudden ecstasy, Brown utters his dying words: "I know! I have found him! I hear him speak! Blessed are they that weep, for they shall laugh! Only he that has wept can laugh! . ." (374). However lucid the recognition of his total self is, Brown, as did Dion, dies tragically defeated.

The tragedy is further intensified by Cybel's last words uttered with profound pain: "Always spring comes again bearing life! . . . but always, always love and conception and birth and pain again — spring bringing the intolerable chalice of life again!" (375). These words should be taken in context with those she utters after Dion leaves her for the last time: "What's the good of bearing children? What's the use of giving birth to death?" (339). Both remarks indicate Cybel's symbolic nature: that she is the mother of inner life and it is tragic to give birth to the spirit only to have it wither away. The epilogue adds the most intense tragic accent of all: four years later, we see Margaret, alone on the same dock on which she declared her love for Dion eighteen years ago, sending her sons off to dance with their girlfriends, then taking Dion's mask from under her cloak and saying to herself: "My lover! My husband! My boy! . ." (377).

Dion and Brown both die with the words "Our Father Who Art." In Jungian psychology a sharp distinction is made between the self and the *ego*:

> But inasmuch as the *ego* is only the center of my consciousness, it is not identical with the totality of my psyche, . . . I, therefore distinguish between the *ego* . . . [as] only the subject of my consciousness, while the self is the subject of my total psyche which also includes the unconscious.[19]

As an empirical concept, the self expresses the unity of personality as a whole and is imaged as a king, hero, or totality symbol (circle, square, etc.) in myths and dreams. When each of the characters prays the Our Father they have discovered the self: Dion recognizes that the unconscious is not the only reality and must be in unity with the outside world; Brown, through the suffering he experiences from living under Dion's mask, discovers his inner self and realizes that an outer life centered around objects is not sufficient and must be in union with an inner life.

God the Father is an image of the self in the unconscious as well as one of unity and wholeness. Brown, posing as Dion after the drawings are ripped up, says: "This is Daddy's bedtime secret for today: Man is broken. He lives by mending. The grace of God is glue" (370). Dion Brown's problem is a problem of mankind: a divided self. It is Dion's creative energy from the unconscious in one part of the self and Brown's ordered world and organizing principle in the other. The solution is the unity of the two parts in the self. In the play such a unity is absent, and the source of the tragedy is precisely the resultant disunity. The structure of the play supports this theme so obviously, that O'Neill offered the part to John Barrymore, suggesting that both characters be played by the same actor and that Dion Anthony and Billy Brown may be expressionistic objectifications of a multiple personality.[20]

The Nietzschean interpretations essentially address the same theme when interpreting the play in the Apollinian-Dionysian context. The Dionysian then becomes the creative energy of the unconscious and the Apollinian the ordering principle of conscious experience of the outside world. However, there is a tendency in this approach to reduce Dion to a suffering artist whose creative vitality is surpressed by a hostile society symbolized by William Brown or to interpret the play in terms of archetypal patterns of behavior and thereby place the characters on a Procrustean bed.

Yet, many of the Nietzschean interpretations bring out a "significance beyond the recognizable characters of the drama" as does a Jungian approach (and possibly a Goethean one). In all cases, no interpretive approach should be the exclusive "theoretic key to the work" including that of the author.

Notes

1. *The Great God Brown, Nine Plays by Eugene O'Neill* (New York: Random House, 1959), IV, ii, p. 372. Subsequent references to *The Great God Brown* are drawn from this edition and will be cited parenthetically in the text.

2. O'Neill in a letter to Kenneth Macgowan (ca. March 25, 1925). Quoted in *The Theatre We Worked For*, ed. Jackson R. Bryer (New Haven: Yale University Press, 1982), p. 91.

3. Barrett Clark, *Eugene O'Neill: The Man and His Plays*, rev. ed. (New York: Dover, 1947), p. 106.

4. O'Neill in a letter to the *New York Evening Post*, Feb. 13, 1926. Quoted in Clark, pp. 104–06.

5. From *The American Spectator*, December 1932; reprinted in Toby Cole, *Playwrights on Playwriting* (New York, 1961), p. 68.

6. H. Steinhauer, "Eros and Psyche: A Nietzschean Motif in Anglo-American Literature," *Modern Language Notes*, 64 (April, 1949), p. 226.

7. Edwin A. Engel, *The Haunted Heroes of Eugene O'Neill* (Cambridge, Mass., 1953), pp. 174–175.

8. Egil Törnquist, *A Drama of Souls* (New Haven: Yale University Press, 1969), p. 124n.

9. Michael Hinden, "*The Birth of Tragedy* and *The Great God Brown*," *Modern Drama*, 16 (Sept. 1973), p. 137.

10. Linda Ben-Zvi, "*Exiles, The Great God Brown*, and the Specter of Nietzsche," *Modern Drama*, 24 (Sept. 1981), p. 266–67.

11. Törnquist, p. 127.

12. Oscar Cargill, "Fusion-Point of Jung and Nietzsche," *O'Neill and His Plays*, ed. Cargill et al. (New York: New York University Press, 1961), pp. 408–10.

13. Doris Falk, *Eugene O'Neill and the Tragic Tension*, (New Brunswick: Rutgers, 1958), p. 108.

14. The work, *Psychology of the Unconscious*, trans. into English by Beatrice M. Hinkle (New York: 1916; London: 1917), is now included in volume 5 of the Bollingen series of Jung's works entitled *Symbols of Transformation* (Princeton, N.J.: Princeton University Press, 2nd ed., 1967). *Psychological Types* was originally published in 1921 in Switzerland, translated into English by H. G. Baynes and published in 1923 under the title, *The Psychology of Individuation*. It is now included in the Bollingen series as volume 6, and entitled *Psychological Types*, (Princeton, N.J.: Princeton University Press, 1971). Quotations from these works will be made from the Bollingen volumes and referred to by volume number and page.

15. Bollingen, Vol. 6, p. 54.

16. Bollingen, Vol. 6, p. 138. Jung cites *The Birth of Tragedy* (trans. Haussmann), p. 26.

17. Bollingen, Vol. 6, p. 467.

18. His anima (for a woman animus). The "soul-image" is a specific image produced by the unconscious which images the unconscious. In the case of a man, the unconscious is pre-

sented as a woman (at first, a mother); in a woman, the image is a man. c.f. Bollingen, Vol. 5, pp. 388–89; Vol. 6, p. 470.

19. Bollingen, Vol. 6, p. 425.

20. Mardi Valgemae, "Eugene O'Neill's Preface to *The Great God Brown*," *Yale University Library Gazette*, 43 (July 1968), p. 28n.

Eugene O'Neill: The Drama of Self-Transcendence

Carl E. Rollyson, Jr.

Louis Sheaffer reports that Eugene O'Neill's "entrance into the world, according to stories that came down in the family, was achieved with difficulty."[1] He was born of an apprehensive mother who did not want another child and grew up in a family beset by acrimony, mistrust, and misunderstanding. He suffered from his father's peripatetic acting career and never felt he had a home. He became an arrogant loner who nevertheless longed for acceptance by others. He had a strong death wish, but at the same time he desired recognition for his remarkable individuality. When he turned to writing plays in his mid-twenties, O'Neill had scarcely learned how to control his enormous rage at having been born at all, and his earliest work is deeply flawed by his morose self pity. But his experience at sea, his travel to South America, his aborted suicide attempt and rebirth, his work as a reporter, and his convalescence as a tubercular patient in a sanitarium, gave him abundant material to cast about for suitable ways of objectifying his grievances against the world. O'Neill always had an ax to grind, a grudge to bear, so that even in his mature years he could produce dreadful self-serving plays, yet his persistent explorations of dramatic form often drove him to go well beyond special pleading. At its best, his writing is itself an act of self-transcendence, so that the divisions in his own character are enlarged to encompass those of the whole world.[2] Perhaps only a man who felt so at odds with the particulars of life would attempt to dramatize existence in its entirety, as if within the enclosure of a play like *Lazarus Laughed*, for all of its faults, he could finally contain the ebb and flow of his own contradictions.

O'Neill's early life before playwriting seems predicated on thwarting his father's faith in self-improvement and material success, and his plays, as I have argued elsewhere, not only repudiate the nineteenth century vision of heroic possibilities expressed in his father's profitable stage vehicle, *The Count of Monte Cristo*, they systematically invert that vision in order to attack the autonomy of O'Neill's characters.[3] For example, Brutus Jones loses much more than his title of Emperor; he loses himself. Like the Count of Monte Cristo, Jones believes that the world is his, but he is reduced to "stumbling and crawling through the undergrowth" of the forest in a futile attempt to elude his deposition, and he becomes fused with the collective experience of his race,[4] an incipient example of the general truth enunciated in *Lazarus Laughed*: "Man slowly arises from the past of the race of men that was his tomb of death" (I. 359–60). Ponce De Leon in *The Fountain* is similarly humbled but also elevated when he ecstatically embraces not his individuality but his place in the unity of all things (I. 442). Yank in *The Hairy Ape* exults in his power to command his men in the fireman's forecastle. He "represents to them a self-expression, the very last word in what they are, their most highly developed individual" (III. 208). Nevertheless, he is displaced and does not belong: "I ain't on oith and I ain't in heaven, get me? I'm in de middle tryin' to separate 'em, takin' all de woist punches from bot' of 'em" (III. 253). O'Neill, the young man who boasted that he would become more famous than his father,[5] surely sympathizes with his dethroned characters, but he also has them share his lament that he was ever born at all. Characters in *All God's Chillun Got Wings* and *The Great God Brown* explicitly raise the question of whether life is worth living (II. 319, III. 265), and *Lazarus Laughed* poises its complete structure on just that question.

Many of the plays leading up to *Lazarus Laughed* bear the heavy strain of O'Neill's preoccupation with self-transcendence, with the way to be himself and more than himself. Yank's dialect, for instance, is a cover for O'Neill's precarious suspension between heaven and earth, and for his suspicion that his salvation could not be won in either human society or an afterlife. Sheaffer's biography is replete with incidents that reveal the playwright's inability to accept the solace of either religious or social solutions to his self-turbulence.[6] This is Tiberius's dilemma in *Lazarus Laughed* (I. 352–53). Like the Emperor Jones, Tiberius Caesar hears and fears "Death dancing round me in the darkness, prancing to the drum beat of my heart!" (I. 353). Jim Harris in *All God's Chillun* and Dion Anthony in *The Great God Brown* strive against a human community that cannot incorporate them and cannot appreciate their desire for an ideal shaping of themselves. Jim fails more than his law exam, and Dion fails at more than his art, for both men are attempting to raise themselves above their society's dichotomies of artist and materialist, of black and white, in order to become what O'Neill once claimed he was seeking in a woman, "who will combine in the same proportion in which I have them spirit and body; who will not be wholly of the earth earthly or the spirit spiritually . . . who will practice not deadening restraint but exultant freedom."[7] The blacks and whites in *All God's Chillun* are precursors of the divided choruses, separate races, and personality types in *Lazarus Laughed*. In the former play, the stage setting is bifurcated by a street leading left, where the faces are white, and a street leading right, where they are black (II. 301). In the latter play, there is a doorway on the left opening on a road "where a crowd of men has gathered," and on the right, there is another doorway "leading to the yard where there is a crowd of women" (I. 273). Later, characters are split apart by their religious beliefs just as O'Neill felt divided about his family's Catholicism.[8]

Like O'Neill, Eben in *Desire Under The Elms*, reacts to "each day [as] a cage in which he finds himself trapped but inwardly unsubdued" (I. 203).[9] Eben's "defiant, dark eyes" are reminiscent of O'Neill's and of many other characters in *The Emperor Jones*, *The Hairy Ape*, and *The Great God Brown*, who chafe under their sense of imprisonment in a world that psychologically and sometimes physically crushes them (III. 198, 207, 265). O'Neill's plays are dominated by rooms and other places with low ceilings, cramped spaces, and other cages for human inhibition. Each of these constricted environments also typify their characters' lack of a refuge. Characters as diverse as Abbie Putnam in *Desire Under The Elms*, Yank in *The Hairy Ape*, and Caligula in *Lazarus Laughed*, are homeless and replicate O'Neill's own longing for a home, for a way to root and periodically regain his sense of belonging to the world.

Desire Under The Elms, one of O'Neill's most explicit portrayals of the deracinated person's search for a "hum," as Abbie calls it, embodies his sense of futility over identifying home with a piece of ground, with a single set of family relationships, with what the characters obsessively call "mine" throughout the play (I. 217, 221, 232–33, 237–38, 253, 260–62). What O'Neill had learned on the sea — that he could only feel at one with all of the elements of life, not just with some of them — became an increasingly obtrusive theme in the plays that culminated in *Lazarus Laughed*. No single living character could embody his craving for an absorption in wholeness — the splitting up of William Brown and Dion Anthony had proven that to him. Instead, Lazarus, one who had died and who had been recalled to his integral function in the life cycle, appeared to present O'Neill with a way of fully expressing his urge toward an identity with all things, an urge that lay dormant, he firmly believed, in all human beings. In *Desire Under The Elms*, the characters are most relaxed and free when they praise nature's beauty, when they open their eyes and their arms to the sky and the sun. In these moments they are possessed by their link with the world rather than trying to possess it, and thus they are following the course of self-transcendence that Lazarus offers to Tiberius, who thinks he can own the earth (I. 352).

In the plays that precede *Lazarus Laughed*, characters struggle to be individuals and want to be marked out from the crowd even as they are drawn to love others and embrace the world. Their very individuality makes them dominant, alienates them from others, perverts their own best instincts, and separates them from themselves. Dion Anthony cries:

> Why am I afraid to dance, I who love music and rhythm and grace and song and laughter? Why am I afraid to live, I who love life and the beauty of flesh and the living colors of earth and sky and sea? Why am I afraid of love, I who love love? Why am I afraid, I who am not afraid? (III. 265)

Abbie Putnam covets the Cabot farm as "mine" yet diminishes the power of her possessiveness by evoking "Nature—makin' thin's grow—bigger 'n' bigger—burnin' inside ye—makin' ye want t' grow—into somethin' else—till ye're jined with it—an' it's your'n—but it owns ye, too,—an makes ye grow bigger—like a tree—like them elums" (I. 229). She feels the pull of her own history, of her desire to be as solidly rooted as the elms, but she also responds to another kind of pull the elms enforce: the energy of growth itself that is bigger than her tenacious individuality. Eventually she surrenders to her love of Eben and of nature but not before her own and every other character's overriding sense of ego wrecks the conditions that are right for rebirth.

In *Lazarus Laughed*, O'Neill turns his characters' yearning for self-transcendence into a full scale treatment of what becomes a cosmic paradigm of rebirth. The play is his *Eureka*, for like Poe, he probes the origin and direction of the universe.[10] He goes far beyond the plotted lives of the individuals in his previous plays in order to dramatize a heuristic schema that is comparable to the complex studies of mythic and religious experience by Mircea Eliade and William James. The dialogues of *Lazarus Laughed* exemplify the debate Eliade identifies in *Cosmos and History*: "the modern world is, at the present moment, not entirely converted to historicism; we are even witnessing a conflict between the two views: the archaic conception, which we should designate as archetypal; and the modern, post Hegelian conception."[11] Eliade's belief that there is an unresolved conflict between archaic man, who feels himself "indissolubly connected with the Cosmos and cosmic rhythms," and modern man, who "insists that he is connected only with History,"[12] is virtually the same unresolved conflict that informs *Lazarus Laughed*, in which man's ontological confusion, his uncertainty about where he stands in the universe, is exposed.

In the play, modern man, personified by the Romans, is bound by a linear, historical conception of movement from life to death, whereas archaic man, represented by Lazarus and his followers, denies that life and death are separate categories of experience and affirms that both are but aspects of one whole cycle. Lazarus, a man who has died, uses self-contradictory phrases obsessively ("Death is dead!") to accomplish what other mystics, described by William James, also aim for: a demolition of the logical patterns of conceptual speech.[13] Lazarus employs the language of paradox to suggest that life can cohere by the joining together of what only seem to be the opposites of life and death. Furthermore, he declares that man cannot find a secure position in life by the use of argument or reason; he cannot, in other words, establish his own sequence of events, his own autonomous history.

Lazarus himself is the incarnation of life as an organic paradox. He is remarkable for his "detached serenity" and for a face still marked by "former suffering" which has "never softened into resignation" (I. 274). While his oneness with nature is suggested by his dark complexion, "the color of rich earth upturned by the plow" (I. 274), he retains a "bitter and mocking" tone (I. 289), reminiscent of Dion Anthony's sardonic pose, but Lazarus surmounts Dion's inner confusion with "an infinite disdain" and sadness (I. 289) that reflect his deep identification with and separation from the guilt, the loneliness, the weariness, and the fear of human beings. Like "rich earth upturned by the plow," he has emerged from the depths, from the tomb of the ground upon which life is sustained. He has not come to speak of his personal experience; he becomes, simply, the cynosure of the gathering who are drawn to hear him express the collective and elemental experience of mankind.

Lazarus resembles Eliade's description of archaic man who participates in the reality of eternal growth that transcends the historical conception of human life as having an irretrievable beginning and an inevitable end.[14] His rebirth is neither a product of his will to life nor the outcome of an historical event. An historical event, James notes, has an "autonomous intrinsic value."[15] Lazarus's rebirth, on the other hand, is just another repetition of the cosmic rhythm of renewal.

The opening dialogue of Act I presents an array of attitudes toward Lazarus that emphasize the modern need to rationalize rebirth, to say that it has somehow come from within him, or that it is a miracle performed by Jesus, or that Lazarus never died (I. 274). For others the rebirth is genuine because they have witnessed it, or were close to the man or to the experience (I. 276). None of the reactions address the mystery of rebirth itself, however, for each speaker takes refuge in a private and personal response. The weighing of probabilities, the indulgence in speculation—these characteristics of modern man divorce him from any direct connection with the phenomenon of rebirth.

Lazarus's extraordinarily condensed rendering of the moment of his rebirth tells us that this transformation was immediate, intuitive, and emotional:

> I heard the heart of Jesus laughing in my heart: "there is Eternal Life in No," it said, "and there is the same Eternal Life in Yes! Death is the fear between!" and my heart reborn to love of life cried "Yes!" and I laughed in the laughter of God! (I. 279)

As a dying man Lazarus has said "No" to life as he knew it, yet paradoxically this "No" gave him relief and allowed for the affirmation of a newer, greater life, the saying of "Yes" to all of existence. For him the real death is not the death of the body, but the death of the human heart or spirit which fears the extinction of the self. Lazarus laughs in the laughter of God because he has attained the all embracing quality so typical of mystical experiences, and which R. M. Bucke calls "cosmic consciousness": an understanding of "the life and order of the universe," a sense of immortality, and a conviction that eternal life is already achieved.[16]

Lazarus's laughter expresses a relaxed state of mind, a letting go or release from the cares that had saddened him and made him fearful, a giving way to the fundamental conditions of rebirth as James understands them.[17] In the act of letting go, of dying, Lazarus discovers that he has had to experience the whole cycle of life in order to be at peace with himself. As a refrain to his wonderful exultant "Yes!" the chorus chants:

> The stone is taken away!
> The spirit is loosed!
> The soul let go! (I. 278)

Lazarus, the father who lost all of his children, the man who was a bad farmer, breeder, manager, and bargainer, who could never forget his sorrows, vanishes into the chorus of celebration, which in its expressions of relief dramatizes a collective version of rebirth remarkably similar to the individual cases James summarizes:

> Give up the feeling of responsibility, let go your hold . . . be genuinely indifferent as to what becomes of it all, and you will find . . . that you gain a perfect inward relief. . . . To get to [this relief] a critical point must usually be passed, a corner turned within one. Something must give way, a native hardness must break down and liquefy; and this event . . . is frequently sudden and automatic, and leaves on the Subject an impression that he has been wrought upon by an external power.[18]

Lazarus's rebirth is sudden and automatic; and he associates it with the external power of Jesus. The moment of death is the critical point he must pass, so that the sorrows and disappointments of his previous life are not only overcome they are accepted as a necessary part of existence. His laughter is the liquefying element that breaks down the rigidity of his former self. He does not rely on his personal strength; he has no pride in himself as an individual and is able to rest in the relinquishment of a private self.[19]

That prolonged laughter should be the primary vehicle of Lazarus's self-transcendence is particularly striking in view of Sheaffer's report that O'Neill "was practically never known throughout his life to laugh aloud."[20] Yet, like Lazarus, O'Neill was capable of exorcising his somber spirits: "when he smiled . . . his face became transformed, radiant, his eyes seemed literally to sparkle."[21] Moreover, Sheaffer suggests that O'Neill's suicide attempt was a way of driving out his "devils,"[22] just as surely as Lazarus welcomes death as the jettisoning of his cares. Lazarus sustains the inner and outer light that O'Neill maintained only fitfully, as if Lazarus is a reverse image of his author, seldom sinking into the low spirits that dogged O'Neill all his life, even though he saw his writing career as a sign of his "second birth."[23]

The recurrence of suffering that tormented O'Neill is balanced in the play by the recurrence of rebirth, of the moment of Lazarus's self-transcendence, a moment which becomes for him the exemplary model of his new life. As he struggles with his grief over the deaths of his parents and sisters (I. 293), he looks up to the stars and, as if answering a question, says simply and quietly "Yes!" (I. 293) His laughter in this scene is the same laughter he heard and expressed in his tomb, for the experience of death and life are simultaneous for him. In several scenes (I. 277, 279–80, 289) he repeats the same paradigmatic gestures, for, like Eliade's archaic man, he recognizes that "reality is acquired solely through repetition or participation; everything which lacks an exemplary model is 'meaningless,' i.e., it lacks reality."[24]

In his meeting with Jesus, Lazarus has found his exemplary model; in his repetition of and participation in Jesus's laughter he has also become an exemplary model.[25] To the modern mind, Lazarus's behavior is truly paradoxical because, like archaic man, he "sees himself as real only to the extent that he ceases to be himself . . . and is satisfied with imitating and repeating the gestures of another. In other words, he sees himself as real, i.e., as 'truly himself,' only, and precisely, insofar as he ceases to be so."[26] The sense of history, of duration, of the development of a unique human personality is entirely absent from his ontology; and so for Lazarus there is no state of becoming.

Lazarus's urge to repeat himself, like Yank's insistent belief that he "belongs," and like the indefatigable refrains of all the characters in *The Iceman Cometh* — a work that brilliantly sums up O'Neill's fixation on repetition — is indicative of O'Neill's hostility to history, to the conviction that man's actions amount to a consecutive and cumulative achievement. Thus he rejects the historicism of the Jews in *Lazarus Laughed* who argue over whether Lazarus is the Messiah who will positively intervene in history, the savior who will come only once to set things right. And he approves of the Greeks who accept Lazarus as an archetypal figure and exemplary model in their own mythology: the "Son of Man and a God!" (I. 298) who is part of an endlessly repeating cycle.

In many ways, Caligula is the prime representative of the historicist state who is torn apart by the conflicts Lazarus transcends. He articulates the tensions and torments that thwart the crowds of various races, religions, ages, and personality types who are fascinated by Lazarus but who cannot quite master their fears to follow him. Caligula's laughter, like their's, is "harsh, discordant, frenzied, desperate, and drunken" (I. 281). It recalls the harsh, barking laughter of *The Hairy Ape* that is meant to emphasize man's alienation from his natural strengths. He is a collection of contradictions: bony and angular but also broad and powerful, long arms and hands but short, skinny hairy legs, "a prematurely wrinkled forehead" but "the curly blond hair of a child." He is masculine and feminine, animal and human. He wavers between outright declarations of love for Lazarus and fierce denunciations. He is "spoiled, petulant and self-obsessed, weak but domineering" (I. 299). He sways from one emotion to its opposite in the matter of a moment. He is proud and humble, anxious to claim the glories of Caesar, dubious that his own reign as Caesar will bring him the security and happiness that is promised in Lazarus's laughter. Incredibly cruel and brutal he nevertheless reveals a childish innocence and vulnerability before Lazarus and openly admits his confusion. At the same time, he wants to preserve his miserable confusion rather than hazard a fundamental reversal in his behavior. Torn in so many different directions and divided by so many different impulses, he stands as a peculiarly fascinating example of the conflicting views of archaic and modern man, and of O'Neill's own psychology which Sheaffer cites for its "excess of adolescent emotion."[27] Caligula desperately demands his unique place in history and wants to believe that he is a maker and manipulator of events, the cynosure of all that he governs. Nonetheless, he is not prepared to accept the anxiety that accompanies the assumption of an historical role or the inexorable loss of vigor and control over events that are not subject to the repetition of a cosmic paradigm. Like the early O'Neill, Caligula evades his responsibilities.

Caligula is caught in a debilitating contradiction: as long as he acts to protect himself, he feels less and less free to be truly himself. He senses this impasse, but as a youth brought up in army camps, schooled in bragging and self-defense, he is without parents and without any sustained connection with the suffering or the joy of others. He acts in a vacuum, which makes him extraordinarily susceptible to Lazarus as a father figure who can be imitated, but which also deprives him of any notion of how to emulate the example of another. In contrast to Tiberius, Caligula has to somehow create himself as a Caesar; and he is baffled by the complexities of autonomy. Like O'Neill, who could not follow the example of his father, Caligula rejects Tiberius as old and outmoded.

It should be clear, then, why Caligula is given the role of anticipating the responses of the crowd to Lazarus. He stands for mankind that is without direction, but which persists in pursuing the illusion of autonomy while dreading the chaos of events provoked by individual actions, and lured to an exemplary model that would lift the burdens of individual responsibility. The crowd stirs as Caligula gives out his first intense declaration of love to the approaching Lazarus. The simultaneous stimulation of the crowd and Caligula enact the abandonment of self-obsession and self-reliance that constitutes Lazarus's rebirth (I. 303–05). The crowd that chants "in a deep, rhythmic monotone like the rising and falling cadences of waves on a beach" (I. 303) calls to mind James's metaphor of the "inner man" who "rolls over into an entirely different position of equilibrium, lives in a new center of energy."[28] The illusion that is created of the movement and sound of a great body of water emphasizes the mesmerizing force of an experience in which the crowd and Caligula are taken out of themselves. In this ritualistic and ceremonial movement we have the re-creation of a cosmos in harmony with itself, so that all of its members are united.

This re-creation of the world's harmonic rhythms is similar to Edmund's memory in *Long Day's Journey into Night* of "a lazy ground swell and a slow drowsy roll of the ship"[29] that totally absorb him in the elements of the sea. For both O'Neill and his characters, the sea is home, a perfect blend of self and cosmos.[30] The sea is, to once again borrow James's words, a liquefying medium that breaks down the person's native hardness. Throughout *Lazarus Laughed*, O'Neill also attempts to evoke this liquefying medium by having the laughter of the choruses and the crowds follow the rising and falling rhythm of the sea, and by having the singing and dancing of groups and individuals mimic the musical soaring and diving, the loud and quiet voice, of Lazarus himself. In sum, the ensemble of sound is designed to blur the integrity of single responses. As Travis Bogard observes, "on the page, the chorus lines appear to follow sequentially, cue-to-cue. In the theatre, however, they overlap the speeches of the protagonists, their sound and their words echoing what is said, elaborating, emphasizing, and augmenting the dialogue."[31] O'Neill attempted a more modest version of this concert of sound in *The Hairy Ape*, but in *Lazarus Laughed* the effect upon the play's characters and audience is meant to be much more symphonic—so much so that when Caligula tries to reassert his will to dominate, it is as if he is struggling to turn back the ocean itself, or the tides of life, rather than just subduing an unruly mob. Lazarus's affirmative laughter is "like a strain of music receding into the silence over still waters" (I. 324). This quiet moment—the pure acceptance of existence in and for itself—balances the chorus's fear of life expressed earlier in the play (I. 295–96) and maintains the alternating rhythms of the sea, of life, intact.

Those rhythms, however, are disrupted by the massive marble walls and triumphal arch that advertize the Roman ambition to fashion its own history. The Romans confer value on their own effort to renew themselves. Yet O'Neill shows an uneasiness in this "outstandingly historical people," as Eliade calls them.[32] They dread death and dissolution, the end of things, of the material world which they have so successfully built. By treasuring their role in the shaping of history they have also departed from the regularity of nature. Consequently, there are signs of decay everywhere as their greed for self-fulfillment degenerates into mindless and perverse entertainments. We hear a "confused drunken clamor of voices" (I. 326) and see in the masculine women and effeminate men "sex corrupted and warped, inverted lusts and artificial vices" (I. 336). As Miriam, Lazarus's wife, says, "these columns and arches and thick walls seem waiting to fall, to crush men and then to crumble over the bones that raised them until both are dust. . . . Its will is so sick that it must kill in order to be aware of life at all" (I. 329–30). Nothing is sacred except the human will to power. Yet a world deprived of a sense of the sacred turns in upon itself; eager to contrive "novelties" in place of the steady, undeviating periodicity of nature, modern man betrays himself. Without a cosmic paradigm in which to participate the actions of individuals are arbitrary and easily devalued—as we see in Caligula's contorted behavior.

In contrast to the Romans who are caught up in the terror of history, Lazarus seems almost lethargic, like Nietzsche's Dionysus, who has looked "truly into the essence of things [and] gained knowledge." For him action cannot "change anything in the eternal nature of things."[33] Lazarus is, however, without the nausea that Nietzsche attributes to Dionysian man and which was manifested in Dion Anthony. Indeed, Tiberius is attracted to Lazarus because "once I laughed somewhat like that" (I. 339). Tiberius searches for a method that would replicate Lazarus's rebirth, but there is no technique or exercise or magic potion that would help him to attain self-transcendence. It is only in those moments when he forgets his skepticism, his questioning, his rigid control over himself and stares into Lazarus's eyes that Tiberius loses himself: a "dreamy smile softens his thin, compressed mouth" (I. 342).

Such moments closely resemble the paradigmatic meeting of Jesus and Lazarus, but they easily elude Tiberius who blinks away his reverie that comes uncomfortably close to his anticipation of death (I. 343). Along with Pompeia he demands that Lazarus prove his power and the authenticity of his rebirth, thereby ignoring the proof of his own briefly altered state of consciousness: "Yes! A cloud came from a depth of sky—around me, softly, warmly, and the cloud dissolved into the sky, and the sky into peace!" (I. 342) This movement away from earth and time confuses and enrages him, so he tests Lazarus's serenity by consenting to Pompeia's request that Miriam be poisoned, but Miriam's own self-abnegating laughter preserves the precedent of her husband's rebirth (I. 348).

Lazarus devoutly upholds the regenerative power of the laughter he first heard in the tomb because it is man's unique answer to defeat and death. Since it comes from himself it is also a means of mastering his terrified reaction to his vulnerability. Laughter is an expression of the human imagination that unifies the tragic world "falling into pieces, all props awry, 'all coherence gone.' "[34] Lazarus's laughter is the acceptance of a world without props. When the props are kicked out from under us or others, we either laugh or cry; sometimes we do both—as is the case with the choruses in the play who shift so swiftly from laughter to tears, from saying "Death is dead!" to "Life is Death" (I. 297). We cry at human loss, and yet we often laugh because laughter offers us "*a sense of regain*," that replenishes the loss.[35] That is why all of the characters in the play, sooner or later, are called to laugh with Lazarus. Pompeia, for example, throws herself into the flames with him, for she is caught in that laughter "heard for a moment, rising clear and passionately with that of Lazarus" (I. 367). She has finally experienced that union with life, that sense of completeness unfulfilled by her desire for a meeting of the flesh. Her death, moreover, enacts the essential paradox of the rebirth pattern that Lazarus says men cannot remember: only by dying can the individual feel truly alive and secure in the vast scale of things. Caligula, on the other hand, finds himself the master of an empty stage, beset by imagined foes, and striking out, ultimately, at himself—just as the young O'Neill blamed others but injured himself. Like the "hairy ape," Caligula closes the play suspended between heaven and earth, "straining upward to the sky," and "groveling" on the ground, begging for and bemoaning both an individual and universal fate: "Forgive me, Lazarus! Men forget!" (I. 371)

Lazarus Laughed suggests that modern man's historical consciousness has fostered the illusion of self-sufficiency, yet that illusion also provokes a terror of the finality of history, the irreversibility of events. Man cannot undo or dissociate himself from that which he has created. As Hayden White says in his summary of Nietzsche's view of history: "the past is constantly before man as an image of things done, finished, complete, unchangeable. The intractibility of this past is the source of man's dishonesty with himself and is the motive power behind his own self-mutilation."[36] At the end of Act III (I. 349) O'Neill graphically dramatizes this dishonesty and self-mutilation that prevent man from projecting beyond what he regards as his fixed past.

The way out of this determinism, Lazarus stresses, is through direct contact with the elements of the universe out of which man has arisen. More important, however, is Lazarus's notion that man can have a vision, a consciousness of his reabsorption in nature, which will allow him to abolish his unalterable past and recover, like Eliade's archaic man, "his virtualities intact."[37] In Eliade's words, "nature recovers only itself, whereas archaic man recovers the possibility of definitively transcending time and living in eternity."[38]

Lazarus's exhortatory language is itself an example of how it is possible to live in eternity. Each speech excites sheer wonder in the multiplicity and dynamism of existence:

Throw your gaze upward! to Eternal Life! to the fearless and deathless. The everlasting! To the stars! (I. 289)

Are you a speck of dust danced in the wind? Then laugh, dancing! Laugh yes to your insignificance! Thereby will be born your new greatness! (I. 309)

Out into the woods! Upon the hills! . . . Out with you under the sky! (I. 310)

Once as squirming specks we crept from the tides of the sea. Now we return to the sea! Once as quivering flecks of rhythm we beat down from the sun. Now we re-enter the sun! (I. 324)

Millions of laughing stars there are around me! And laughing dust, born once of woman on this earth, now freed to dance! New stars are born of dust eternally! The old, grown mellow with God, burst into flaming seed! The fields of infinite space are sown — and grass for sheep spring up on the hills of earth! (I. 349)

Go out under the sky! Let your heart climb on laughter to a star! (I. 360)

Lazarus follows Nietzsche's advice that man must once again learn to
" 'frolic in images' without hardening those images into life-destroying 'concepts.' "[39] Lazarus's words constantly evoke a universe that is re-creating itself by periodically purifying itself; and through his vision he, like archaic
man, "takes part in the repetition of the cosmogony, the creative act *par
excellence.*"[40] The biography of an individual ("born once of woman on this
earth") is subsumed in this creationistic conception. Each successive speech
is necessarily a repetition of Lazarus's initial speech, and the landscape of
sun, sky, sea, and earth, the images of laughing, dancing, and flaming, all
emanate from an unvarying cosmic paradigm of rebirth.

The presentation of this cosmic paradigm overwhelms and discredits
the historical view of human potentiality in such a way that the tension and
excitement of the play is sometimes diminished. Louis Sheaffer speaks for
many critics when he finds the play overdone and too much the product of
O'Neill's mysticism.[41] He might have rectified the play's imbalance by por-
traying more sophisticatedly the significance of the historicist view in order
to enrich the dialectic between Lazarus and Tiberius, for example. Instead,
Tiberius is easily dismissed because his view is simply mechanistic and is
itself destroyed by his foolish and cynical superstition. Contrary to what
Lazarus Laughed implies, the historicist view need not be regarded as
merely rational and logical, a system of thought that sets up a terrifying
"contradiction between consciousness and its object."[42] Missing from the
drama is any sense that historicism (as it was developed by Hegel) approaches an organic interpretation of the consequences of human action, an
organic interpretation that attempts to show that self-motivated human
actions are not simply arbitrary.

Lazarus is an especially appealing character in those moments when he
gives way to grief, when we can see him as a human being struggling with
and overcoming his sorrow. He is also awe inspiring in his close identification with nature, yet his unassailability seems inhuman, almost distasteful,
the mark of a fanatic pursuing a programmatic philosophy silencing the
slightest deviation. As Eliade observes, "modern man, who accepts history
or claims to accept it, can reproach archaic man, imprisoned within the
mythical horizon of archetypes and repetition, with his creative impotence,
or, what amounts to the same thing, his inability to accept the risks entailed
by every creative act."[43] By re-identifying himself with nature archaic man
reveals "a fear of movement and spontaneity."[44] With every human gesture
under the rigid control of a paradigm archaic man retreats from responsibility for his own actions; and by revering the paradigm he soothes the guilt
that follows from freely willed actions.[45]

Had O'Neill been willing to modify his intention of presenting the cosmic paradigm as an unquestionably superior model, he might have improved the dramatic form of the play by proposing the parallel choices of
repetition and variation, as does Kierkegaard in *Repetition*, where he asks
"whether a thing gains or loses by being repeated."[46] Should man immerse

himself in the creative flow of things, try to recapture a sense of himself as part of the larger whole of nature, or should he stake everything on the development of self-awareness, on an extreme effort to preserve human autonomy by searching out the unity that might be perceived in the diversity of experience? Although *Lazarus Laughed* ambitiously addresses the dilemma of historicism and aptly evolves out of O'Neill's earlier dramas of self-transcendence, it does not permit us to ask such an open-ended question.[47]

Notes

1. Louis Sheaffer, *O'Neill: Son and Playwright* (New York: Little Brown, 1968), p. 4.

2. For one of the most recent explorations of the ties between O'Neill's life and art and the world, see Michael Manheim, *Eugene O'Neill's New Language of Kinship* (Syracuse: Syracuse University Press, 1982).

3. See "O'Neill's Mysticism: From His Historical Trilogy to *Long Day's Journey into Night*," *Studies in Mystical Literature*, 1 (Spring 1981), 220.

4. Eugene O'Neill, *The Emperor Jones*, in *The Plays of Eugene O'Neill*, (New York: Random House, 1955), III 199-202. Unless otherwise noted, all references to O'Neill's plays are to the three volume Random House edition and are incorporated in the text by volume number and page within parentheses.

5. Sheaffer, pp. 225, 264.

6. Sheaffer, pp. 67-68, 102, 121, 247, 300.

7. Sheaffer, p. 282.

8. Sheaffer, pp. 76, 154, 272.

9. Sheaffer, p. 351, could easily be describing one of O'Neill characters as well as the author himself in this observation: "the unfriendly universe pressed down on him in the dark and filled him with the forebodings of naked primitive man."

10. Sheaffer, p. 56, notes that Sarah Sandy, the family nurse, read Poe to the young O'Neill, and that the older O'Neill "felt a personal identification with the haunted author" (p. 304). Given O'Neill's interest in doubles, in divided personalities, and in a mystical yearning for a merger between self and world, his affinity with Poe seems very deep and enduring.

11. Mircea Eliade, *Cosmos and History: The Myth of the Eternal Return* (New York: Harper Torchbooks, 1959), p. 141. I use the term "archetype" throughout this essay in the same way Eliade does: as a synonym for "exemplary model" or "paradigm." No reference to Jung's conception of the "archetype" is intended. Similarly, I employ the term "historicism" in Eliade's sense to mean a concern with the uniqueness of historical phenomena and persons, with their independence and integrity, and their inimitable character. Douglas Day, "Amor Fati: O'Neill's Lazarus as Superman and Savior," in *O'Neill: A Collection of Critical Essays*, ed. John Gassner (Englewood Cliffs, N.J., 1964) has pointed out the usefulness of *Cosmos and History* for a study of *Lazarus Laughed*.

12. Eliade, p. 141.

13. William James, *The Varieties of Religious Experience* (New York: Collier Books, 1961), p. 330.

14. Eliade, p. 5.

15. James, p. 319.

16. James, p. 313. Several critics have attributed the form of Lazarus's rebirth, and especially his exultant laughter, to O'Neill's profound absorption of Nietzsche's *The Birth of Trag-*

edy and *Thus Spake Zarathrustra*, but the laughter and many other aspects of O'Neill's drama of self-transcendence can be documented in the literature of mysticism. For example, James, p. 302, quotes Tennyson speaking of his individuality dissolving and fading away into "boundless being." Lazarus's laughter is an expression of "boundless being," of a clear and sure state comparable to Tennyson's evocation of what is "utterly beyond words—where death was an almost laughable impossibility—the loss of personality (if so it were) seeming no extinction, but the only true life."

17. James, p. 101.

18. James, p. 101.

19. James, p. 102, refers to this stage of rebirth as "giving your private convulsive self a rest."

20. Sheaffer, p. 95.

21. Sheaffer, p. 95.

22. Sheaffer, p. 214.

23. Sheaffer, pp. 252, 289.

24. Eliade, p. 34.

25. I am not suggesting, however, that Lazarus becomes a disciple of Jesus. Douglas Day and Frank R. Cunningham, "*Lazarus Laughed*: A Study in O'Neill's Romanticism," *Studies in the Twentieth Century*, 15 (1975), 54, maintain that Jesus is converted to Lazarus's joyful acceptance of man's participation in an eternal present. Their interpretation is hard to credit, since it is Jesus's laughter that awakens Lazarus, and it is Lazarus who kneels before Jesus. It is true that Jesus, with a questioning look in his eyes, seems to take comfort from Lazarus's "Yes" but their relationship seems reciprocal. They share each other's laughter as equals and create a timeless paradigm of rebirth. They are brothers in the sense that both of them have experienced the sadness and joy of life and each of them—through very different interpretations of existence—reach an affirmative vision of man's wholeness.

26. Eliade, p. 34.

27. Sheaffer, p. 124, quotes Walter Kaufmann on Nietzsche, but it is clear that Sheaffer thinks the phrase applies to O'Neill as well.

28. James, p. 257.

29. Eugene O'Neill, *Long Day's Journey into Night* (New Haven: Yale University Press, 1956), p. 153.

30. Sheaffer, p. 167, titles one of his chapters "Home to the Sea," and makes clear that O'Neill felt he belonged to the sea. Other passages in Sheaffer, pp. 59, 65, 69, 316, 351, 458, mention his powerful attraction to the water, his impressive swimming, and his seeming oneness with the sea itself. Sheaffer, *Son and Artist* (Boston: Little Brown, 1973), p. 229, reports a friend's memory of O'Neill "telling me the story of *Lazarus* one day while swimming sidestroke."

31. Travis Bogard, *Contour in Time: The Plays of Eugene O'Neill* (New York: Oxford University Press, 1972), p. 283.

32. Eliade, p. 75.

33. Friedrich Nietzsche, *The Birth of Tragedy*, in *Basic Writings of Nietzsche*, ed. Walter Kaufmann (New York: Modern Library, 1968), pp. 59–60.

34. Harold H. Watts, "Myth and Drama," in *Myth and Literature: Contemporary Theory and Practice*, ed. John Vickery (Lincoln: University of Nebraska Press, 1966), p. 79.

35. Watts, p. 82.

36. Hayden White, *Metahistory: The Historical Imagination in Nineteenth Century Europe* (Baltimore: Johns Hopkins University Press, 1973), p. 347.

37. Eliade, p. 158.

38. Eliade, p. 158.

39. White, p. 335.

40. Eliade, p. 158.

41. Sheaffer, *Son and Artist*, pp. 201–02.

42. White, p. 128.

43. Eliade, p. 156.

44. Eliade, p. 155.

45. Eliade, p. 155.

46. Søren Kierkegaard, *Repetition: An Essay in Experimental Psychology* (New York: Harper Torchbooks, 1964), p. 33.

47. In "O'Neill's Mysticism," pp. 232–34, I argue that in *Long Day's Journey into Night* he arrived at a style and structure that could dramatically encompass the conflict between repetition and variation.

Eugene O'Neill as Social Historian: Manners and Morals in *Ah, Wilderness!*

Ellen Kimbel

It is exactly half a century since the first production of Eugene O'Neill's only major comedy, *Ah, Wilderness!* and an appropriate time for a reassessment. Although it is one of O'Neill's most performed plays, its critical history has been odd, to say the least. It has been variously: dismissed as too false and sentimental to be worthy of serious consideration;[1] judged as having substance only insofar as it is the sunny counterpart of *A Long Day's Journey into Night*, that is, as wish fulfillment fantasy;[2] assessed as a nostalgic family comedy whose true meanings exist in the currents of evil and despair beneath its bright and sparkling surface.[3] While these approaches to *Ah, Wilderness!* differ from one another, it is interesting to note that they share a certain common assumption: that is, they suggest that the play's real value, when there at all, is found in its subtle evocation of the tragic vision expressed in the rest of the O'Neill canon. In short, critics of O'Neill's work have not known quite what to make of this unprecedented and atypical sampling of good cheer.

The dramatist was himself aware of the play's anomolous relationship to the rest of his work. He referred to it as a "dream walking" and admitted it was "out of [his] previous line." And, he had this to say about the work's focus:

> My purpose was to write a play true to the spirit of the American large small town at the turn-of-the century. Its quality depended upon atmosphere, sentiment, an exact evocation of the mood of a dead past. To me, the America which was (and is) the real America found its unique expres-

sion in such middle-class families as the Millers, among whom so many of
my own generation passed from adolescence into manhood.[4]

This statement shows O'Neill to be the most cogent of the play's commentators, most of whom, eager to avoid committing the intentional fallacy, have
paid scant attention to O'Neill's view of the play and have insisted on its
correspondence to *Long Day's Journey*. Such interpretations, while illuminating the dramatist's psychological development and/or his personal history, do not take sufficiently into account the play's final effect, both as read
and performed. And that effect, particularly from the perspective of the
nineteen-eighties, is one of affirmation tinged with nostalgia for a time of
innocence, simplicity, and safety — a time long gone but summoned up and
revitalized with great poignancy in *Ah, Wilderness!*

That it has always been a hugely popular work is in itself revealing. It
had a long run on Broadway in 1933, its first production; it has been filmed
twice (once with music as *Summer Holiday*); it was made into a Broadway
musical as *Take Me Along*; it has been adapted for television; and even at
this writing it is playing in New York. Indeed, it seems that the number of
productions of *Ah, Wilderness!* accelerates even as the time and spirit it recreates recede into the ever more distant past. It should be obvious that its
ongoing success is due not to its reworking of the intricate O'Neill family
relationships or to its place in the dramatist's technical or thematic evolution but rather to its clear and convincing representation of the cultural milieu of middle-class small town America at the turn of the century, in fact,
to what O'Neill had all along claimed for it.

There are a number of ways in which the work is firmly anchored to the
period which is its setting. First, the conventions and beliefs of the Miller
family are to a great extent characteristic of that large, increasingly powerful business and professional group that was to become the mainstream of
American culture and it is these attitudes, genteel and conservative, that
shape the broad plot outline of the play. Further, the details of O'Neill's
stage directions (painstakingly accurate here as in all his plays), recreate the
look and feel of the period, contributing to the authenticity. The Miller
home, for example, is furnished in the "medium-priced tastelessness" of the
period: there are sliding doors and portières, a front parlor, a back parlor, a
piazza, and an open front porch. The hotel bar has at least two items that
have since disappeared from view: a "family entrance" and a brass cuspidor.
There are several references to the popular ballads of the day: in the bar, the
player piano grinds out "Bedelia," Arthur Miller sings "Then You'll Remember Me," "Dearie," and "Waiting at the Church" and Sid refers to performances at Hammerstein's Victoria theater in New York. There are, too, a
number of contemporary colloquialisms; and if O'Neill's critics have judged
the language of his plays to be less than felicitous (the dramatist himself
frequently complained that he had no ear for dialogue), here, the use of
long forgotten phrases is less clumsy than essential to the play's periodicity.
Thus, Sid, when funny is "a caution," Waterbury is a "nifty old town," a

spanking is a "good hiding," and a prostitute is a "tart" or a "swift baby." The play then, is rather remarkable in its capacity to catch and hold for a few brief hours a whole constellation of manners and morals redolent of a bygone age.

This should not be construed as a reductive view of *Ah, Wilderness!* Clearly, the play by the very nature of its genre — nostalgic family comedy — lacks the philosophical, mythic, and poetic suggestiveness of the tortured dramas for which O'Neill is justifiably famous. However, it does have some interesting things to say about adolescence and the nature of the family unit early in the century, and in so doing, it acts as a reflecting lens for these same areas of experience in the high-tech, media-saturated, coolly cynical present.

The values by which the Miller family is defined, the old traditional ones of home and family, respectability and success have been judged by some readers to suggest a Philistine view, one embracing all that O'Neill's major works reject as patently false and hollow.[5] But this is either an objection to the form itself (compare, for example, the beliefs, behavior, and goals of the families in *Our Town, Life With Father, I Remember Mama,* or the Andy Hardy movies), or is a response to the known facts of the author's own very different life. Neither of these is a valid basis for judging *Ah, Wilderness!*, which is either a success or a failure entirely on its own terms.

The values dramatized and implicitly endorsed by the play are those of affirmation: there is, in the main, approval, even admiration of the Millers and the patterns of experience they represent, and of the kind of adulthood toward which Richard moves at the work's conclusion. When there is irony, it is gentle and it is directed toward the follies of adolescence — the theatrical posturing, the self-aggrandizement, the tendency to see the world in extremes of black and white. And when there is psychological probing — as there is in Sid's obdurate need to fail, in Lily's prim self-righteousness, and in Nat's painfully inhibited approach to sex in his "man to man" talk with Richard — it is accomplished with a most delicate and compassionate scalpel. These are — these men and women in a "large small town" in Connecticut early in the century — good and decent people who are regarded by their creator with tenderness and not a little wistfulness.[6]

The play's fundamental optimism is in evidence from the beginning. It is suggested by the description of the set — a bright sitting-room, cheerful in the morning sunlight, comfortable rockers and armchairs around a table, and books everywhere (books, the stage directions assure us, "the family really have read") and it is enhanced by the animated buzz of conversation from an unseen dining room; and then by the appearance of a blond, sunburnt boy who is "bursting with bottled up energy."[7] The day is July Fourth, the year is 1906, a period of time when Americans still believed in the promise and the dream and when that holiday gave the signal to families all over the country to join in celebration — on picnics, on day-long journeys to a relative for the annual barbecue, and of course for the ubiquitous fireworks.

In *Ah, Wilderness!*, the day is of more than usual significance, for it symbolizes Richard's own personal, if short-lived revolution. That which he rebels against is to some extent that which his parents represent: this, of course, makes him not only typical, but healthy. But since his parent's values are those espoused by the work as a whole and since, by implication, they become his own, they must be given particular scrutiny.

Nat and Essie Miller are neither idealized nor flat and predictable. Their weaknesses — Nat's tolerance of Sid's drinking, his insensitivity to his sister's unhappiness, his occasional boorishness; Essie's needless prolonging of the bluefish joke, her snappishness under stress — make them credible, convincing. Their great strengths, and it is these that the play emphasizes, is in their essential relationship to one another, and in their attitude toward their children. They function in their attributes as that against which other relationships are measured — throwing into bolder relief, for example, the loneliness of Sid and Lily, becoming the normative pattern for Richard to emulate. And, tangentially, but not insignificantly, they provide a perspective on turn-of-the-century middle class mores.

It was customary in that period of our history for men to be alternately protective and patronizing of their women. That we now regard such behavior as a ritual of deference and *politesse* masking a very real, if unconscious oppression, is both beside the point and after the fact. It is historically accurate and the play catches this attitude perfectly in the relationship of Nat to his wife. Thus, the contents of the books Richard is now reading (Swinburne, Ibsen, Carlyle, Shaw, Wilde, *The Rubaiyat*) remain secreted from Essie; she is expected not to be present during the "birds and bees" dialogue; and it is presumed she will not mind when her husband, in full view of the family, "slaps her jovially on her fat buttocks." Her retaliation (like that of millions of women like her) is subtle but effective: the perpetuation of the bluefish joke; her own cherished belief that "men are weak" and her unblinking announcement to Nat that her mother had never thought him "overbright."

But that which most often distinguishes Nat and Essie Miller in their relationship to one another is their capacity for loving. During much of the play, they manifest real awareness of and concern for each other's feelings. For example, Nat, sensing his wife's distress over Richard's absence, tries to keep her mind off the lateness of the hour and encourages Mildred and Arthur to provide some distracting entertainment. And when Sid taunts Nat about his annual retelling of a story of his youthful heroism, Essie comes to her husband's defense. That they are still romantically involved is demonstrated in the famous last scene, a moment at least quietly suggestive of the mood of lovers:

Mrs. Miller: . . . I'm going to turn out the light.
All ready?
Miller: Yep. Let her go, Gallagher. (She turns out the lamp. In the ensuing darkness the faint moonlight shines full in through the screen door. Walk-

ing together toward the front parlor they stand full in it for a moment, looking out. Miller puts his arm around her. He says in slow voice) — There he is — like a statue of Love's Young Dream. (Then he sighs and speaks with a gentle nostalgic melancholy) What's it that *Rubaiyat* says

> "Yet Ah, that Spring should vanish with the Rose!
> That youth's sweet-scented manuscript should close!"

(Then throwing off his melancholy, with a loving smile at her) Well, Spring isn't everything, is it Essie? There's a lot to be said for Autumn. That's got beauty, too. And Winter — if you're together.

Mrs. Miller (simply): Yes, Nat. (She kisses him and they move quietly out of the moonlight, into the darkness of the front parlor.)

And there is the sense throughout of a genuine and tender comradeship, particularly in evidence in their unified response to their children.

It is, of course, the relationship of parents to their children that is the cornerstone of the play; for if *Ah, Wilderness!* is the story of a young boy's painful and precipitous growing up, the process takes place within the context of the family, whose adult members counsel, berate, support, or punish, all the while establishing the group's expectations and values. In fact, even Lily and Sid are part of this pattern: she is the auxiliary mother to the Miller children, offering wisdom to Richard, instruction to Mildred, and love to all: "I feel the same love for yours as if they were mine," she tells Essie. And Sid is, throughout, the wayward child, unable to control his drinking or to keep a job, or to make a commitment to Lily, overly reliant on slapstick humor to attract attention, and openly self-pitying.

The work begins by establishing the solidarity of the Miller family — an extended family with its inclusion of Lily and Sid[8] — whose bonds are genuine and unquestioned. This cohesiveness is continually felt so that even when there are lapses (Nat and Essie's raw nerves while waiting anxiously for Richard's late night return, Sid's drunken gaucheries, a few moments of privately experienced nostalgia at the sound of old beloved ballads) we know that a harmonious balance will once again be achieved. This is the state of being toward which all elements of the play strain and which is established, however conditionally, at its conclusion. That Sid and Lily remain on the periphery of the charmed circle, Lily sadly resigned to the distinctions, Sid, too self-involved and self-justifying to make the distinctions, adds to the play's verisimilitude.[9]

The two day period of *Ah, Wilderness!* is Richard's rite of passage. Indeed, it is his brief flirtation with rebellion (expressed in his daring new enthusiasms for poetry, philosophy, love, sex, and alcohol) and his family's efforts to restrain him that give the work its structure. While his "radical" reading habits have been established before the play begins, his open disaffection is precipitated by his mistaken belief that his girl, Muriel, has rejected him and his conviction that his family's attitudes toward him are unimaginative and cloddish. His reaction is to spend an evening with a prostitute in a disreputable and seedy bar. The event is pivotal. It functions thematically as the "fall" from which Richard must emerge chastened in order to be accepted once again by the social group that defines him, which is to say, his family and community. And it functions socio-historically as a view — albeit a symbolic one — of adolescence in that post-Victorian period, making abundantly clear the changes that have taken place in the conception of childhood from then to now.

Stage directions for this scene are explicit in suggesting the sordidness of the places:

> The back room of a bar in a small hotel — a small dingy room, dimly lighted by two fly-specked globes in a fly-specked chandelier suspended from the middle of the ceiling. . . .In the middle of the right wall its window with closed shutters. Three tables with stained tops. . . . a brass cuspidor is on the floor by the table. The floor is unswept, littered with cigarette and cigar butts. The hideous saffron-colored wallpaper is blotched and spotted.

This is, given the general tone of the play and the warmth and graciousness of Richard's home, a kind of hell. And Belle, with whom he sits awkwardly at a table, is his Satan. That he fails to adapt to this environment is central to the meaning of both his character and the play, but the degree to which he fails provides some of the work's most humorous moments. He is, throughout the course of the scene alternately guilty, embarrassed, flustered, humiliated, shy, shamefaced, defensive, shocked, and finally, sickly drunk, and if this were not enough misery, he is at the scene's conclusion, kicked and pushed out by the bartender. What the scene promotes, in addition to his terrible discomfort, is the extraordinary inexperience of Richard Miller, his utter inability to understand the code of the underworld in which he finds himself. (At first he doesn't drink, then he both drinks too much and tips too much; and in a sudden flush of benevolence, he tries to convert Belle from her sinful ways.) His awkwardness is the predictable response of one who has been sheltered from the vicissitudes of life; and his repugnance at the idea of sex with Belle is perfectly consistent with the background that shaped him (deny it though he will) and his own sensitive nature. Like the many young men of his generation for whom he is here the representative figure, Richard's notions of sex are inextricably bound to the emotion of love. It is this view and his consequent unblemished chastity that reunites him with Muriel and returns him to his approving and very much relieved parents.

The beach scene, that of his reunion with Muriel, is the structural and thematic counterpart to the bar-room scene: in the bar he is initiated into the world of evil with Belle as his guide; on the beach, he achieves redemption through Muriel, his young and innocent dispenser of grace. The saloon is dark and claustrophobic and filthy and is peopled by tough, street-wise types who represent a corrupt, if unfortunate, element of humanity. Everything that takes place within the scene works toward creating feelings of guilt and self-loathing in Richard. The beach represents his paradise, the "paradise enow" of *The Rubaiyat*. It is an oasis of beauty with white sand shimmering in the moonlight, and Richard, purged of worldly temptations and nearly overwhelmed by the loveliness of the night and by his own romantic impulses, achieves a moment of transcendence: "Gee, it's beautiful tonight . . . as if it was a special night . . . for me and Muriel. . . . Gee, I love tonight. . . . I love the sand, and the trees, and the grass, and the water and the sky, and the moon. . . .It's all in me and I'm all in it. . . . God, it's so beautiful!"

The scene between Richard and Muriel is, in more worldly terms, an enormously effective rendering of the behavior that characterizes young love: the vulnerability masked by an air of bravado, the alternating displays of timidity and brashness, and, of course the great waves of desire. Thematically, the scene constitutes for the young lovers an identification with Nat and Essie and the values that define them, a correspondence reinforced by the concluding scene of the play with Nat and Essie holding hands in the moonlight and Nat quoting from *The Rubaiyat*. The two couples are almost replications of each other, the children in the process of becoming what the parents are. Or nearly so, for in Richard's attitudes, his cultural interests, his special kind of perceptiveness, and in the initial description of him, O'Neill makes clear that for all the characteristics he shares with his parents, there are distinct and critical differences: "In appearance he is a perfect blend of father and mother, so much so that each is convinced he is the image of the other. . . . But he is definitely different from both of his parents, too. There is something of extreme sensitiveness added — a restless, apprehensive, defiant, shy, dreamy, self-conscious intelligence about him." These qualities insure that while the foundation of Richard's character is shaped in the image of his parents, he will move beyond them to something even better, something more imaginative and more wise. But whatever that new kind of being is, it will have been fired in the twin crucibles of love and discipline, those forces most at work in the Miller family; and Richard's short-lived emancipation will potentiate a more mature, more authentic freedom for him later: "I don't think we'll ever have to worry about his being safe — from himself — again," Nat tells Essie, "And I guess no matter what life will do to him, he can take care of it now." There is a sense then, in which the play is about the socialization of the young during a far more innocent time than our own. It makes clear the incontrovertible distinctions that existed between parents and their children, parents setting carefully circumscribed limits, children expected to understand and comply. The reward for acquiescence was in the continued support (we call it nurturing, today) of the young by the adults in the family, who assumed, or at least hoped, that the children would eventually embrace their own cherished values. Young people were sequestered from much of life's brutality then — from violence, evil, human misery, injustice, and death. They are certainly less so today — through perpetual exposure to television and through their increased involvement in their parents' troubled lives. It is a questionable enrichment; for we seem to be losing much that had earlier characterized childhood and our young people seem to be too old too soon.

O'Neill knew from his lack of it, the advantages to the child of the kind of family he gives us in *Ah, Wilderness!* The play, he said, represented what he wished his youth had been. That it is a play of fantasy makes it no less authentic, no less convincing a work, for if he did not experience so wholesome a childhood as Richard Miller's he was at least witness to it.[10] Few American writers have written of the glories of the middle-class; the assumptions upon which it is based are, as though by edict, dismissed or derided. In *Ah, Wilderness!* our most distinguished and truth-telling dramatist explores the conventions of this sector of our culture and finds many of its values life-enhancing. In its nostalgic journey back through time, O'Neill's comedy not only shows us how it was for many American families at the turn of the century, but suggests as well what we have lost.[11]

Notes

1. Both Ruby Cohn in *Dialogue in American Drama* (Bloomington: Indiana Univ. Press, 1971), pp. 40–42, and Edwin A. Engel in *The Haunted Heroes of Eugene O'Neill* (Cambridge, Mass.: Harvard Univ. Press, 1953), pp. 270–77, find the play inconsequential, a falsification of experience that conceals a smug acceptance of superficial values.

2. Arthur and Barbara Gelb in *O'Neill* (New York: Harper's, 1962), p. 81 and Travis Bogard in introduction to *The Later Plays of Eugene O'Neill* (New York: Modern Library, 1967), p.xxiii.

3. Louis Sheaffer in *O'Neill: Son and Artist* (Boston: Little, Brown, 1973), pp. 405–06; John Henry Raleigh in *The Plays of Eugene O'Neill* (Carbondale: Southern Illinois Univ. Press, 1965), pp. 80, 139; John T. Shawcross in "The Road to Ruin: The Beginning of O'Neill's Long Day's Journey" *Modern Drama*, 3 (1960), 295–96; Frederic I. Carpenter, *Eugene O'Neill* (New York: Twayne, 1964), pp. 136–38, 145–47. Thomas F. Van Laan in his "Singing in the Wilderness: The Dark Vision of Eugene O'Neill's Only Mature Comedy," *Modern Drama*, 22 (1979), 9–18, takes the most extreme view among those critics who see the play as more dark than bright. It is, he says, about life as a wilderness, its characters face a "desolate reality," and O'Neill's attitude toward them is part regret and part contempt.

4. Quoted by Barret H. Clark in *Eugene O'Neill: The Man and His Plays* (New York: Dover, 1947), p. 138.

5. See especially Ruby Cohn, pp. 40–41 and Thomas F. Van Laan, pp. 10–11, 17.

6. O'Neill responded to the play's success by asserting that it proved that "emotionally we still deeply hanker after the old solidarity of the family unit." Quoted in Sheaffer, p. 423.

7. Although commentators have referred to the correspondences in the stage sets of *Ah, Wilderness!* and *Long Day's Journey* in support of a dark reading of the comedy, there are significant distinctions. The front parlor in *Journey* has "the appearance of a room rarely occupied." There is a "dark, windowless back parlor never used" and furniture is "formally arranged." As Mary and James Tyrone enter the living room her "extreme nervousness" and his "sentimental melancholy" are in evidence.

8. This expanded family structure has disappeared in American culture and with it the

enlarged slice of the world, the additional ways of being and doing that were available to the young.

9. There is a very real sense in which Sid and Lily perpetuate the relationship exactly as it is; that is, neither really wishes (or is able) to go beyond the safe parameters they have established.

10. For the families O'Neill knew in New London, Connecticut, at about the same time as the setting of the play and who served as models for the Miller family, see Sheaffer, pp. 404–05.

11. I attended the Roundabout Theatre production in New York City (July, 1983) after the completion of this essay. The performance emphasized precisely those qualities in the play that I have suggested are essential to an accurate reading. Interviews with John Stix, the director, and with Philip Bosco and Dody Goodman who play Nat and Essie Miller with extraordinary sensitivity revealed that from the beginning they had determined that O'Neill wrote *Ah, Wilderness!* as a warm, nostalgic comedy and that they would play it that way. It was felt that the tone of the work and the authentic representation of turn-of-the-century America would allow modern theatergoers to accept its admittedly dated conventions. The enormous enthusiasm of the audience on the day I attended proved them correct.

The Transcendence of Melodrama in O'Neill's *The Iceman Cometh*   Michael Manheim

When one talks about melodrama from the perspective of Robert B. Heilman in his two books on the subject,[1] one is mainly talking about two closely connected characteristics. The first is intrigue, the often stock melodramatic plot with its deceptions, complications, crises, and denouements. The other is the simple polar opposition of good and evil (often as dictated by the popular culture of a period), and the struggle within the framework of that opposition between clearly defined protagonists and antagonists. Heavily dependent upon melodrama in his earlier plays, despite an oft-stated antipathy to it, Eugene O'Neill in his later plays successfully transcended melodrama. In *A Moon for the Misbegotten*, the playwright seemingly made intrigue the central dramatic interest of the play, then displaced that intrigue with a far deeper interest, one which announced his concern not with the surfaces of human experience, but with its wellsprings.[2] In that play, the age-old comic intrigue of a farmer trapping a wealthy suitor into marrying his daughter is displaced half way through by a drama of deep confession and self-recognition. In *The Iceman Cometh*, on the other hand, the use of melodrama does not emphasize intrigue. Rather, the play is built around the polar opposition of good and evil, on the identification of protagonists and antagonists — and the displacement takes the form of denial of that opposition, of the very existence of protagonists and antagonists. Moreover, in *The Iceman Cometh*, the polar oppositions of melodramatic experience are identified with the past, with what characters recall about what has brought them to their present circumstances. The transcendence of melodrama is then identified with what the audience and certain characters are brought to realize about the present.

There is, of course, one set of melodramas of the past in *The Iceman Cometh* which I have already explored.[3] Those are the recalled melodramas implicit in the encounters of Larry Slade and Don Parritt, and they lead directly to Parritt's suicide in the play. This action is in part an enactment of O'Neill's exorcising of his own fears and hostilities, those hidden feelings that kept pushing him toward a suicidal perspective throughout much of his earlier writing. But the transcending of melodrama in this play cannot be associated solely with the author's personal experience. Larry's confusions about his past are relevant to the entire process by which melodrama is transcended in the play. Having been the lover of a woman who was the leader of a radical political "movement" — Rosa Parritt — Larry left that woman and came to live the life of a derelict at Harry Hope's saloon. His reactions to what he has done are deeply contradictory. Sometimes he feels he was betrayed by Rosa because her new political ideology had led her to take other lovers. Thus he feels he was the betrayed protagonist in a melodrama in which a faithless woman was the antagonist. At other times, however, he feels he was the antagonist, a guilty betrayer of a woman who was in her fashion faithful to him. The division in his feelings is quite intense and reflects itself in the division in his feelings toward her son. At times he feels a guilty loyalty toward Parritt, and at other times he violently rejects Parritt. In fact, Larry seems trapped between two irreconcilable melodramatic images of himself associated with his past experience. Until Parritt's suicide, he cannot stop being the betrayer or the betrayed; and this confusion on Larry's part begins to suggest the means by which the simplicities of the melodrama are explored and rejected in this play.

Larry's confusion about his past leads us to think about the past lives of the play's other characters, lives which in fact create a deep resonance of past melodramatic experience repeated again and again. These are figures about whom Larry is objective. He looks at them with detachment and sympathy, understanding them even while he has not fully understood himself. Larry, functioning as a sort of narrator early in the play, relates something of what has brought each figure to his present state. Each has lived through an experience from which he has emerged in defeat. It would appear at first that these men, all of course alcoholics, turned to alcohol as the result of their personal failures. But as we learn more about their stories, it becomes apparent that whether the alcohol was cause or effect is unclear. Did it result from the failure, or did it cause the failure? All we know with certainty is that they have all been alcoholics for a long time.

As with the alcoholism, so with other aspects of the past experiences of these men, we find we cannot distinguish cause from effect. The failure in each case seems actually to have been a conclusion on the individual's part that the worse, or "evil," side of his nature became dominant in a crucial experience; and its having become dominant made him believe that his value as a human being was irrevocably lost. That belief accounts for much of his reaction in the present. Each character, fearing what that loss might do to his personal stability, attempts to keep at bay the panic which might result from its total acceptance. Hence the drink (which continues unabated, whether originally cause or effect), and hence the pipe dreams. Each character keeps feeding himself with the illusion that he will reform, take up a life he imagines once having lived as a productive human being. Yet, as we with Larry's help become familiar with details of the past episodes which were so crucial to these people, we become aware of many obscurities, obscurities which resemble the uncertainty about the alcohol. We begin to realize that the "failure" these people have experienced is rooted not so much in actual evidence as in the individual's assessment of the key event, and that an opposing assessment is equally plausible. He might not have been the "evil" person he concluded he was.

The stories or scraps of stories we hear about or from these individuals are melodramatic. They all hint at intrigue, and they all assume a fixed ethical framework and a struggle between protagonists and the antagonists. The character first presents himself as the protagonist in his story, and those who opposed him as the antagonists. But no sooner do we get this view than a countering view emerges. The character, we learn, was "really" the antagonist and is currently drinking and pipe-dreaming to escape that role. That might seem sufficient on the face of it: the man is living a lie, while we know the truth. But O'Neill does not let the countering view of the character's action stand. In fact, we know nothing. The possibility that the person was in deed the protagonist he thinks he so crucially failed to be lingers. Our impressions feel tugged at from either side by the opposing melodramatic constructions — both of which have fictive life, neither of which (the character's own statements notwithstanding) can quite outweigh the other. Rather than the idea of the past as a shaping force, then, the idea of the past as ambiguous is suggested to us — a not uncommon theme in contemporary literature.

These observations need to be spelled out, of course, through the specific experience of the characters; but before they are, one more general observation needs to be made. As I observed earlier, melodrama in this play refers to the past, not the present. When they are not struggling with the conflicting melodramas of their pasts, these characters live in an unmelodramatized present. As we shall see, the protagonist/antagonist divisions associated with the past dissolve in the present into the complexity of the individual persona we see before us. Melodrama, of course, does not ordinarily allow for complexity in its characters. Its conflicts are between simple roles representing a clear struggle between good and evil, and the assumption is that such struggle has really ended for residents of the "end-of-the-line" cafe. Except for the Larry-Parritt action, where the conflicting melodramas of Larry's past become part of the present in the person of Don

Parrit, there is no real melodrama in the saloon.[4] In the present in which we see these people, they have all been cleansed of hope for the triumph of any clearly definable good over any clearly definable evil. Despite their pipe-dreaming claims, they have been freed of hopes and roles. In the day-to-day life of the saloon, they are essentially roleless, complex personalities existing in an ethically indeterminate world. Divided for the most part into groups determined by national or professional origin, these individuals resemble families whose members alternately lacerate and nurture one another. They deny the viability of melodrama because they live in moral flux amid constantly shifting emotions.

Let us look at a few of these characters through the detail we are provided. Most detailed, and most obviously melodramatic, is the story of James Cameron (known as Jimmy Tomorrow), the journalist of the Kipling stripe who feels he has been defeated by his wife's betrayal of him. Based on a journalist who actually did commit suicide at Jimmy-the-Priest's while O'Neill was there in 1912, Jimmy Tomorrow is a hypersensitive, affectionate man whose loyalty to his friends is expressed in the most open terms. He recognizes that the seemingly cynical Larry is "the kindest man among us," and he is a regular peacemaker between Cecil Lewis and Piet Wetjoen, who are eternally at odds. But Jimmy is also weak, sentimental, and muddle-headed. When drunk, he is nothing short of a cry-baby. Jimmy tells the story of his having been destroyed, driven to drink, by the discovery that his wife has become the lover of a hated rival. Larry reminds Jimmy, however, that his wife probably betrayed him because he was already an alcoholic. This leads to an apparently irresolvable dilemma. Yes, Jimmy had long been an alcoholic; but yes, Jimmy did turn to alcohol in response to his wife's betrayal. Neither account can be denied. Jimmy was both betrayer and betrayed.

What we have in effect here is, again, not one melodrama, but two melodramas, each effectively cancelling out the other. In the first, Jimmy has been the protagonist and his betraying wife the antagonist. This is a melodrama of disaster, since the "evil" wife has been victor, and Jimmy has become a despairing derelict. But there is the opposing melodrama, the one in which the wife has been the victorious protagonist, presumably living "happily ever after," and Jimmy has been the antagonist now receiving his "just desert." There is no evidence as to which melodrama is the "true" melodrama. One is tempted to say the truth lies somewhere in between, but the fictive truth does not lie somewhere in between. If it did, that in-between-ness would have to be provided us through some third fiction of the past, which is not. We are provided only with the two stories, both of which have literary viability, both of which have a "moral," both of which must be accepted. Thus the past melodramas, being mutually exclusive, can serve in no cause-and-effect relationship to the present, Jimmy's decision that one of them does notwithstanding. Jimmy says he believes in the story in which he was the protagonist, but with Larry's help he sporadically admits that he really believes in the other story and in himself as antagonist. That is why he continues to drink and that is why he has his pipe dreams of rehabilitation. In fact, the melodrama in which he was antagonist is no more the truth than its opposite, if Jimmy could but accept this — that is, if Jimmy did not need to see life in melodramatic terms. Larry's "wrong kind of pity" is really right because in being compassionate, he is encouraging Jimmy the complex man to reveal himself in place of the craven, foolish antagonist. He is recognizing the sensitive, thoughtful Jimmy who really does exist.

Larry's compassion leads us to the present, the present in which we see Jimmy residing and functioning. That present involves no melodrama. That present, in the saloon, involves the many sides of Jimmy Tomorrow, not as protagonist or antagonist but as a single, complex human being living among others. His personality as we see it includes the sentimentally muddle-headed Jimmy and the compassionate peace-making Jimmy — and also a good many other Jimmy's: the arrogant Jimmy, the jovial Jimmy, the boisterous Jimmy, the patriotic Jimmy, the flaccid Jimmy. In what we see of him there are no melodramatic alternatives. There is only the man in the process of being his various selves in response to shifting stimuli. That is the man we recognize and remember.

Jimmy's story is the sole set of events out of a character's past described for us in full-blown melodramatic terms. About the other characters, we get only hints of old stories, not enough to make up detailed or even coherent plots, but enough to suggest that in each case there was an event that affected the individual so strongly that he attributes his present state to it. At the same time, ambiguities about these events quickly present themselves. There are bold contradictions implicit in their stories that suggest the kind of conflicting melodramas associated with Jimmy's past. We see opposing sides of their personalities that certainly fit their self-contradicting stories; but, then, we also see other qualities in their natures having little to do with their conflicting past melodramatic roles. That Joe Mott has at one time been an independent entrepreneur, the owner of a successful Black gambling house, suggests a self-secure independence of the restrictions placed upon Blacks in the early twentieth century by the White establishment. Here is the Black protagonist, the defender of the honor of his down-trodden people. Yet Joe tells us about his kow-towing to the party boss in order to obtain permission to operate the gambling house, and we quickly are aware of an opposing story (not detailed) and an opposing personality. He has not only been a sychophantic lackey of the very society he has been defying but also an emulator of its corruption. He might have been hypocritical in his role as Black protagonist, of course, or merely manipulative in his relations with the party boss; but we are provided no fictions of the past to justify such in-between interpretations. All we are told is of his conflicting roles, and we thus have no way of knowing who the *real* Joe was. Joe thinks he was the sycophant and so pipe dreams that he was the successful entrepreneur, but the facts we are provided support the contradiction.

In the present, on the other hand, we see many sides of Joe's nature. In his relationships with the two bartenders, with the battling Briton and Boer, even with his one trusted friend, Larry, he flatters, he debases himself, he fawns, he is cowardly. Yet at the same time, a genuine defiance is as daring as ever, especially when he breaks a whiskey glass he has been drinking from — to Rocky's consternation:

> I's on'y savin' you de trouble, White Boy. Now you don't have to break it, soon's my back is turned, so's no white man kick about drinkin' from de same glass. . . . I's tired of loafin' 'round wid a lot of bums. I's a gamblin' man. I's gonna get in a big crap game and win me a big bankroll. Den I'll get de okay to open up my old gamblin' house for colored men. Den maybe I comes back here sometime to see de bums. Maybe I throw a twenty-dollar bill on de bar and say, "Drink it up," and listen when dey all pat me on de back and say, "Joe, you sure is white." But I'll say, "No, I'm black and my dough is black man's dough, and you's proud to drink wid me or you don't get no drink!"[5]

Joe's speech calls attention to precisely those attitudes on the part of White society that have hurt most, and which his story of the past never did call attention to. Despite its allusions to the past, Joe's speech is very much part of the present in that it makes us genuinely empathize with his defiance. But his present personality is also that of the fawning hypocrite, as I have suggested. And it is also that of the ready helper, the curious observer, the courageous fighter, and the amiable accommodator. What constitutes the unique, recognizable, and familiar Joe Mott is more elements than can be listed. And there is no one conception of good and evil that can serve as a moral guide to Joe's behavior, or to the responses of others to him. Despite the apparent evil of the bartender's racism, for example, Rocky and Chuck suffer in their failures precisely as Joe suffers in his; and Joe has moments not only of defiance or pusillanimity but of genuine harmony with them, as with everyone else. He is a man who, quite apart from his pipe dreams, recoils when hurt, who strikes back, who is compassionate and nurturing when allowed to be.

Another figure with a strikingly contradictory past is the old she-beenkeeper himself, Harry Hope. That past is tied up with Harry's activities as a Tammany Hall politician and with his much-lamented late wife, Bessie. Harry says the party wanted to run him for office, and his cronies in the play attest to the fact that he once had a political following. And he certainly played the role of the steadfast husband. Then we learn that in fact Harry was a hack the organization was going to run for office in a year in which they expected to lose, and we learn that in fact Bessie was a "nag" who made Harry's life miserable. In this case, it is more tempting than ever to say that the truth lay somewhere in between. Harry could have been both a popular politician *and* the hack the organization took him for; and he could have been both strong and henpecked as a husband. Those contradictions could simply make for an early complexity in his character. But the

Harry of the past is not a character in this play. Harry sees himself in the past as playing contradictory roles in contradictory melodramas: one in which he was the popular politician and good family man unreasonably victimized by an indifferent organization, the other in which he was the corrupt hack who was henpecked to boot. We never directly encounter the Harry of the past; we are only told about him. And what we are told supports only two mutually exclusive interpretations — both of which are oversimplified versions of the man we see in the present.

In the character we do encounter, we are made acquainted with the contradictory aspects of his personality suggested by his contradictory melodramas, and we are made acquainted with much more. We meet a man who is genuinely compassionate, genuinely giving, genuinely unfeeling, and genuinely selfish. He cares for others even as he abuses them; he is taken advantage of even as he is loved. The contradictions here end in complexity, not oversimplification. When he looks back, Harry runs from one past melodramatic role to another which is more acceptable to him. But neither role really characterizes the volatile, irate Harry we know, who gives affection when people need it, whiskey when people need it, cheap morality when people need it, shelter when people need it. This Harry, who is actually free of the melodramatic images his view of the past creates, is the figure who is genuinely suited to the name O'Neill gives him, even with its ironic overtones. More than any character but Larry, Harry in his concern for others represents this play's kind of hope.

And so for the assumptions of the others about themselves. They each seem caught between conflicting melodramas in their lives. Hugo Kalmar championed the masses in a disastrous melodrama of revolution, but he fears he was really an aristocratic oppressor of the masses. Both melodramatic images have equal validity, and we are told nothing about his past to suggest the complex individual we see on stage. Willie Oban was a brilliant, witty law student who was at the same time a father-hating ne'er-do-well. Cecil Lewis dreams of returning to his position of honor in the British military establishment, while he recalls all too well the story of his having been discovered to be a petty crook and probable coward. And his inseparable companion and eternal adversary Piet Wetjoen dreams of being the brave Boer fighter he really was to obscure the story of his equally undeniable cowardice. Pat McGloin and Ed Mosher, whose shadowy pasts linked them respectively to the police department and the circus, are similarly caught between opposing melodramatic images. McGloin was a shrewd, successful grafter or gullible fall guy, depending on the melodramatic perspective from which he views himself. Ed was the barker who turned to drink because he lost his job, or lost his job because he turned to drink — the basic contradictory story of the play. At the same time, in all these figures, we see spontaneous qualities that exist quite apart from their fears and dreams. And it is the whole image for which we chiefly remember them.

In the case of the outsiders, those characters who have not taken refuge at the saloon but practice their "trade" in it, past and present are less separable. As with the derelicts, however, they seem caught between self-images associated with conflicting interpretations of their experiences. In this sense, they extend the play's vision to the outside world to those who have not taken permanent refuge in the "No Chance Saloon." As bartenders, Rocky and Chuck pride themselves that they are protagonists in a war against cheating and violent drunks, while they flee the equally accurate label of "pimp," a surefire antagonist's label in any melodrama. Cora, Pearl, and Margie must similarly see themselves as "tarts," protagonists in a world where lustful men and pimps are the antagonists, while they flee the label "whore," which turns them into antagonists in the melodrama of the wicked woman. As tarts the girls can be simply flirtatious, while as whores they are cheats, thieves, and debasers of men. As bartenders, Rocky and Chuck can be protective and brotherly toward the girls — Chuck can actually be Cora's suitor — while as pimps they are the worst of scavengers in regard to the girls. Yet what can we say actually characterizes these people? We see both aspects of their personalities, their good versus evil views of themselves; but more important, we also see in each a nature that is free of either label. They are whole human beings, not melodramatic simplifications. Rocky has a natural altruism quite apart from his bartender role-playing, while Cora and her friends display a motherly benevolence at times that exists quite independent of the business they engage in. These qualities are evident especially when these characters are involved with the figure they each trust most in the play, Larry Slade — and the greater openness and complexity when with him is evident in all the play's minor figures.

Which brings us back to Larry, and the first problem we must again address is why he shows these people what Hickey calls "the wrong kind of pity." Unlike Hickey, Larry recognizes that these people have totally accepted what they claim to have denied, their "failure." Thus he does not badger them, as Hickey does, about their refusal to admit that failure. While he reminds Jimmy of the contradictions in his story, he spares Jimmy the humiliation of actually living out the hopelessness of his pipe dream of rehabilitation. He spares Harry the agony of admitting he cannot take his walk around the ward. He spares Hugo the pain of having to explicitly acknowledge his aristocratic pretensions. Larry knows he need not elicit these all-out statements and gestures of despair because the men know all too well how true and inevitable they are, even if they do not represent the *whole* truth. And Larry knows that once made, such statements and gestures can only make the men feel truly "licked," which is the way they return to the bar following their attempts to confront "reality" in Act IV.

But neither does Larry believe his friends capable of rehabilitation in the usual sense. Although he knows their secret despair, he by no means accepts their pipe dreams, their visions of themselves in their lost protagonist's roles. In fact, Larry is dubious of all the opposing images with which these people are obsessed. He no more believes in Jimmy or Harry or Hugo as protagonists than he accepts their despair when they see themselves as antagonists. Larry has rejected all melodramatic divisions. He is "cursed," he says, with being able to see all sides to all questions. Hence, the past, with its conflicting melodramas, is for Larry meaningless as a guide to the present. The Jimmy that Larry accepts is neither the bankrupt nor the wronged husband but an individual made up of constantly changing moods and outlooks. Larry will not classify Jimmy into the opposing roles Jimmy classifies himself into on the basis of his past. Jimmy is simply a being who responds to Larry, who affects Larry, and who is served by Larry. And so with each member of the club, Larry has a unique, significant, and unconditional relationship. Larry's outlook earlier in the play, of course, is somewhat colored by the struggle with his own past, by counterpulls of his own melodramatically conceived roles in his relationship with Rosa Parritt. But Larry from the start is recognized by Jimmy explicitly and the others implicitly as "the kindest man among us," and by the time Larry is able to cast off the demons of his past, as he does in experiencing Parritt's suicide, Larry's acceptance of his associates has become as bedrock as the bar he inhabits.

Parritt's suicide and Hickey's great confession remain central problems, however (with or without their autobiographical implications for O'Neill); and since these events are so crucial to the play's development, before the final word is spoken about Larry, those events must be examined from the perspective of their relationship to melodrama. The first point to be observed is Hickey's immediate recognition that he and Parritt have something deeply in common. Both have lived out a melodrama that places them among the great antagonists of popular culture. They have sold out motherhood. Hickey has betrayed the virtuous wife-mother, and Parritt has betrayed his heroic mother and the social cause she is devoted to. Thus, any possibility of their being able to pipe dream for a past in which they are protagonists seems remote.

To look at Parritt first, Larry knows that a counter-image of the boy once did exist. There was a melodrama in which Parritt loved and revered his mother, but wanted to be loved and revered in return. Since, because of Rosa's Movement, her love and approval were withheld, Parritt became, in his view of himself, the protagonist son who took revenge on his evil mother. But the crime was too great for Parritt to take refuge in his pipe dream. (He makes a feeble attempt when he talks about his "patriotism," but he fails abysmally.) Unlike the derelicts, who punish themselves in little ways for their actions as antagonists in the past but whose crimes necessitate no large-scale punishment, Parritt cannot avoid large-scale punishment. He literally cannot live with himself.

Parritt's dissimilarity to the others goes beyond the seriousness of his crime, however. O'Neill has also made him faceless. The residents of the saloon find him repellent chiefly because he reveals nothing with which they can empathize. Even his suffering is antisocial. He keeps living only in the single, desperate melodrama in which he is the antagonist who committed the greatest of crimes. It is as though Parritt has no existence in the present and thus can draw no understanding or compassion. We see in him none of the spontaneous, ever-changing quality that makes for the complexity and humanity of the living others. Only Larry and the audience are fully exposed to him; and all we and Larry hear is the repetition of haunting fears, arrogant denial, and feverish appeal for sympathy. It is the mood associated with haunting fear that sets the Parritt episodes apart from the rest of the play — a fear that is part of Larry's persona as well, since he is struggling to understand his reactions to the same woman and to a parallel pair of past melodramas. It is the fear that ends for the audience and Larry alike only with Parritt's terrible plunge — that plunge which as it ends Parritt's existence ends also both melodramatic effect and the recall of melodramas in the play. Following that plunge, the present, with all its complexity, is allowed finally to dominate.[6]

Like Parritt, the Hickey we see in the play is living in a single melodrama; but he cannot allow himself to see himself as antagonist, but must rather see himself in a twisted way as protagonist. Throughout his past, he has been the stock antagonist in an old-fashioned melodrama — the wastrel husband of the long-suffering wife. His pipe dream in this role, of course, was that he would reform; but that dream, like those of the derelicts, proved impossible to fulfill. Like them, he really did accept his role as antagonist, although he would not acknowledge it. His false promises to reform, as he tells us, built up such guilt in him that he came to hate himself, the hatred finally becoming so unbearable that he could no longer live with himself. Suddenly, however, he says, he came to acknowledge his role as antagonist. He came, he says, to accept the fact that he would not reform and simply performed an act, murdering his wife, which would spare her further suffering. In doing so, Hickey had actually come to see himself as protagonist in a new melodrama, a melodrama of self-acceptance, in which the wife became the new antagonist in her patience and hope. And it is in this new role as protagonist of self-acceptance that Hickey came to reform his friends in the saloon. That this new view was in fact just an opposing melodrama is what he seems to become aware of in the last moment of his long confession:

> . . . I remember I heard myself speaking to her, as if it were something I'd always wanted to say: "Well, you know what you can do with your pipe dream now, you damned bitch! (He stops with a horrified start, as if shocked out of a nightmare, as if he couldn't believe what he had just said. He stammers) No! I never — !
>
> . . . .
> No! That's a lie! I never said — ! Good God, I couldn't have said that! If I did, I'd gone insane! Why, I loved Evelyn better than anything in life.[7]

In killing Evelyn, Hickey did not come to accept himself, as he claims. He has indulged in a new pipe dream, this one being that his wife "deserved" to die. The minute Hickey realizes this, at the end of his speech, he realizes at once the counter-truth of the old melodrama. Of course he loved Evelyn. Of course he was insane, if insanity means total failure to perceive reality. He was criminally insane. The failure to perceive the reality that he both loved and hated his wife resulted in the ultimate crime of violence. And like Parritt, he now sees clearly the true need for his punishment. In coming to understand the nature of his insanity, Hickey is ready to assume genuine responsibility for his action. His new melodrama disappears into true self-acceptance.

The difference is that Hickey is hardly the faceless Parritt. Like the derelicts, he has a quite distinct existence apart from his conflicting melodramatic roles. He lives in a vivid present as well as a haunting past, as Parritt cannot. Aside from his efforts to reform the others, which are a function of his new melodrama of self-acceptance, Hickey has a direct, personal relationship with each of them, as Larry does. He gives to others, and is given to by them. Hickey is basically a "lord of misrule," a bringer and receiver of pleasure, "not only witty in himself but the cause of wit in others."[8] Beyond his melodramatic confusions, Hickey is an infinitely complex man, a figure of great strength and gargantuan flaws. And his sudden coming to self-awareness at the end of his speech is of tragic magnitude. Through the true confrontation with his contradictory selves which closes his great confession, he achieves understanding beyond that of others, and he accepts death. He becomes, in short, a tragic hero.

If, then, in the classical sense, O'Neill intends Hickey to be the tragic hero of the play, the strong man who lives out his ultimate agony in public, where does that leave the play's other hero, the introspective Larry Slade, who lives out his personal agony in private? Part chorus and part raisonneur, Larry is the strongest man of all, the one who can live on without pipe dreams, the one survivor capable of seeing life in other than melodramatic terms. Through Parritt, he comes to realize the contradictions of his own melodramatic past — the utter indeterminateness of Rosa Parritt and her "Movement," and the absence of anything to be learned from his loving/hating relationship with her other than that it once existed. The condition in which we find Larry at the play's conclusion embodies the significance O'Neill intends for the entire work. The derelicts are happily returning to their rotgut and their melodramatic pipe dreams; Parritt and Hickey have met their "just deserts." Larry, having transcended his personal melodramas, reaches his point of stasis, that absolute middle which many heroes of later twentieth century drama attain. Amidst the cacophony and dissonance of the newly *un*reformed derelicts, "Larry stares in front of him, oblivious to their racket."

We must review just what O'Neill has Larry do and say in the few moments between Parritt's suicide and this final, enigmatic scenic image. Larry's posture, it cannot be stressed enough, implies no emulation of Parritt. There is no suggestion whatsoever that he will follow Parritt up that fire escape.[9] His immediate reaction following Parritt's leap is actually more re-

vealing of his mental state than the final image referred to above. Though
often alluded to in part, that immediate reaction is by no means a single
simple response:

> Poor devil! (*A long-forgotten faith returns to him for a moment and he
> mumbles*) God rest his soul in peace. (*He opens his eyes* — with a bitter self-
> derision) Ah, the damned pity — the wrong kind, as Hickey said! Be God,
> there's no hope! I'll never be a success in the grandstand — or anywhere
> else! Life is too much for me! I'll be a weak fool looking with pity at the
> two sides of everything till the day I die! (*With an intense bitter sincerity*)
> May that day come soon! . . . Be God, I'm the only real convert to death
> Hickey made here. From the bottom of my coward's heart I mean that
> now.[10]

What is usually referred to in this speech is Larry's "real" conversion to
death,[11] but that is only one of the moods out of which he speaks. His first
response is one of compassion, a compassion rooted in a "long-forgotten
faith." Larry's attitudes at this point recall those of the late Con Melody
referred to by his daughter Sara in the recorded version of O'Neill's *More
Stately Mansions* (written shortly before *Iceman*). Sara speaks admiringly
of Con for his "defiance of a God he denied but really believed in."[12] The
contradictions implicit in this observation, obliterating as they do any kind
of melodramatic view of existence, parallel the contradictions of Larry
Slade in this speech. Obviously and not surprisingly overwrought at what
has just happened, Larry speaks of his compassion, then of his wrong kind
of pity, then of his inability to hold a fixed view of things, then of his "real"
conversion. There is no reason to believe that he will stop seeing all sides to
all questions, that he will cease showing compassion, that he will cease believing intermittently in a long-forgotten faith, or cease defying a God he
has long since denied. A new attitude toward death in the speech is present,
but it is the attitude that finds death the one certainty amidst so much uncertainty. The speech is not a suicidal statement, any more than is his oft-
quoted Sophoclean/Nietzschean sentiment that "best of all were never to
have been born." Larry awaits the certainty of death, but his final stage
image contains nothing of the haunted quality which accompanies Parritt's
genuinely suicidal statements in the play. Larry now awaits death with a
determination about life that is made all the stronger by his triumph over
illusion of any kind.[13] Thus do we understand the play as a commitment to
the complexity of the present.

In the meantime — and that is a large meantime since it includes the
ongoing lives of Larry and all his friends — Larry goes on. And there is no
way of imagining Larry existing in any fashion other than that we have already seen. He will continue to be a nurturer of others. Perhaps Larry will
parallel in his fashion the enigmatic doctor in the parable with which Ed
Mosher closes the first act of the play. This great physician, says Ed, spent a
lifetime providing useless medicine and giving meaningless counsel — except
that there was a medicine to his person that saved, and the meaninglessness

of his counsel was the only thing which had "meaning." He was, says Ed, a lazy good-for-nothing who died of overwork at the age of eighty:

> The saddest part was that he knew he was doomed. The last time we got paralyzed together he told me: "This game will get me yet, Ed. You see before you a broken man, a martyr to medical science. If I had any nerves I'd have a nervous breakdown. You won't believe me, but last year there was actually one night I had so many patients, I didn't even have time to get drunk. The shock to my system brought on a stroke which, as a doctor, I recognized was the beginning of the end." Poor old Doc! When he said this he started crying. "I hate to go before my task is completed Ed," he sobbed. "I'd hoped I'd live to see the day when, thanks to my miraculous cure, there wouldn't be a single vacant cemetery lot left in this glorious country." . . . I miss Doc. He was a gentleman of the old school.[14]

The point of the anecdote, so evocative of the American vaudeville image of the drunken doctor, is its discontinuity — what some would call its absurdity. Ed's doctor is impossible to assess rationally. There are too many gaps and implicit contradictions in his story. There is no logical way to understand his past. What precisely do we do with a doctor who preached the avoidance of work and who at the age of seventy-nine was so busy he did not have time to get drunk? Too many implied contradictions are present here for us to do much more than smile, which is of course what we are intended to do. His medical career was a haphazard sequence of indeterminate actions leading his patients to recovery or death, or both, and himself to endless inebriation, endless laughter, and a youthful death — at the age of eighty. There was obviously no melodramatic perspective in any phase of Doc's existence. He is the one figure referred to in the play of whom it might be said that his remembered past was characterized by the same chaos as his present — and that he embraced that chaos.

Hickey, of course, the Hickey of better days, is the character who most resembles Doc in personality; but Hickey is gone forever, and the only creature left with Doc's perspective must now be the introspective Larry.[15] Larry now really believes that the past cannot be a guide to the present, that there can in fact be no past but only conflicting interpretations of it. And we have been brought to see what Larry sees, that, in the words of a recent well-known literary theorist, the past can only be "experienced as a picture with gaps or as two pictures side by side which cannot be reconciled."[16] The two pictures for us have been the contradictory melodramas, and we have learned that the only reality is a present which in its complexity denies all melodramatic perspective. We too are cursed in having to look at all sides of all questions and all people.

Larry will continue to live suspended between his poles of faith and denial — like a good many mature thinkers before him — and he will fill his days ministering to others. He will live in the unmelodramatizable mercury of the present. He, like the play he speaks for, in transcending the melodramatic view of existence, leaves us with an image of existence in flux.

Notes

1. *Tragedy and Melodrama* (Seattle: University of Washington Press, 1968); and *The Iceman, the Arsonist, and the Troubled Agent: Tragedy and Melodrama on the Modern Stage* (Seattle: University of Washington Press, 1973).

2. See my article "O'Neill's Transcendence of Melodrama in *A Touch of the Poet* and *A Moon for the Misbegotten*," *Comparative Drama*, 16 (Fall 1982), 238–50.

3. See my book *Eugene O'Neill's New Language of Kinship* (Syracuse, N.Y.: Syracuse University Press, 1982). I discuss the play as a whole on pp. 113–56, concentrating specifically on the Larry-Parritt action on pp. 138–41.

4. Heilman, countering this view, sees *The Iceman Cometh* as a "drama of disaster," a melodrama in which evil triumphs rather than good, the evil in the play coming in the form of Hickey's perfidy and the weakness of the derelicts, and the good in the form of a never-achieved self knowledge. See *Tragedy and Melodrama*, pp. 49–55. I disagree with Heilman's conclusions about the play, both as to characterization and theme.

5. Eugene O'Neill, *The Iceman Cometh* (New York: Random House, 1946), p. 170.

6. This shift at this point suggests that Parritt is not a living character like the others, but what Jamie in *Long Day's Journey* calls "the dead part of myself."

7. *The Iceman Cometh*, pp. 241–42.

8. The phrase, of course, paraphrases Falstaff's description of himself in Shakespeare's *Henry IV, Part 2*: 1. 2. 11–12.

9. Mary McCarthy led the way in seeing Larry's outlook as suicidal at the play's conclusion in her review of the original production, "Dry Ice," *Partisan Review* (November-December 1946) 577–79.

10. *The Iceman Cometh*, p. 258.

11. Most critics recognize Larry's "conversion to death" as the only point of the passage. See, for example, Winifred Dusenbury Frazer, *Love as Death in 'The Iceman Cometh'* (Gainesville: University of Florida Press, 1967), especially pp. 31–32; Doris V. Falk, *Eugene O'Neill and the Tragic Tension* (New Brunswick, N.J.: Rutgers University Press, 1958), pp. 161–62; Leonard Chabrowe, *Ritual and Pathos — the Theatre of Eugene O'Neill* (Lewisburg, Pa.: Bucknell University Press, 1976), pp. 85–86; and Cyrus Day, "The Iceman and the Bridegroom," *Modern Drama* 1 (May 1958), 5. But several critics also recognize the sense of release, of a deep trouble having past, implicit in Larry's speech. See, in particular, Edwin Engel, *The Haunted Heroes of Eugene O'Neill* (Cambridge, Mass.: Harvard University Press, 1952), p. 285; and Normand Berlin, *Eugene O'Neill* (New York: Grove Press, 1982), p. 138.

12. From the recording of *More Stately Mansions*, ed. and abridged, as produced on Broadway, by Elliot Martin (New York: Caedmon Records, TRS 331).

13. Of Larry's final posture in the play, Normand Berlin says that he "seems to be staring directly at man's *existence*." (*Eugene O'Neill*, p. 142)

14. *The Iceman Cometh*, pp. 89–90.

15. In real life, of course, this idea suggests the image of the introspective Eugene having to become the embodiment of the long-dead extraverted Jamie.

16. J. Hillis Miller, "Ethics of Reading," in *American Criticism in the Poststructuralist Age* (Ann Arbor: University of Michigan, 1981), pp. 19–41. The quotation is taken from p. 31.

Empty Bottles, Empty Dreams: O'Neill's Use of Drinking and Alcoholism in *Long Day's Journey Into Night*

Steven F. Bloom

One of the most pervasive critical comments about much of Eugene O'Neill's drama is that it is repetitious. Some critics recognize that this repetitiousness is essential to the dramatist's vision, especially in the late plays, yet few seem to appreciate the vital connection between the repetitiousness, the vision, and alcoholism. The life of an alcoholic, after all, is very much defined by repetitious behavioral patterns, and it is in these patterns—in the symptoms and effects of alcoholism—that O'Neill finally discovered a realistic context in which to dramatize his vision of life.

In *Long Day's Journey Into Night*, the realities of alcoholism are vividly depicted in the behavioral patterns of the Tyrone family, collectively and individually, and especially in the dissipation of Jamie Tyrone and the disintegration of Mary Tyrone. Edmund is the romantic idealist, whose visions of transcendence are pointedly couched in terms of romantic notions of blissful intoxication. In the contrast between this romantic myth of intoxication and the realistic symptoms and effects of alcoholism, O'Neill captures the despairing paradox of the human condition, as he sees it.

Three of the four major characters in *Long Day's Journey* become intoxicated by Act IV; the fourth character is under the influence of morphine throughout most of the play. The only other character, Cathleen the servant, is actually drunk most of the brief time she is on stage. Everyone in the play, then, ingests some kind of intoxicant, and the four major characters are, to varying degrees, addicted. This pervasive dependence on chemical substances inevitably affects the behavior of the characters and their interactions in various ways, some subtle and some blatant.

It is important that the symptoms of alcoholism are commonly identified with the symptoms of addiction to chemical substances in general,[1] and that the term "chemical dependency" is used interchangeably with "alcoholism" and "addiction." Furthermore, many of the symptoms of "opioid intoxication" (and morphine is an opioid) are often easily confused with those of alcoholic intoxication.[2] So although Mary Tyrone is addicted to morphine rather than to alcohol, she can still be considered the central addictive figure within the family, and the behavior of this family can be viewed as typical of families of chemically-dependent individuals.

The Diagnostic and Statistical Manual of Mental Disorders (DSM-III) describes the behavioral disorders caused by opioid dependence as being "marked by remissions while in treatment or prison or when the substance is scarce and [by] relapses on returning to a familiar environment where these substances are available and friends or colleagues use these substances."[3] Mary Tyrone is at just such a juncture when this play begins; we eventually discover that she has recently returned from a sanatorium, and that her addictive behavior has been in remission. Her home environment, however, is clearly established as one that is highly conducive to relapse. The Tyrone men may have a different "substance of choice," but their dependence on alcohol obviously reinforces Mary's inclination to return to morphine. In addition, the apparent isolation of the Tyrones from external influences of any kind increases the chances of relapse for Mary.

Within this environment, however, the family has successfully created a façade of calm and pleasant normality. It is in the elaborate system of denial with which they have fostered this smooth surface that the Tyrones initially appear to fit the mold of the "alcoholic family." In an article called "The Progression of Alcoholism and the Family," Don and Nancy Howard point out that in the constant attempt to deny that there is a problem in the family, the alcoholic and his or her relatives will "establish themselves in routines and patterns of communication that appear to work on the surface."[4]

So effective are the patterns and routines established by the Tyrone family that when one first views or reads the play, the true nature of the situation can go unnoticed for a while. Nobody drinks during the first act; there are only are only a few references to drinking and drunkenness, and these seem rather innocuous; and certainly, all references to morphine are oblique and evasive. Thus *Long Day's Journey* begins as a pleasant, peaceful domestic drama might begin, quite obviously similar, in fact, to O'Neill's own domestic comedy *Ah, Wilderness!* As Henry Hewes remarked in his review of the original New York production of *Long Day's Journey*, "one might assume that this was going to be a comedy about two 'regular fellers' and their happily-married mom and dad."[5] It is morning; the family has had breakfast; Tyrone and Mary enter together smiling and teasing each other quite lovingly, with the two sons heard laughing in the dining room. Little is missing, it seems, from the scene of domestic tranquility. As the act progresses, however, we notice hints that all is not well beneath the surface, and that the three men are desperately trying to sustain the calm façade.

The earliest indications of tensions are not directly, explicitly, connected to alcoholism. There is apparently a generational conflict between the father and his two sons, but at first this hardly seems remarkable; there is also obvious concern for Edmund's health and Mary's "nervousness," but the latter is not necessarily drug-related. There is cetainly a pattern of defensiveness within the family, as hardly a comment goes by without provoking a defensive reaction from someone. Even Edmund's story about Shaughnessy and the pigs — the kind of story O'Neill often uses in his plays to promote an atmosphere of camaraderie — here leads to an argument with the father pitted against his two sons. For the most part, however, the men make concerted efforts to contain their arguments and to sustain a jocular and amiable atmosphere. That it *is* an effort to do so becomes clear as soon as Mary exits; then, the façade falls and the mood changes drastically.

The anger and defensiveness beneath the surface are now released in a confrontation between father and son that consists of bitter accusations and counteraccusations. The contrast between this scene and the previous one when Mary was present illustrates a pattern within the alcoholic family that the Howards describe as typical:

> If the problem drinker appears to be in a pleasant mood and is sober, no one would dare mention anything unpleasant or any drinking behavior, fearing that such a communication would rock the boat and the pleasant mood would be drowned in the resulting anger and defensive response.[6]

Thus, the anger and defensiveness that are suppressed in Mary's presence later emerge, displaced into other issues and other relationships. So, rather than discussing their feelings about Mary's addiction and the family's problems in any sustained and meaningful way, the two men argue about other matters. Jamie blames his father for Edmund's illness because, he says, Tyrone has hired the doctor who charges the least to treat him; and Tyrone responds to this by admonishing his son for wasting his life and for being ungrateful. Once again, the observations of the Howards are germane:

> Each person keeps the cycle revolving with denial, fear, guilt, blame, confusion and belief in myths. In this kind of family, communication is vague, unclear, and indirect; roles are upset and inconsistent and rules are unspoken and broken; self-worth is negative and low; and the total atmosphere is distrustful and closed.[7]

This description seems made to order for the interactions we observe among the Tyrones throughout Act I.

An important example of the lack of communication in the Tyrone family occurs in this scene between Jamie and Tyrone. Tyrone accuses his son of ingratitude in the following terms: "The only thanks is to have you sneer at me for a dirty miser, sneer at my profession, sneer at every damn thing in the world except yourself." Significantly, Jamie denies this: "That's not true, Papa. You can't hear me talking to myself, that's all" (*LDJ*, p. 32).[8] Jamie's wry confession of his self-hatred is a clear indication of what lies beneath the sneering persona he presents to the world; it is a glimpse of the self-loathing that he will confess painfully in Act IV. Most significantly here, however, it is a comment that goes virtually unnoticed by his father, who merely "*stares at him, puzzledly, then quotes mechanically*": " 'Ingratitude, the vilest weed that grows'!" Tyrone does not hear the self-hatred in his son's words; he hears only what he customarily expects to hear — ingratitude. In addition, Jamie's response to his father's quotation further confirms the impression that their argument conforms to a pattern, even down to the details of the literary allusions: "I could see that line coming! God, how many thousand times—! *He stops, bored with their quarrel, and shrugs his shoulders*. All right, Papa. I'm a bum. Anything you like, so long as it stops the argument" (*LDJ*, p. 33). The pattern is predictable and they barely feel the need to listen to each other anymore.

Within this pattern of hostile defensiveness, however, there are moments of genuine, mutual concern and compassion. O'Neill describes one of these moments of "understanding sympathy": "It is as if suddenly a deep bond of common feeling existed between them [James and Jamie] in which their antagonisms could be forgotten" (*LDJ*, p. 36). Although it is only momentary, this shared sympathy does exist, and it should remain a constant factor beneath all of the arguments and accusations. These peaceful moments of mutual compassion, and the suggestion that these feelings always exist, should establish the bonds that tie these people together. Although they are unable to live with each other in tranquility, they are even less capable of living without each other. This familial loyalty is certainly not an uncommon feature in alcoholic families: although they cause each other tremendous suffering, the family members remain loyal at each other. The problem is not whether or not they care about each other, but rather, the difficulty they have expressing the caring feelings and acting on them in a helpful way.

So it is also typical that these moments of compassion inevitably give way to continuation of hostilities, as we observe here in the case of the Tyrones. After the resumption of hostilities between father and son, we are reminded of the extent to which their behavior revolves around the central addictive personality—the wife-mother. When she enters the room, the men's hostility changes to feigned heartiness and cheer. The goal again becomes to avoid upsetting Mary, as the family "joins together in an effort to hide the problem," according to the Howards:

> The cover-ups and outbursts of anger produce guilt and the family begins to choose its responses in reply to the problem drinker's actions, a continuation of the initial patterns to maintain functioning and perhaps a moment of peace. In other words, family members, the spouse and children, wait to see and assess how the problem drinker will act or speak and respond in likewise manner in order to maintain harmony. The problem drinker becomes a mood setter and controller in the center of the cycle of reinforcement. The family members step to the music in an effort to keep things from getting worse. . . . The pattern emerges then as a series of hills and valleys. The hills represent the crisis situations and the valleys the smoothing over and burial of problems. If no changes in behavior or communication occur, the valleys become a period of pretending, of "walking on egg shells."[9]

Both images in this unfortunately mixed metaphor apply to *Long Day's Journey*. As James and Jamie increasingly suspect Mary's relapse, they try to cover up any indications of hostility between them that might upset her. It quickly becomes evident, however, that the attempt to sustain the calm atmosphere, given the feelings of guilt and blame, is a formidable task. Certainly, the movement of much of the first three acts of *Long Day's Journey* follows this path over these hills and into the valleys, and they are the same hills and valleys traversed again and again. In terms of the accompanying image, the "egg shells" in the Tyrone family are pervasive; they surround each character. Indeed, Act I could appropriately be subtitled, "Walking on Egg Shells."

An important factor in the cycle, of course, is the behavior of the addict—in this case, Mary. Throughout the first act, her behavior is rather mysterious; she is clearly troubled, yet her sons and husband do not acknowledge this impression in any explicit way. They attempt only to ignore it, or to put a positive light on what they, and we, see:

> JAMIE *With an awkward, uneasy tenderness.* We're all so proud of you, Mama, so darned happy. *She stiffens and stares at him with a frightened defiance. He flounders on.* But you've still got to be careful. You mustn't worry so much about Edmund. He'll be all right.
> MARY *With a stubborn, bitterly resentful look.* Of course, he'll be all right. And I don't know what you mean.
> JAMIE *Rebuffed and hurt, shrugs his shoulders.* All right, Mama. I'm sorry I spoke.
>
> (*LDJ*, pp. 41–42)

The denial system is illustrated here quite clearly, both on the level of Jamie's denial of their fears about what seems to be happening to her, and on the level of Mary's denial. Even when presented with the indirect concern for her in terms of Edmund's condition, she is stubbornly resistant to acknowledging any problem at all. Her bitter resentment confirms the sense of necessity that the men feel to avoid even the most oblique reference to her condition. And Jamie's attempt to express concern actually suggests his own desire to believe that his mother is not experiencing a relapse. Her denial that there is anything for her to "be careful" about obviously implies that indeed there is: the denial is symptomatic of the disease.

In the following scene between Mary and Edmund, we move closer towards perceiving the truth about the situation. Naturally, mother and son attempt to sustain the façade of pleasant amiability, which inevitably evolves into the usual cycle of accusation, guilty defensiveness, and counteraccusation. As Mary becomes increasingly desperate, she finally attempts to blame the cycle itself:

> MARY Oh, I can't bear it, Edmund, when even you—! *Her hands flutter up to pat her hair in their aimless distracted way. Suddenly a strange undercurrent of revengefulness comes into her voice.* It would serve all of you right if it was true!
>
> (*LDJ*, p. 47)

These words suggest that Mary is looking for the justification she feels she needs to resume her drug addiction. This is, of course, typical of the rationalization process observed in alcoholics. At this point, Mary manages to turn the men's suspicious concern for her around and make it a reason for her relapse. Her revengefulness now becomes part of the pattern; she now has a way to blame *them* for the current situation.

The physical symptoms that Mary has exhibited throughout the first act are of unspecified origins; it is clear that she suffers from some kind of disorder that has been under control for about two months, but it is not explicitly defined as morphine addiction and withdrawal until later in the play. Our first opportunity to observe Mary when she is alone reveals an obvious sense of fright and desperation, which compounds the nervousness that is apparent in her scenes with the others. The cause of this behavior is not yet explicitly revealed. In retrospect, however, it is evident that O'Neill has carefully incorporated effects of "opioid withdrawal" that are, in fact, identifiable from the outset. According to the *DSM-III*, "common associated features include restlessness, irritability, depression, tremor, weakness, nausea, vomiting, and muscle and joint pains."[10] Except for the nausea and vomiting, all of these features are indicated to some extent during Act I, and as the effects of opioid intoxication take over, these withdrawal symptoms will recur at those times when the drug's effects wear off. Although Act I ends without a drink consumed and barely a mention of the subject, it seems clear that chemical dependency is a controlling factor within this discordant familial environment.

During the next two acts, the signs of Mary's relapse become more definitive, and our interest turns to the reactions of the three men. Within the system of the addictive family, as we have seen, denial is a prominent behavioral characteristic; we have seen that it is operative for the Tyrone men. All three continually deny responsibility for their own lives, and since Mary's condition is a concrete reminder of their failures and disappointments, each has a vested interest in denying the fact of her relapse. O'Neill endows each of them with a different capacity for denial, and these differences are consistent with each character's philosophical stance: Edmund is the romantic idealist; Jamie is the cynical realist; and Tyrone is the resigned pragmatist.

Accordingly, Jamie gives up hope for his mother much sooner than Edmund does. Edmund's investment in trusting his mother is not only indicative of his desire that she not return to her addiction; it is also consistent with his romantic philosophy. Thus, as Mary's symptoms become increasingly apparent, Edmund's denial becomes more desperate. When she enters for the first time in Act II, for instance, her demeanor is noticeably changing, however slightly; "She appears to be less nervous, to be more as she was when we first saw her after breakfast, but then one becomes aware that her eyes are brighter, and there is a peculiar detachment in her voice and manner, as if she were a little withdrawn from her words and actions" (*LDJ*, p. 58).

The diagnostic criteria for "opioid intoxication" are described in the *DSM-III* as follows:

> Psychological signs commonly present include euphoria and dysphoria, apathy, and psychomotor retardation. Pupillary constriction is always

present. . . . Other neurological signs commonly observed are drowsiness, slurred speech, and impairment in attention and memory. The maladaptive behavioral effects may include impaired judgment, interference with social or occupational functioning, and failure to meet responsibilities.[11]

These symptoms will become increasingly observable in Mary as the play progresses; the impaired judgment and interference with social functioning will be particularly important indicators of the extent of her intoxication. At this point in Act II, however, the detachment and "bright eyes" are noticeable changes to which the two sons have significantly different responses:

> She kisses [Edmund]. He stops coughing and gives her a quick apprehensive glance, but if his suspicions are aroused, her tenderness makes him renounce them and he believes what he wants to believe for the moment. On the other hand, Jamie knows after one probing look at her that his suspicions are justified, his face sets in an expression of embittered, defensive cynicism.
>
> (*LDJ*, p. 58)

In the following scene with their mother, then, Edmund attempts to sustain "normal" interaction with his mother, accepting her comments about feeling "rested" with no visible signs of suspicion. Jamie's responses, however, carry clear double messages, implicitly rejecting her façade of normalcy, as well as Edmund's. As if she suspects and feels Jamie's recrimination, she attacks him — but indirectly — for his lack of respectfulness towards his father, which leads him to blame her, while Edmund lashes out at both of them. And thus, the pattern is perpetuated.

Mary's only escape from the cyclical recrimination is a fatalistic contemplation of life:

> It's wrong to blame your brother. He can't help being what the past has made him any more than your father can. Or you. Or I.
>
> (*LDJ*, p. 64)

Mary's attitude denies the possibility for change — it is one of hopelessness; at the center of her cycle of blame and guilt is a sad, impotent feeling that no one is to blame, and nothing can be done. Jamie's cynical pessimism derives from his mother's fatalistic attitude, whereas for Edmund, his mother's view is a challenge to his optimistic illusions.

When Tyrone is confronted with the undeniable evidence of his wife's relapse, his countenance noticeably changes and he appears to be a "tired, bitterly sad old man." In his anger and disappointment, he turns to alcohol; the intense stress of confronting the truth is apparent as he pours his second drink and Mary comments that he never has "more than one before lunch":

> MARY . . . . I know what to expect. You will be drunk tonight. Well, it won't be the first time, will it — or the thousandth?
>
> (*LDJ*, p. 69)

The circular nature of their predicament is reiterated here: Tyrone uses Mary's relapse as an excuse to drink, while she uses his drinking as an excuse for her relapse. The rationalization process is typical, as are the pleas for help and defensive denials that operate in the scene between husband and wife as they seek and find more justification for their addictive behavior.

By the beginning of Act II, Scene ii, Mary has clearly resumed taking the morphine and the others know it. When they enter, therefore, although the situation is parallel to the opening scene of the play, the contrast is striking. Now, they are merely going through the motions of domestic normalcy. Tyrone enters behind his wife, not with her, and he "avoids touching her or looking at her." The sons are no longer joking and laughing, but rather, "Jamie's face is hard with defensive cynicism," and Edmund is "heartsick as well as physically ill." Mary is discussing domestic matters, but this time nobody listens to her, and she herself seems "indifferent." While Mary continues to deny her relapse, the others find it increasingly difficult to do so; thus, they fluctuate between bitter denial and resigned acceptance, with Edmund the most resistant. All attempts to sustain the semblance of domestic tranquility of Act I have been dropped.

As Mary becomes increasingly intoxicated, she retreats further into the past, where she finds familiar disappointments to weave into the pattern of guilt and blame. For instance, she blames James for not providing a home for her, suggesting that this deprivation has been a cause of her addiction; in response, James blames her addiction for rendering it impossible to maintain a "real home." Neither of them accepts the other's accusations, on the surface, yet their defensiveness implies at least a subconscious sense of responsibility. Mary claims, though, that she is not bitter, that it is not James' fault; however, she does not accept the responsibility herself. Instead, the implication is that nobody is responsible, which means, of course, that there is nothing anyone can do about the situation. The addictive personality typically relinquishes responsibility for his or her behavior, which fosters the addiction. As we see again and again, this attitude defines life for Mary Tyrone.

Meanwhile, the beliefs of the father and sons are increasingly tested by Mary's retreat to addiction. Jamie is increasingly cynical, at this point accepting his mother's relapse as total: "They never come back." On the other hand, Edmund remains desperately optimistic: "It can't have got a hold on her yet. She can still stop." It is typical of Tyrone's misunderstanding of his sons that he rejects both of their philosophies as being equally "rotten to the core," when, in fact, they are different.

Edmund continues to speak of communicating with Mary, while his father and brother are prepared to accept the next stage of her progression:

JAMIE *Shrugs his shoulders.* You can't talk to her now. She'll listen but she won't listen. She'll be here but she won't be here. You know the way she gets.

TYRONE Yes, that's the way the poison acts on her always. Every day from now on, there'll be the same drifting away from us until by the end of each night —

(*LDJ*, p. 78)

Edmund cannot tolerate this challenge to his beliefs, so he characteristically avoids any additional disturbing conversation by leaving the room. This allows the other two — Jamie and James — to confront each other and the situation, about which they seem to agree. In spite of their awareness of the facts, however, their confrontation again becomes an occasion for the expression of disappointment and anger that is displaced onto each other rather than directed towards Mary, or towards themselves. Each feels guilty about Mary's relapse, and each also blames the other. The feelings are played out, however, in terms of Edmund's illness and what will be done for him now that the doctor has diagnosed consumption. Jamie accuses his father of putting monetary considerations before Edmund's best interests, and Tyrone retaliates by insinuating once again that it is Jamie's influence on Edmund that has made him vulnerable to the disease. This argument allows them to avoid the issue of Mary's addiction, and eventually it redirects their attention to Jamie's drinking, a related issue, but one that is regarded as a less serious one by this family.

There is, of course, sufficient evidence in the play that the Tyrone men are alcoholics. The description of Jamie when he first appears mentions "signs of premature disintegration," and "marks of dissipation," key words in O'Neill's descriptions of alcoholic characters in his other plays. Jamie, then, seems to be the most visibly affected by his addiction, on a physical level. There have been other signs, though, of dependency in all three of them. The drinks before lunch, the sneaking of drinks behind Tyrone's back, Cathleen's comments about their drinking habits, all clearly indicate alcoholic dependence. Furthermore, Tyrone's constant refrain that he has "never missed a performance" sounds very much like the typical attempt by the alcoholic to convince others that he has no drinking problem. Whether or not he has ever missed a performance is irrelevant. There is sufficient evidence that he drinks heavily, and behaves irresponsibly because of it, as Mary's story of their honeymoon suggests. The fact, however, that he feels the need to "prove" that he does not have a problem is his indictment. And when he says that "no man has ever had a better reason [to get drunk]," this is the symptomatic rationalization system of the addictive personality.

It is interesting, then, that the first actual drunkenness that we observe on stage does not involve the Tyrone men. Rather, it is Cathleen who becomes increasingly "tipsy" as she sits listening to Mary's rambling. This is significant for several reasons. First, O'Neill often uses drinking in his late plays to foster an atmosphere realistically conducive to monologues in which characters reveal their inner thoughts and feelings. In this scene, for instance, while Cathleen complains about Smythe the chauffeur, Mary contemplates her love for the fog and her hatred of the foghorn and reminisces about her life, without the difficulties presented by her family when she rambles in this fashion. Cathleen does not respond to Mary in any meaning-ful way, and that is just what Mary wants — company (because she does not want to be alone), not companionship (because she *is* alone). We observe Mary talking to herself in the course of the play, which we accept as part of her intoxicated behavior. That she would speak of such personal matters to Cathleen, however, reiterates the seriousness of her condition in that it suggests "impaired judgment." Coupled with her rather unkempt appearance, which suggests "impaired functioning," her behavior in this scene with Cathleen in Act III becomes a vivid depiction of the effects of morphine.

Cathleen is also obviously used to provide contrast to the Tyrones. She regards drinking as "a good man's failing," and she suggests that a drink makes Bridget the cook "cheerful." Bridget "loves her drop," Cathleen says. Her attitude towards drinking is that it is an acceptable outlet, a healthy release,[12] and that it lifts the spirits. In contrast, she has a low regard for teetotalers: "I wouldn't give a trauneen for a teetotaler. They've no high spirits" (*LDJ*, p. 101). Abstinence is thus viewed as a less admirable trait than indulgence. This may be a healthy attitude for some people, but the irony here is that it is blatantly inappropriate in the case of the Tyrones. Indeed, they have no "high spirits" at all; their indulgence leads only to depression and dissipation. In Cathleen's eyes, though, drinking in the Tyrone family may seem like "a good man's failing"; she is only aware of the symptoms, not the disease. She is ignorant of the anguish that exists beneath the surface of this family environment, having been conned by the persuasive appearances that they try so hard to sustain. She sees only the good in Tyrone, and even in Mary; she is not at all aware of Mary's drug addiction even though she is the one who obtains the latest supply of morphine from the pharmacy. She mistakes Mary's behavior for drunkenness, which puzzles her since she knows that Mary has not had anything to drink. Although Cathleen's innocence about drug addiction is believable because it probably would be far removed from her experience, yet it would be difficult to accept her complacence when confronted with Mary's increasingly mysterious behavior if Cathleen were not under the influence of alcohol.

Another contrast provided by Cathleen's rather innocuous tipsiness becomes apparent when Edmund and James enter and we see the effects of drinking that they suffer from:

> Tyrone has had a lot to drink but beyond a slightly glazed look in his eyes and a trace of a blur in his speech, he does not show it. Edmund has also had more than a few drinks without much apparent effect, except that his sunken cheeks are flushed and his eyes look bright and feverish.
>
> (*LDJ*, p. 108)

These are the indications of the more subtle effects of drinking that alcoholics might exhibit, as opposed to the more visible effects in Cathleen's behavior. While the effects of drinking on the Tyrones are less apparent, however, they run much more deeply and have greater long-term consequences. Seasoned alcoholics, they are able to "hold their liquor," but contrary to what alcoholics often imply by this, it does not mean that they are not affected by it.

As the subsequent scene progresses, and the drunk men confront the wife-mother who at this point is highly intoxicated with morphine, the "unfulfilled promises and lost expectations" that are frequently observed at the heart of the "strained and tense" relationships among members of alcoholic families, emerge.[13] This confrontation affects Tyrone deeply, so that by the end of Act III, with all his defenses broken down, he appears to be very much like the spouse of the alcoholic as described by the Howards: "believing [he] truly possesses all the inadequacies that have been heaped upon [him]," he "waits within the loneliness of his . . . own mind confined by fear and doubt, waiting for the next crisis."[14]

In Act IV, O'Neill turns his attention to the three drunk men, and Mary does not appear until the end (although her presence is felt, which is true for these men always). Under the influence of substantial quantities of alcohol, and within the context of the hopeless cycle of guilt and blame that defines their collective and individual plights, the three men achieve a directness in communication that had been previously impossible, when some hope and sobriety had existed. Now, their hopelessness (and for Edmund, the onslaught of hopelessness) provides fertile ground for the alcohol to cultivate uninhibited contemplation and expression of regrets, without the customary defensiveness. The only voice of hope that remains is Edmund's, but in spite of the "native eloquence" with which O'Neill endows that voice, it is ultimately muted by the cries of desperation reverberating around it.

At the start of the fourth act, O'Neill describes the effects of drink on Tyrone in more detail than previously:

> He is drunk and shows it by the owlish, deliberate manner in which he peers at each card to make certain of its identity, and then plays it as if he wasn't certain of his aim. His eyes have a misted, oily look and his mouth is slack. But despite all the whiskey in him, he has not escaped, and he looks as he appeared at the close of the preceding act, a sad, defeated old man, possessed by hopeless resignation.
>
> (LDJ, p. 125)

The acknowledgement that he has "not escaped" is crucial here, because it prohibits one from perceiving the character as obliviously drunk, and it defies the notion that drinking does provide escape. As is so often the case with O'Neill's alcoholic characters, intoxication only increases Tyrone's sense of defeat and loneliness.

Edmund, too, is described as somewhat more discernibly drunk than before:

> He is drunk now, too, but like his father he carries it well, and gives little

sign of it except in his eyes and a chip-on-the-shoulder aggressiveness in his
manner.

(*LDJ*, p. 126)

In the scene that follows, the fact that these men are intoxicated obviously
contributes to the movement and tone of their confrontation. The scene follows the established patterns, at first, with guilt, accusations, and defensiveness prompting many of their words; but the scene is also characterized
by a softened affection. In their drunkenness, both men crave company;
they dread the thought of being alone this night with Mary wandering
through the past upstairs. They need each other for distraction from that,
but the events of the day have also made them somewhat more sympathetic
to each other, and more inclined to listen. Several comments that in the first
three acts would have resulted in a bitter fight are now qualified, and even
retracted. This kind of interaction enables them to engage in an extended
dialogue that leads to renewed appreciation of each other. Not insignificantly, the stage directions throughout this scene refer to their drunkenness,
which is clearly the enabling factor. The effects of alcohol enable the father
and son to relate warmly towards each other for the first extended period of
time in the play.

　This scene is more important in terms of Edmund's lyrical expression of
his philosophy than in terms of the relationship between father and son that
evolves. As Edmund begins to ruminate on the significance of the fog for
him, the stage directions explicitly indicate that he "*sounds more tipsy and
looks it*" (*LDJ*, p. 130). Edmund's contemplation on the meaning of the fog
sounds much like his mother's in Act III. They both love the fog because it
protects them from truth and reality. But Edmund is more of a romantic
than is his mother, and he proceeds accordingly, beyond the oblivion of the
fog to the oblivion of death:

> It was like walking in the bottom of the sea. As if I had drowned long ago.
> As if I was a ghost belonging to the fog, and the fog was the ghost of the sea.
> It felt damned peaceful to be nothing more than a ghost within a ghost.
>
> (*LDJ*, p. 131).

Edmund has experienced such peaceful feelings only while at sea, and now
it is only a memory; escape is unattainable in his present reality, as it is for
his brother and for his father. Mary, however, does live "as a ghost" by re-
treating into the fog of her drugged, death-like state; she escapes from the
present, but she does not forget.

　Edmund would like to forget. His response to his father's quotation
from *The Tempest* is significant. Tyrone implores Edmund to remember
that Shakespeare has said everything "worth saying," including what he
thinks Edmund is getting at: "We are such stuff as dreams are made on, and
our little life is rounded with a sleep." Edmund replies:

. . . Ironically. Fine! That's beautiful. But I wasn't trying to say that. We are such stuff as manure is made on, so let's drink up and forget it. That's more my idea.

(LDJ, p. 131)

Edmund would like to find some transcendental meaning in life, but he certainly does not believe he can find it in Shakespeare's "dreams." This exchange highlights the misunderstanding that characterizes the father-son relationship, but the mode of communication brings them together; there is a genuine sense of mutual satisfaction in this exchange since it challenges both men's imaginations.

Edmund's impulse to "drink up and forget it" derives from his despair at achieving transcendence of the kind he claims to have experienced at sea. The sad truth, however, is that drinking does not even allow Edmund to forget, let alone transcend, his reality. Everything that happens in the course of this day, in fact, has reinforced the sense that it is impossible for this family to forget, and that intoxication exacerbates the problem.

In spite of his sense of the real, depressing effects that intoxicants have on him and his family, or perhaps *because* of it, Edmund turns to Baudelaire to advocate the romantic vision of drunkenness. Edmund desperately wants to believe that one can be "so drunk you can forget," as Baudelaire's prose poem promises:

> "Be always drunken. Nothing else matters: that is the only question. If you would not feel the horrible burden of Time weighing on your shoulders and crushing you to earth, be drunken continually.
>
> Drunken with what? With wine, with poetry, or with virtue, as you will. But be drunken.
>
> And if sometimes, on the stairs of a palace, or on the green side of a ditch, or in the dreary solitude of your own room, you should awaken and drunkenness be half or wholly slipped away from you, ask of the wind, or of the wave, or of the star, or of the bird, or of the clock, of whatever flies, or sighs, or rocks, or sings, or speaks, ask what hour it is; and wind, wave, star, bird, clock, will answer you: 'It is the hour to be drunken! Be drunken, if you would not be martyred slaves of Time: be drunken continually! With wine, with poetry, or with virtue, as you will.' "

(LDJ, p. 132)

Ultimately, there is considerable irony in Edmund's evocation of Baudelaire's exhortation: the Tyrones are seen to be "drunken continually," and yet they clearly do not escape the crushing "burden of Time." In direct opposition, in fact, to the ramifications of Baudelaire's prescription is the reality of the Tyrones' lives, which is best defined by Mary when she denies the possibility of forgetting the past: "Why? How can I? The past is the present, isn't it? It's the future, too. We all try to lie out of that but life won't let us" (*LDJ*, p. 87). Do what they may, the Tyrones are continually demonstrating that they are enslaved by Time, and their enslavement seems to be intensified by their intoxication.

As for Edmund himself, he does not experience transcendence for the audience to see; he merely reports about it in his past:

> . . . When I was on the Squarehead square rigger, bound for Buenos Aires. . . . I lay on the bowsprit . . . with the water foaming into spume under me. . . . I became drunk with the beauty and singing rhythm of it, and for a moment I lost myself — actually lost my life. I was set free! . . . I belonged, without past or future, within peace and unity and a wild joy, within something greater than my own life, or the life of Man, to Life itself! To God, if you want to put it that way.
>
> (*LDJ*, p. 153)

This is undeniably a romantic vision, this "oneness," "beyond life," and significantly, in terms of Baudelairian drunkenness, "without past or future," which means beyond the "burden of Time." And Edmund builds further to a hyperbolic climax in which he experiences an ecstatic moment of revelation:

> . . . For a second you see — and seeing the secret, are the secret. For a second, there is meaning! Then the hand lets the veil fall and you are alone, lost in the fog again, and you stumble on towards nowhere, for no good reason.
>
> (*LDJ*, p. 153)

His analogy of life as "stumbling" through the "fog" implies his awareness that the chemically-induced intoxication that he and the others experience is a different kind of fog from the one he dreamt of previously; this fog does not allow transcendence. While it may protect one from present reality, it is still only "stumbling." Edmund's moment of revelation at sea has been shattered for him on land, where the best he can do is attempt to lose himself in an alcoholic fog:

> It was a great mistake, my being born a man. I would have been much more successful as a sea gull or a fish. As it is, I will always be a stranger who never feels at home, who does not really want and is not really wanted, who can never belong, who must always be a little in love with death.
>
> (*LDJ*, pp. 153–154)

The ecstasy he recalls experiencing at sea is foreign to his life as a man; it is beyond the human condition to find this meaning for life.

When Tyrone responds to Edmund's poetic expressiveness in this scene, he remarks that Edmund has the "makings of a poet," which Edmund aptly qualifies:

> I couldn't touch what I tried to tell you just now. I just stammered. That's the best I'll ever do, I mean, if I live. Well, it will be faithful realism, at least. Stammering is the native eloquence of us fog people.
>
> (*LDJ*, p. 154)

Thus, human beings are characterized by Edmund as stammering and stumbling in the fog, never transcending it. Certainly, this is the picture of the alcoholic, constantly seeking to escape his problems, or in the romantic vein, to transcend them, but always ending up drunk, depressed, and debilitated, stumbling and stammering through a bleary-eyed haze.

It is especially appropriate, then, that the sounds of Jamie stumbling and falling on the front steps follow immediately after Edmund's romantic ruminations. Edmund is awakened from his romantic musings by the hard realities of drunkenness. Just as he has reached the intoxicated, lyrical heights of his romantic idealism, he is forced to confront his drunken brother stumbling into the house:

> Edmund watches with amusement Jamie's wavering progress through the front parlor. Jamie comes in. He is very drunk and woozy on his legs. His eyes are glassy, his face bloated, his speech blurred, his mouth slack like his father's, a leer on his lips.
>
> (*LDJ*, p. 154)

This passage is unusually descriptive, for O'Neill, of some of the stereotypical, external signs of drunkenness. Even in the dialogue, O'Neill has Jamie drop letters from words and slur his "s's." And yet, it is inconsistent: Jamie drifts in and out of this speech pattern, and he sometimes shows more of the external signs of drunkenness, and sometimes less. Given O'Neill's use of the effects of intoxication, it is apparent that this is intentional. We know that Jamie has consumed a large quantity of alcohol, and he comes home here with the intention of playing the role of the drunken profligate son, the happy-go-lucky young swell, on whom the day's traumatic events have had little effect. Beneath this performance, however, we can detect some of the more subtle signs that O'Neill usually uses. For instance, the extreme mood changes are striking, as Jamie vacillates between loudly singing lewd songs and softly contemplating his profound sense of personal failure. He is desperately attempting to conceal his despondency and sustain his performance, but he ultimately cannot endure. Given the situation that he enters into, with Mary wandering further into her past upstairs, and Edmund and Jamie having just candidly aired their deepest disappointments, these traditionally comic external signs of drunkenness become potentially tragic, and considerably poignant in terms of Jamie's desperation.

As Jamie relates the story of his evening's adventures, appropriately quoting Wilde and Kipling as accompaniment to the image of cynical detachment that he strives to sustain, Edmund is an attentive, intoxicated listener. During Jamie's monologue, he drops his drunken façade, as hopelessness triumphs. The external signs of intoxication at the beginning of the passage — the nodding head, the slurred speech, the bravado — gradually give way to the more subtle manifestations of intoxication, such as the sudden, extreme mood changes mentioned above. The attempt to hide behind romantic literary allusions gives way to the deeper feelings of hopelessness, helplessness, and loneliness. His romanticized tale of the conquest of Fat Violet, the whore, leads ineluctably this time to a confrontation with his feelings about his mother, whom he angrily and with "hatred" calls the "hophead." He then confesses the true nature of his self-esteem:

> . . . I suppose it's because I feel so damned sunk. Because this time Mama had me fooled. I really believed she had it licked. She thinks I always believe the worst, but this time I believed the best. *His voice flutters.* I suppose I can't forgive her — yet. It meant so much. I'd begun to hope, if she'd beaten the game, I could, too. *He begins to sob, and the horrible part of his weeping is that it appears sober, not the maudlin tears of drunkenness.*
> (*LDJ*, p. 162)

With the façade down, Jamie is now confronted with his own intense feelings of self-hatred, which is, of course, at the heart of his alcoholic dependency, and directly opposed to Edmund's romantic visions of drunkenness.

In the ensuing climactic confrontation with Edmund, in which he confesses his conflicted feelings towards his brother, Jamie reveals that he has intentionally lured Edmund into situations that would "make a bum" of him: "Made my mistakes look good. Made getting drunk romantic. Made whores fascinating vampires instead of poor, stupid, diseased slobs they really are. Made fun of work as sucker's game. Never wanted you to succeed and make me look even worse by comparison. Wanted you to fail" (*LDJ*, p. 165). Particularly interesting here is Jamie's remark about having "made getting drunk romantic." Edmund's romantic vision of intoxication is thus seen to have its roots in Jamie's cynicism. Jamie's comment thus confirms what we have already noted: the transcendent escape of intoxication is an illusion; the reality lies in the drunkenness depicted on stage — that is, in Jamie's drunken misery. Thus, Jamie's purgative confession of his love-hate feelings towards his brother, which is really a confession of his own self-loathing, serves as yet another blow to Edmund's romantic aspirations.

The impact of Jamie's confession on Edmund is evident in the virtual absence of Edmund's usual efforts to deny the sordid reality. He becomes much more complacent than usual, suggesting his sense of defeat. Furthermore, when Jamie finally falls asleep, succumbing to the loss of consciousness that comes with the final stages of intoxication, Edmund's response is to bury his face in his hands, "miserably." This is certainly the response of a defeated man; Edmund seems to share his brother's misery here, and perhaps he even recognizes it as a reflection of his own.

Thus, to conclude that Edmund's transcendental idealism is triumphant in this play, as some commentators have done, is extremely misguided. The confrontation with Jamie, coming as it does, *after* Edmund's transcendental monologue, emphatically reminds us that Edmund's transcendence is merely a memory, and a fleeting one at that, especially when contrasted, as it is, with the very real, concrete, and inescapable effects of alcoholism that he must confront in his brother. The other important reminder of the realities of intoxication is the irretrievable immersion of Mary into her morphine addiction, which not insignificantly, returns to our consciousness at the end of the play, as Mary finally descends to join the others.

Some critics have argued for an optimistic interpretation of this play based on new love and understanding that enters into the relationships between Edmund and his father and brother. Indeed, alliances have shifted somewhat, as we see Edmund defend his father against his brother in the final moments, but it is certainly not clear that these are permanent realignments; given the nature of this family, in fact, that seems highly unlikely. There is no convincing evidence that the interactions in the final scene represent a conclusive picture of the family. It is, rather, quite likely that their responses to the day's words and occurrences may change as they become incorporated into the family's collective and individual memories; we have certainly witnessed enough strange discrepancies in their recollections of other past events. At the very least, it is difficult to see in the very final moments the "love arising out of the men's tolerance towards each other," which Rolf Scheibler claims is a sort of beacon of hope for the Tyrones.[15] Whatever light shines in Act IV is dimmed by the final images on the stage.

After each of the men attempts to reach Mary one last time, James futilely attempts to blame her beha·ior on the "damned poison," acknowledging that she has never been "in it as deep as this." This refers both to the extent of her intoxication as well as to its causes. To the extent that their lives have brought them to this point, and Mary to the depths of her chronic condition, it can be said that the family has never been this "far gone." The "damned poison," of course, be it alcohol or morphine, is not the cause of their misery; it is merely a symptom. Tyrone, however, stubbornly clings to his beliefs. He would still turn to the same words to explain life as he had done earlier: "The fault, dear Brutus, is not in our stars, but in ourselves that we are underlings" (*LDJ*, p. 152). He would argue with Edmund's derisive laughter at life for being "so damned crazy." And so, he can blame the morphine, and blame the alcohol, and insist that there is "nothing wrong with life." Tyrone may still find comfort in this viewpoint, but his sons, with their modern sensibilities, cannot, and certainly, O'Neill does not; the action of the play clearly defeats this view of the human condition.

As for the hopefulness some find in the relationships among the men, it is important to note that the last drink of the play eludes them:

Jamie pushes the bottle toward [Tyrone]. He pours a drink without disarranging the wedding gown he holds carefully over his other arm and on his lap, and shoves the bottle back. Jamie pours his and passes the bottle to Edmund, who, in turn, pours one. Tyrone lifts his glass and his sons follow suit mechanically, but before they can drink Mary speaks and they slowly lower their drinks to the table, forgetting them.

(*LDJ*, p. 175)

They never have this final drink. In the last moments of the play, the device that was supposed to enable them to forget is itself forgotten, overwhelmed by the presence of Mary, in her current condition representing everything that they would like to escape from. Contrary to suggesting any feelings of togetherness among the men, the denial of even this small token of a drink together emphasizes the feeling of being alone that each man actually experiences.

The play ends, significantly, with *Mary's* words:

> That was in the winter of senior year. Then in the spring something happened to me. Yes. I remember. I fell in love with James Tyrone and was so happy for a time. *She stares before her in a sad dream. Tyrone stirs in his chair. Edmund and Jamie remain motionless.*
>
> CURTAIN
(*LDJ*, p. 176)

Perhaps the men are listening; perhaps each is contemplating his own sense of lost happiness, lost opportunities, lost dreams. The final image, though, is clear: the withdrawn Mary, shrouded within a drugged trance, whose regression into her past inevitably returns her to the present, surrounded by three drunken men, also unable to attain oblivion, unable to forget where and who they are. It is, finally, a striking image that in no way confirms Edmund's romantic visions, but rather, destroys them. The "meaning of life," described in Edmund's rapturous account, is conveyed in moving, but abstract, language, while the hopelessness that all the Tyrones feel is presented palpably on stage as the curtain falls.

This final scene, with the characters tied together immovably, almost inevitably recalls the closing moments of *Waiting For Godot*. The dramatic mode is quite different, but O'Neill's characters' existential plight is quite similar to that of Beckett's. Like Vladimir and Estragon, the Tyrones are trapped by the emptiness of their isolated existence, and impotent to effect any change. Like Vladimir and Estragon, the Tyrones would like to leave, but there is nowhere to go; there is no escape. Unlike Beckett's characters, however, O'Neill's characters are haunted by the past. Drugs and alcohol cannot protect them from the emptiness of their lives; these only intensify the feelings of hopelessness, and keep them trapped in circles of behavior and interaction that ultimately leave them all alone. Happiness has only lasted "for a time," and in the distant past; meaning has only been glimpsed for a moment. Now, the transitory, abstract nature of that glimpse of life's meaning is emphasized as it fades quickly in contrast to the concrete reality of these four miserable human beings. They do not even have the unqualified sense of devotion to each other that Vladimir and Estragon have. Vladimir and Estragon are comic figures in that in spite of their plight, they maintain hope; the Tyrones are sad, pitiful figures in that because of their plight, they have no hope.

In *Long Day's Journey Into Night*, O'Neill captures his vision of the human condition in the figure of the alcoholic who is constantly and repeatedly faced with the disappointment of his hopes to escape or transcend present reality. As the effects of heavy drinking and alcoholism increase, the alcoholic, in his attempt to attain euphoric forgetfulness, is repeatedly confronted with the painful realities of dissipation, despondency, self-destruction, and ultimately, death. This is the life of an alcoholic, and for O'Neill, this is the life of modern man.

Notes

1. George A. Mann, M.D., *The Dynamics of Addiction* (Minneapolis: Johnson Institute, 1983), p. 1.

2. *Diagnostic and Statistical Manual of Mental Disorders*, 3rd ed. (Washington, D.C.: American Psychiatric Association, 1980), III, p. 143.

3. *DSM-III*, p. 172.

4. Don and Nancy Howard, "The Progression of Alcoholism and the Family," in *A Family Approach to Problem Drinking: The Four-Week Family Forum* (Columbia, Miss.: Family Training Center, 1976), p. 46.

5. Henry Hewes, "Long Day's Journey Into Night," in *O'Neill and His Plays: Four Decades of Criticism*, ed. Oscar Cargill, N. Bryllion Fagin, and William J. Fisher (New York: New York University Press, 1961), p. 220.

6. Howard, p. 47.

7. Howard, p. 51.

8. This and all future references to *Long Day's Journey Into Night* (*LDJ*) are to Eugene O'Neill, *Long Day's Journey Into Night* (New Haven: Yale University Press, 1955).

9. Howard pp. 46–48.

10. *DSM-III*, p. 144.

11. *DSM-III*, p. 142.

12. Monica McGoldrick Orfanidis and John K. Pearce, "Family Therapy with Irish Americans," in *Family Process* 20, No. 2 (1981), 236. "Alcohol, 'the good man's weakness' has long been the major Irish outlet for disallowed feelings. It is for the Irish their universal disqualifier. . . . One group of researchers, commenting on the very low rate of neuroses found among American Irish, noted that, 'It is remarkable that the Irish can find an outlet for so many forms of psychic conflict in this single form of escape.' " This explanation of behavior in terms of cultural norms within ethnic groups can help us understand Tyrone's attitude towards drinking, in part, and it certainly puts Cathleen's attitude in perspective. Her views are "typically Irish," and so much of O'Neill's use of intoxication in his drama defies these views. Part of her function in *Long Day's Journey* is obviously to voice this attitude so that it can be seen for the fallacy that O'Neill sees it as.

13. Howard, p. 48.

14. Howard, pp. 48–49.

15. Rolf Scheibler, *The Late Plays of Eugene O'Neill* (Bern: Francke, 1970), p. 131.

Hughie: Pipe Dream for Two   Laurin Roland Porter

O'Neill's one-act drama, *Hughie*, following close on the heels of its predecessor, *The Iceman Cometh*, can be read as a condensed version of its better known counterpart. Although the particulars of time, place, and personae differ, the theme that structures the action of both plays is identical. To survive, O'Neill insists, men must cling to a pipe dream to protect him from reality. In *Iceman* the collective dream-swapping occurs in fairly elaborate fashion among the dozen-odd denizens of Harry Hope's saloon. In *Hughie* we are presented with a much simpler but equally devastating pipe dream for two.

The cultural backdrop of both plays reveals a society laced with corruption. *The Iceman Cometh* focuses its attention on a seedy bar in New York's West Side in 1912; *Hughie*, on a run-down hotel near Times Square in 1928. They are worlds equally devoid of hope or potential. Because the traditional structures fail to provide a viable alternative to society's indifference, the boarders at Hope's saloon form a family of their own to ward off the desperation that threatens them; Erie Smith seeks a similar comfort in the companionship of a new night clerk, Charlie Hughes. The common denominator in each case is the need for a pipe dream, since life cannot be endured without a protective shield of illusion.

The only obstacle to happiness in this scheme of things arises when a member of the "family" refuses to play by the rules, challenging the validity of the dream and breaking its soporific spell. For Harry Hope and his crew in *Iceman*, this occurs when the salesman Hickey arrives, newly converted and peddling a return to reality. For Erie Smith, the game threatens to break down with the death of Hughie, the previous night clerk, who participated in his fantasies of excitement and glamour. Since the pipe dream is communitarian in nature and must be shared to be believed, Smith must find a replacement for his feckless pal.

It is not surprising that the two plays have so much in common. O'Neill completed *Hughie* within two years after writing *The Iceman Cometh* (probably by June of 1941).[1] It was one of the projected series of from six to nine plays to be collectively entitled *By Way of Obit*.[2] The plays, which were to cover a period of eighteen years, from 1910 to 1928, were each to be named after someone recently deceased. According to a letter O'Neill wrote to George Jean Nathan at this time, the protagonist of each play was to speak at length about his dead friend to

> a person who does little but listen. Via this monologue you get a complete picture of the person who has died — his or her whole life story — but just as complete a picture of the life and character of the narrator. And you also get by another means — a use of stage directions, mostly — an insight into the whole life of the person who does little but listen.[3]

Although he outlined scenarios for several of the other one-acts, O'Neill destroyed them on February 21, 1944, in the face of his encroaching illness and the prospect of further deterioration; only *Hughie*, the sole completed play, was preserved.[4]

It appears, however, to be fairly representative of the venture as a whole. According to a letter to Nathan in July in 1942, "It [*Hughie*] give [sic] you an idea of how the others in the series will be done."[5] Writing at the height of his power, O'Neill has created in *Hughie* a small gem of a play whose brilliance derives as much from its economy of characterization as from its poetic use of language. And as in *The Iceman Cometh*, the result reflects both O'Neill's cultural insights and his personal experience of life.

Because on at least one level the play's concerns are cultural in nature, both the setting and the personae of *Hughie* are described in cultural terms. The action takes place in the lobby of a run-down hotel in midtown New York between 3 and 4 A.M. of a day in the summer of 1928. Built as a "respectable second class" institution in the decade 1900–10, the hotel, like many others, was "forced to deteriorate to survive" following the First World War and Prohibition. The stage directions, in extremely cynical tones, remark that even the "Great Hollow Boom" of the twenties — The Everlasting Opulence of the New Economic Law — has passed it by.[6] As the capitalized labels imply, if society is not to blame for the demise of this world, it certainly has been no help. The hotel limps along merely by "cutting the overhead for service, repairs, and cleanliness to a minimum" (*Hughie*, p. 7).

O'Neill's choice of a 1928 time-frame further reinforces the impoverishment of the culture at large. The action takes place at the height of the boom years, an era of excitement and optimism, of free-flowing money and champagne. To quote its best known chronicler, the Jazz Age, like Jay Gatsby, had "something gorgeous about [it], some heightened sensitivity to the promises of life."[7] Yet amidst this abundance we see life stripped down to a few bare essentials. The seedy hotel lobby is equipped only with shabby chairs, the usual, impersonal tiers of mailboxes, a desk and telephone switchboard, a clock. Its denizens, a night clerk and a guest, are depicted in equally dismal terms. The seeming-success of American society at this juncture in history is called into question by the microcosm on stage — a world which, as the stage directions make clear, is not unique, but typical. A further irony, of course, lies in the audience's awareness that the boom years led only to the crash of '29.

Both Charlie Hughes, the night clerk, and the guest, Erie Smith, are stock characters from this seamy world. Charlie, sallow and pimply with dandruff and a protruding Adam's apple, is, according to O'Neill, the "essence of all the night clerks I've known in bum hotels."[8] In the cast of characters he is simply "A Night Clerk." In his early forties, he is tall and thin, his face long and narrow and greasy with perspiration; "his nose is large and without character. So is his mouth. So are his ears. So is his thinning brown hair" (*Hughie*, p. 8). His blank physiognomy reflects the vacuum in which he exists. His "blank brown eyes," we are told, "contain no discernible expression." His mind and senses dulled by routine, Charlie has gone beyond boredom to a state of suspended animation. His response to Erie, who intrudes on his isolation, consist of stock phrases. So accustomed is he to his routine that he can maintain his end of a conversation with whatever guest insists on talking while his mind is elsewhere, listening for the el or following the footsteps of the cop on his beat. Occasionally one of the standard jokes or off-color remarks breaks through the barrier, but even then the response is automatic.

It was not always so. When Smith makes the usual crack about Charlie's three children ("That's what comes of being careless"), the clerk returns the expected smile, recalling that he had been mildly offended the first time he heard it a dozen years ago. But this half-hearted emotion has long since been squelched. The last time he was able to feel anything as strong as despair, we are told, "was back around World War days when the cost of living got so high and he was out of a job for three months" (*Hughie*, p. 17). The only excitement in the clerk's pathetic existence comes from the night sounds outside the hotel lobby — the ambulance, the fire engine, the streetcar. And even they serve merely to mark time as another night dies.

Erie Smith, "an oldtimer in this fleabag" (*Hughie*, p. 10), is, like the clerk, a type, one well known to O'Neill from his days at the Garden Hotel. According to the playwright himself, " 'Erie' is a type of Broadway sport I and my brother used to know by the dozen in far-off days. I didn't know many at the time the play is laid, 1928, but they never change. Only their lingo does."[9] The lingo O'Neill refers to identifies Smith as a small-fry Broadway gambler and horse player, "living hand to mouth on the fringe of the rackets. Infesting corners, doorways, cheap restaurants, the bars of minor speakeasies, he and his kind imagine they are in the Real Know, cynical oracles of the One True Grapevine" (*Hughie*, p. 9). He and Charlie, cultural prototypes, attest to the myriads like them in the cheap hotels and side streets across the country.

His appearance, as we would expect, reflects his status. He shares with the clerk a pasty, night-life complexion; they are, after all, inhabitants of the same world. But there the similarity ends. While Charlie is tall and thin, Smith is stout. He has fat arms and legs; a large, round, snub-nosed face; beefy shoulders. He wears "a light grey suit cut in the extreme, tight-waisted, Broadway mode" (*Hughie*, p. 9); his shirt is made of expensive silk, but it is faded and of a blue that "sets teeth on edge." His red and blue foulard tie is stained with perspiration; his red and blue silk handkerchief is used to mop his sweating forehead. His "small, pursy mouth is always crooked in the cynical leer of one who possesses superior, inside information" (*Hughie*, p. 9). He imitates the character he imagines himself to be — the Broadway big-shot, the man about town.

Both Charlie and Smith are not native New Yorkers. Like their soul-brothers everywhere, they came to the big city seeking excitement and a fast buck—the clerk, from Saginaw, Michigan; the gambler, from Erie, Pennsylvania (hence, his nickname). As Smith says, "Nearly every guy I know on the Big Stem—and I know most of 'em—hails from the sticks" (*Hughie*, p. 14). Hughie, the dead night clerk, also fits this pattern. Originally from "a hick burg upstate," he decided to try his luck in New York. "He'd read somewhere," Erie says,

> —in the Suckers' Almanac, I guess—that all a guy had to do was come to the Big Town and Old Man Success would be waitin' at the Grand Central to give him the key to the city. What a bag that is! Even I believed that once, and no one could ever call me a sap (*Hughie*, p. 23).

If Erie is not a "sap," he is certainly down on his luck. Ever since Hughie died a week earlier, Smith has been on a drunk, trying to forget his friend and the fact that he owes a hundred dollars (spent for a gawdy send-off floral arrangement) to several very unsympathetic types who will soon come looking for him. His deepest concern, however, is the run of bad luck he's had ever since Hughie's hospitalization:

> Not a win. That ain't natural. I've always been a lucky guy—lucky enough to get by and pay up, I mean. I wouldn't never worry about owing guys, like I owe them guys. I'd always know I'd make a win that'd fix it. But now I got a lousy hunch when I lost Hughie I lost my luck—I mean I've lost the old confidence. He used to give me confidence (*Hughie*, p. 35).

Erie desperately needs someone to resume Hughie's former role, to believe in him so that he can believe in himself. He seizes upon the new clerk as that person, and the action of the play revolves around his efforts to overcome Charlie's resistance to entering the relationship.

The plot develops two lines of parallel and—except for the play's final pages—nonintersecting action. Smith, ostensibly chatting with the new night clerk, is actually reliving his former conversations with Hughie, trying to recapture the confidence he had derived from these exchanges by drawing Charlie into the familiar routine. At the same time, Erie is fighting a desperate interior battle. His life, like his luck, seems to be running out. As he lingers at the desk, "glancing around the deserted lobby with forlorn distaste" (*Hughie*, p. 17) but unable to tear himself away, it becomes increasingly clear that, given his desperation, to return to his room is to invite suicide. The room key he clings to becomes a visible symbol of his despair. At first he jiggles it, then, momentarily encouraged, he clacks it "like a castanet" (*Hughie*, p. 20). Finally, when it seems he can neither revive Charlie nor pry himself away from the desk, he "twirls his key frantically as if it were a fetish which might set him free" (*Hughie*, p. 28).[10]

Charlie, meanwhile, feigns an interest in Erie's running patter but actually carries on an interior monologue revealed in the extensive stage directions. He, too, fights a silent battle with time, though of a different sort. The stage directions inform us that the clerk is so far removed from emotion that he has even forgotten what it feels like to be bored. However, there are glimmers of life in the fantasies that keep him going through the night. Their violent nature reflects the impotence and repressed rage Charlie clearly feels. He would like to "wake up the whole damned city" with the clanging garbage cans (*Hughie*, p. 17) or even burn it down. As he listens to the footfalls of the cop on his beat, he hopes for a shootout with a gunman — anything to break the monotony and assure him of his existence. For Charlie, life is a series of nights to be lived through, measured by nothing more exciting than the noise of an el approaching and receding. But, although there is something melancholy in the passing of the train,

> there is hope. Only so many El trains pass in one night, and each one pass-
> ing leaves one less to pass, so the night recedes, too, until at last it must die
> and join all the other long nights in Nirvana, the Big Night of Nights
> (*Hughie*, p. 19).

Smith's intrusion in his life represents not a change but an intensification of the monotony. He is merely one more guest who must be endured with simulated interest. The clerk thinks of Erie as his room number "492," recalling Columbus' discovery of America. The allusion is ironic; there are no new discoveries in Charlie's world.

And so the action unfolds, revealing the equally desperate lives of the small time gambler, whose world is defined by horses and poker and crap games, and the grub-like clerk, who ticks off night after endless night. It is Gatsby's world seen from the underside— gambling and petty crime, the "bangtails" and the Follies broads. It is appropriate, then, that this milieu also provide the link which finally allows these two desperate souls to make contact.

Late in the play, when Erie has finally despaired of establishing contact with the night clerk and is merely talking aloud to himself, Charlie, vaguely frightened by the night's death-like silence, rouses himself and tries to recall what Smith has been jabbering about. He remembers talk of gambling, and suddenly it occurs to him that Erie might know his idol, the big shot Arnold Rothstein.[11] Erie's relationship with the gambler is hardly intimate; Rothstein "uses [him] to run errands when there ain't no one else handy" (*Hughie*, p. 34). But it is enough for the clerk, who now sees Smith as "the Gambler in 492, the Friend of Arnold Rothstein" (*Hughie*, p. 37). Erie, sensing Hughes' sudden interest, tentatively tries out his old lines, producing a pair of dice carelessly and saying, "How about shootin' a little crap, Charlie?" (*Hughie*, p. 37). The link has been established. As the play ends, with Erie winning the round, Charlie has taken the place of the dead Hughie, and Smith's luck—and confidence—have returned. His pipe dream, given a believing listener, is once again intact.

It is a mistake, however, to assume that the pipe dream is unilateral. If

Erie uses the clerk, quite consciously, to boost his self-image and shore up his confidence, Charlie, in turn, uses the gambler as a vehicle for his own fantasies. By granting Smith big-shot status, he himself can pretend to be in the action, if only vicariously. As in *The Iceman Cometh*, the dream is communitarian. Life is a game in which both players must engage if it is to continue.

And continue it does. Life wins out over death in this play named after a dead man. Whatever the limitations of the vision of reality with which we are presented — and they are considerable — we must acknowledge the endurance of the human spirit which it insists upon. The tragedy is that it can only endure in the presence of mutual and self deception, each man using his friend for his own purpose. O'Neill's presentation of the new clerk as a parallel to the deceased Hughie, even to the extent of similar names and backgrounds, underlines this point: Charlie merely continues the former clerk's fifteen year relationship with Smith where it left off. This infinitely widens the scope of the play and renders its implications all the more devastating. It is not a pretty picture. Like *The Iceman Cometh*, *Hughie* forces us to consider a world where ideals have failed and cultural supports are sadly lacking. Yet in spite of everything, life goes on, with men huddling together for whatever mutual warmth and comfort they can discover.

If *Hughie* presents us with a portrait of the American culture in the late twenties, it also contains biographical elements drawn from the playwright's personal experiences and relationships. As mentioned earlier, Smith and Hughes are drawn from cultural types that populated the New York world O'Neill frequented in his youth. As such they represent both general types and specific memories.

In addition, the portrait of Erie Smith seems to be at least partially based upon the playwright's older brother. This is suggested, in the first instance, by Smith's Broadway patois. It is a slang characteristic of Jamie O'Neill and thus assigned to his fictional counterpart in *Long Day's Journey*, Jamie Tyrone, where it is used both to express Jamie's cynicism and to camouflage deeper feelings. At one point, exasperated with Jamie's sarcasm, Tyrone snaps at him to hold his "rotten Broadway loafer's lingo," and Edmund, "scornfully parodying his brother's cynicism," chimes in:

> They never come back! Everything is in the bag! It's all a frameup! We're all fall guys and suckers and we can't beat the game![12]

Jamie's seemingly callous exterior, of course, is a shield behind which he hides the intense pain and love he reveals in the play's final act.

The same is true of Smith, a fact which the stage directions suggest from the outset. After describing the "shifty once-over glances [that] never miss the pricetags he detects on everything and everybody" and the "small, pursy mouth . . . always crooked in the cynical leer of one who possesses superior, inside information," O'Neill adds, "Yet there is something phoney about his characterization of himself, some sentimental softness behind it which doesn't belong in the hard-boiled picture" (*Hughie*, p. 9). His genuine sorrow over Hughie's death attests to that fact. Underneath his nonchalant pose, Erie is anything but unfeeling. Though he uses the Broadway tough-guy jargon to suggest the opposite, Smith, like Jamie, is a sensitive, even compassionate human being.

Another link between Erie and Jamie O'Neill is their concern for fashion. The playwright's brother was a fastidious dresser, a fact which is best reflected in his portrait in *A Moon for the Misbegotten*. Jim Tyrone's apparel is described in specific detail upon his first entrance:

> He is dressed in an expensive dark-brown suit, tight-fitting and drawn in at the waist, dark-brown made-to-order shoes and silk socks, a white silk shirt, silk handkerchief in breast pocket, a dark tie. This get-up suggests that he follows a style set by well-groomed Broadway gamblers who would like to be mistaken for Wall Street brokers.[13]

The only difference between the outfits of Tyrone and Smith is that Jim's resembles that of a *well-groomed* Broadway gambler; Erie's reflects less taste and wealth. Like Tyrone he wears a suit "cut in the extreme, tight-waisted, Broadway mode," but his expensive blue silk shirt is old, faded, and offensively bright. His tie, a gay red and blue (unlike Tyrone's conservative dark one), is stained by perspiration. Erie tries to live up to the Broadway big-shot image he has chosen for himself, but lack of funds prevents him from succeeding.

His short, fat legs and arms, round face, and beefy shoulders further complicate matters and link him with Theodore Hickman, still another fictional counterpart of Jamie O'Neill. As the Gelbs have noted, both personae are described in similar terms.[14] Erie is "around medium height but appears shorter because he is stout and his fat legs are too short for his body"; Hickey is "a little under medium height, with a stout, roly-poly figure." Erie has blue eyes, a round face, and a snub nose; his small mouth is characteristically pursed in a cynical leer. Hickey's face is "round and smooth and big-boyish with bright blue eyes, a button nose, a small pursed mouth" (*Hughie*, p. 8; *Iceman*, p. 76). Thematically they are also connected. Both Erie and Hickey are drummers with something to sell; the former, his fantasies of excitement and glamour; the latter, his promise of peace.

Thus the characterization of Smith links him with all three of the other fictional portraits of Jamie O'Neill and suggests that his origin is at least partially biographical. The attitude toward women revealed in *Hughie* also seems drawn from O'Neill's personal history. As in so many of his earlier plays and all of the final ones, women are either whores or, if wives, dream-destroyers. In the first category are the women associated with Erie—the "Follies broads" he brags of. For him, it is a matter of status to associate with "a bunch of high class dolls." When he dreams of talking with Hughie if he were still alive, he says,

I'd tell him I win ten grand from the bookie, and ten grand at stud, and ten grand in a crap game! I'd tell him I bought one of the Mercedes sport roadsters with nickel pipes sticking out of the hood! I'd tell him I lay three babes from the Follies — two blonds and one brunette! (*Hughie*, p. 32)

The "three babes" are lumped together with the Mercedes — and it is no accident that they appear last. In the social stratification of Erie's gambling world, horses (and in this case, cars) are clearly superior to women. "I tell you, Pal," he says to Charlie at one point, "I'd rather sleep in the same stall with old Man o' War than make the whole damn Follies" (*Hughie*, p. 21).

Smith considers himself lucky for not succumbing permanently to any woman's wiles, having narrowly escaped a shot-gun wedding as a youth. Neither Charlie nor the deceased Hughie was so fortunate. We know little about Charlie's wife Jess except that she nags him, but what we learn of Hughie's wife Irma completes the composite. Smith remarks that she was tight with Hughie's money, "keepin' cases on every nickel of his salary" (*Hughie*, p. 16) and only "deal[ing] him four bits a day for spending money" (*Hughie*, p. 21). She only married him, it is implied, because she was "sick of standing on her dogs all day" as a sales girl in "some punk department store" (*Hughie*, p. 23). Erie is clearly biased, of course, but the portrait is nonetheless an unattractive one. "When you call her plain," he says, "you give her all the breaks" (*Hughie*, p. 25).

Women, then, are impediments to dreaming and the freedom with which it is associated. Like Rosa Parritt and Evelyn Hickman, they sap the strength and vitality from their men. The playwright's personal jaded opinion of women is reflected in his fictional portrayals of them.

It is not surprising, then, to see that in *Hughie* as in *Iceman*, the traditional family fails and a surrogate family is substituted in its place.

As in its predecessor, *The Iceman Cometh*, the presentation of the traditional family unit in *Hughie* is extremely uncomplimentary. In the case of Erie Smith, who readily admits that "the family racket is out of my line" (*Hughie*, p. 25), a determination to avoid the entanglements of marriage can be traced back to his youth. His early memories, like those of Hickey, convey a sense of imprisonment. "I don't remember much about Erie, P-a, you understand," he says to Charlie, " — or want to. Some punk burg! After grammar school, my Old Man put me to work in his store, dealing out groceries. Some punk job! I stuck it till I was eighteen before I took a run-out powder" (*Hughie*, p. 14). The "run-out powder" he refers to was prompted by the threat of the shot-gun wedding mentioned earlier.

Hughie and Charlie, though they both have families, provide little evidence in favor of the institution. Both of their wives are depicted as naggers, penny-pinchers, and financial burdens; the children present little hope for change in this dreary outlook.

Thus, as in *Iceman*, the men look to each other for camaraderie, excitement, support. If the family at Harry Hope's is a bit larger, the bond between Erie and Hughie—and the new clerk who takes his place—is every bit as strong.

In this family, Smith serves as outrider. He leaves the hotel in search of money and excitement and returns home at the end of the day to report his successes to the night clerk. The clerk's function is to keep the hearth fire burning, figuratively, if not literally. He must be there when Erie returns, or the day's adventures will lose their savor. As the years have passed, we quickly gather, the actual adventures have diminished to the point where they are created in the telling. But Erie has continued to provide the thrills and the glamour, however contrived; the night clerk's shining-eyed faith made it all seem real. As Hickey needs the validity of Harry and the boarders to believe in his new-found peace, Erie requires the admiration of the night clerk to believe in himself.

The final link between the two plays and perhaps the most important one is that both ultimately present a search for transcendence, a strategy for breaking the stranglehold of time. Erie has managed to survive thus far by virtue of his relationship with Hughie. His nightly return to an admiring audience imposed some sense of meaning or purpose on the trivial events of the day. "Some nights I'd come back here without a buck, feeling lower than a snake's belly," he tells Charlie,

> and first thing you know I'd be lousy with jack, bettin' a grand a race. Oh, I was wise I was kiddin' myself. I ain't a sap. But what the hell, Hughie loved it, and it didn't cost nobody nothin', and if every guy along Broadway who kids himself was to drop dead there wouldn't be nobody left (*Hughie*, p. 19).

It is basically a cyclic experience of life. The mutual pipe dreams of the night give both men the strength to face the coming day. But reality intrudes with Hughie's death, and Erie's luck and confidence abruptly disappear. Time has caught up with him.

Charlie, too, is defeated by the passage of time. The usual comfort he derives from the routines of the night, the els and streetcars passing into oblivion one by one, is suddenly not enough. As he ticks away the slow hours, we are aware that his real battle is not with this guest who won't stop talking or his aching feet or even his humdrum existence, but with time itself. Director Bengt Ekerot of Stockholm's Royal Dramatic Theatre reflected this dimension when, at the play's world premiere, he had the clerk count silently on his fingers as each el passed—a gesture which reviewer Henry Hewes called "the action most essential to the drama."[15]

At Erie's lowest point, when he is "too defeated even to twirl his room key" (*Hughie*, p. 30), the symbolic fetish with which he wards off death, Charlie also reaches his nadir. The stillness of the night closes in on him and reminds him of life's final silence, death:

> The Clerk's mind still cannot make a getaway because the city remains silent, and the night vaguely reminds him of death . . . "I should have

paid 492 more attention. After all, he is company. He is awake and alive. I should use him to help me live through the night" (*Hughie*, p. 30).

Thus he seizes upon Erie in the hope that his rambling chatter will bring him back to life. He recalls Smith's mentioning gambling, and, as it occurs to him that Erie might know his hero, Arnold Rothstein, he "is now suddenly impervious to the threat of Night or Silence" (*Hughie*, p. 32). The link between the two lonely, desperate men is forged and, as Charlie assumes the role of the dead clerk, the old cycle is once again resumed. If linear time has not been defeated, they have at least discovered a way to cheat it a little longer.

As such, the play ends on a positive note; life wins out over death. It is not, however, as John Henry Raleigh suggests, "one of the most optimistic plays that O'Neill ever wrote."[16] It is true that life prevails — at least for the moment, and that a bond is formed between two human beings which will strengthen and sustain them both. But the vision of life with which O'Neill presents us is attenuated at best. There is no possibility of transcendence, no viable means of breaking through the limitations of time and space, no discovery of ultimate meaning or value. O'Neill employs religious language at the point of the clerk's transformation ("Beatific vision swoons on the empty pools of [his] eyes. He resembles a holy saint, recently elected to Paradise"), but it is used ironically. The "rapt hero worship [which] transfigur[es] his pimply face" (*Hughie*, p. 32) is merely for Arnold Rothstein, a gambler associated with the New York underworld as well as Tammany Hall, hence a symbol of the city's corruption. The cycle of mutual and self-deception is merely perpetuated, as Charlie takes Hughie's place and the pipe dream goes on. Life, the play tells us, cannot be borne without illusion, for one fate awaits us all. We live "By Way of Obit."

Notes

1. The general consensus is that O'Neill finished *Hughie* in 1941 (see Egil Törnqvist, *A Drama of Souls* [New Haven, Conn.: Yale University Press, 1969], p. 264), though the Gelbs place its completion in 1942 (Arthur and Barbara Gelb, *O'Neill* [New York: Harper & Bros, 1962], p. 844).

2. There is considerable critical disagreement concerning the number of plays projected in this series. Travis Bogard and the Gelbs place it at six (Travis Bogard, *Contour in Time: The Plays of Eugene O'Neill* [New York: Oxford University Press, 1972], p. 418; Gelbs, p. 843), Louis Sheaffer, at seven (Louis Sheaffer, *O'Neill: Son and Artist* [Boston: Little, Brown and Co., 1973], p. 521), and Tiusanen, at eight (Timo Tiusanen, *O'Neill's Scenic Images* [Princeton, N.J.: Princeton University Press, 1968], p. 316). O'Neill himself wrote under the title of the typewritten version of the first draft of *Hughie*, "A series of one-acters which will include 7, 8, or 9 plays" (Törnqvist, p. 257n).

3. Quoted in Sheaffer, p. 521.

4. Gelbs, p. 854.

5. Gelbs, p. 844.

6. Eugene O'Neill, *Hughie* (New Haven, Conn.: Yale University Press, 1959), p. 7. Subsequent citations in the text refer to this edition.

7. F. Scott Fitzgerald, *The Great Gatsby* (New York: Charles Scribner's Sons, 1925), p. 2.

8. Sheaffer, p. 521.

9. Sheaffer, p. 521.

10. Bogard notes in this regard:

The use of the key is important stage business. It is the only nonverbal sound from within the lobby until the dice roll along the counter at the end of the play. O'Neill marks the turning point in the play, the moment when Erie hits the farthest ebb of his loneliness, with the stage direction *"For a while he is too defeated even to twirl his room key"* (*Hughie*, p. 30). The moment was underscored memorably in the Stockholm production when the actor, Bengt Eklund, dropped the key. In so bare a scene, the action, the loss of the fetish, assumed climactic proportions (Bogard, p. 420n).

11. John Henry Raleigh's discussion of the thematic and historical connections between "Big Tim" Sullivan of *Iceman* and Arnold Rothstein of *Hughie* is worth quoting at some length:

Historically considered, *The Iceman Cometh* and *Hughie* are companion pieces: As "Big Tim" Sullivan is a tutelary presence in the beginning of *The Iceman Cometh*, Arnold Rothstein is an unseen but Olympian presence at the end of *Hughie*; as Sullivan went insane in 1912, the fictional date of *The Iceman Cometh*, so Arnold Rothstein was shot and killed in November 1928, the fictional date of *Hughie*, which takes place some time in the preceding summer of that same year. Indeed the connection in the two plays are [sic] surprisingly close, despite the disparities in their fictional dates. "Big Tim" Sullivan was not only the imaginary benefactor of the imaginary Joe Mott and Harry Hope but was also the real benefactor of the real Arnold Rothstein. Rothstein at the age of sixteen, in 1898, got his first glimpse into the amenities of power, money, and corruption by hanging around the headquarters of Sullivan, who considered him a very promising young man, besides being very useful in dealing with the Jewish constituency (John Henry Raleigh, *The Plays of Eugene O'Neill* [Carbondale and Edwardsville, Ill.: Southern Illinois Press, 1965], p. 75).

12. Eugene O'Neill, *Long Day's Journey Into Night* (New Haven, Conn.: Yale University Press, 1955), p. 76.

13. Eugene O'Neill, *A Moon for the Misbegotten* (New York: Random House, Inc., 1974), p. 24.

14. Gelbs, p. 843.

15. Henry Hewes, "Hughie," *Saturday Review*, October 4, 1958; rpt. Oscar Cargill, N. Bryllion Fagin, William J. Fisher, eds., *O'Neill and His Plays: Four Decades of Criticism* (New York: New York University Press, 1961), p. 226.

16. Raleigh, p. 28.

Concrete Images of the Vague in the Plays of Eugene O'Neill

B. S. Field, Jr.

That Eugene O'Neill had problems as a writer has long been a source of several kinds of critical comment. Among the best is Jean Chothia's *Forging a Language: A Study of the Plays of Eugene O'Neill*, (Cambridge: Cambridge Univ. Pr., 1979), which seeks to show what O'Neill went through and why in his struggle to command an effective dramatic literary style. Chothia's book, however hardly exhausts the topic; rather it opens O'Neill's style to further analysis. One of the issues repeatedly mentioned throughout the book, though never treated as a sub-topic on its own, is O'Neill's fondness for abstractions, for vague terms. The thesis of what follows is that vagueness in O'Neill's style is not merely a regrettable defect. In the long battle described in Chothia's book, O'Neill's struggle to achieve a style, a struggle with language itself, vagueness was both an enemy against him and a weapon for him.

To discuss the style leads to an attempt to explain the man, to psychology, and may also lead to the trendy terminology habitual to adepts in that mystery. The argument that follows here will attempt to take heart from Chothia's example, and to avoid sinking into that abyss, or, at least, to abate that engulfment, by following a strictly literary line: first to define the vague; second to describe some of the guises in which the vague appears in the plays of O'Neill; and finally to suggest why it does so.

The vague, in the language of topography, is a quality of an area or volume with indistinct or unstated boundaries. Its least confusing manifestation is in the merely ambivalent, a statement of limitations which may admit of two contrary interpretations. At the other end of the spectrum is the utterly limitless in volume, density, and duration. It is convenient to describe first some of the examples of the vague in the plays of O'Neill at one end of the spectrum and then some at the other. Many of the purely verbal examples are limitless, that admit of little or no definition. Other examples are merely ambivalent, and admit of two contrary interpretations, and often these are nonverbal, let us call them histrionic, having to do with stage action, with details of the set and lighting. Some examples, however, cannot be so efficiently categorized, and lie between the merely ambivalent and the limitless, between the purely histrionic and the purely verbal. Finally it is convenient to discuss separately a fourth group in which O'Neill embodies the very idea of vagueness itself in concrete objects or in specific terms. The effect of this last on a stage is almost magical, and we will get to that group in connection with the reasons for the appearance of the vague in his plays.

Some obvious examples of verbal vagueness appear in his fondness for grand abstractions, a quality that apparently poisons the style of many of his critics. Death, Life, Romance, Mystery, Love, are all terms that appear in the dialogue as if self-evidently clear. Of course, some lines, like one for Lazarus in *Lazarus Laughed*, are intended to be opaque: "Laughing we lived with our gift, now with laugher give we back that gift to become again the Essence of the Giver." I suppose I could decipher that — the gift, as I take it, is one's life — but in the production of the play I expect that most members of the audience were baffled. A speech in *Great God Brown*, has a similar effect: "The laughter of Heaven sows earth with á rain of tears, and out of Earth's transfigured birthpain the laughter returns to bless and play again in innumerable dancing gales of flame upon the knees of God." One character in *Beyond the Horizon*, O'Neill's first successfully staged full-length play, speaks now and then of Distant Romance, and of an Unknown Beauty over the horizon. Everyone in *Desire Under the Elms* looks at the farm or at the sky and declares it to be "purty." In *Marco Millions* the Chinese court pursues the notion of a soul which Marco brings to them, but no one ever tries to define the term. In *Strange Interlude*, in *Mourning Becomes Electra*, in *Ah, Wilderness!* various characters speak of yearning for some unspecific Peace or Happiness in some secret or faraway place.

It is possible to organize these manifestations of the vague according to their function in a sentence. A small set of adjectives appears in every play throughout O'Neill's career, in the dialogue and in the stage directions: queer, strange, crazy, mad, sick, sick-like, and half-dead-and-alive. Some noun substitutes, like "something," or the pronoun "it" with no referent, appear again and again; in *Desire under the Elms* these last two reappear with incantatory frequency. Various nouns for undefined mental sets appear in play after play: memories, ideas, ideals, illusions, beliefs, dreams, pipe dreams, hopes. A small group of verbs describing vague mental activities form a striking part of his vocabulary: to feel, to belong, to be mixed up, to care, to not care, to "moon," that is, to gaze with empty-headed fatuity. A stage direction in *Dynamo* tells us that one character "moons at the moon."

At the other end of the spectrum of vagueness, down at mere ambivalence, a specimen of histrionic vagueness as well as verbal, is the joke. Jokes are neither truths nor lies. In *Long Day's Journey into Night*, in *Iceman Cometh*, in *Ah, Wilderness!*, in *A Moon for the Misbegotten* at the end of his career, and at the beginning of his career, in some of his one-acts, or in *The Hairy Ape* a little later in his career, characters use jokes to make statements so that they won't be statements. In *Long Day's Journey into Night*, for instance, every character is given the chance to make some cutting quip and then to retract it, to say "it was the booze talking," or "the dead part of me talking." Ambivalence of this kind is also generated histrionically by drunkenness, sickness, rage, all of which are named as causes for behavior, as if that somehow disconnected the character from responsibility for his behavior, like Hamlet's excuse to Laertes in Act V that it was not Hamlet but Hamlet's madness that slew Polonius. A third device that involves this histrionic ambivalence is the machinery of quotation. Characters in O'Neill's plays, especially those figures who in the stage directions are described in terms reminiscent of the looks of O'Neill himself, are always quoting from books. Both Richard Miller and his father in *Ah, Wilderness!* quote from Fitzgerald's *Rubiyat*. Robert Mayo quotes poetry in *Beyond the Horizon*, and the three men in *Long Day's Journey into Night* quote from a variety of sources. The quoting of material allows a character to introduce the idea in the quotation into the debate on stage without having to fear reproaches from other characters, since it is, after all, not he who makes the comment, but Shakespeare or Schopenhauer or Baudelaire. The jokes, the quotations, and the drunkenness or sickness or rage all allow the characters an excuse for irresponsibility that is difficult for a theatre audience to validate or to invalidate.

Slightly more complex than the simple ambivalence of these kinds of mixed verbal and histrionic examples of vagueness is O'Neill's habitual mode of characterization. The characters are all divided people. This dividedness is most strikingly presented in *The Great God Brown*: there are two antithetical and paired central figures in the play, and each so competitive that he cannot cooperate with the other. In addition to the parable of the souls, O'Neill super-added the machinery of masks, which characters sometimes remove, in order to show their true faces to other characters, but which they begin to swap in the middle of the play, a variation that proved fatally confusing to the audiences of its New York production. Clearly the play is one of O'Neill's most deeply felt statements of his model of the personality, and one which has often been deplored by subsequent criticism.

Division and dividedness appear not only in the characters but are also suggested in the settings. O'Neill was always very specific about the sets and stage directions in this plays, sometimes even providing drawings. The typical set is often near or on an edge. It straddles some boundary or divison line, say, on the beach or on the docks, the waterfront, between the sea and the land, or featuring a fence, or a wall; or gratuitously demanding that action occur both inside and outside a house, both upstairs and downstairs, as in *Desire under the Elms*. One of the key scenes in *Ah, Wilderness!* is on a beach; one of the characters sits half in and half out of a rowboat that is partly in the water and partly on the beach, and they talk about how afraid they are of what they want to do. *Beyond the Horizon* is set on a farm that runs down to the seashore, *Anna Christie* and *The Iceman Cometh* and the climactic scene of *Mourning becomes Electra* are on the waterfront, *Long Day's Journey into Night* is in a sea-side summer home, the final scenes of *Strange Interlude* are on the edge of a river and the edge of Long Island Sound, the first and last scenes of *Great God Brown* are on a wharf overlooking the water, and so on. Perhaps the division itself is not the key to the image embodied in all these sets; the key may be in the limitlessness of the two differing prospects that stretch away from the division in either direction.

There is a further kind of histrionic vagueness that cannot be clearly fitted to mere ambivalence, and that is inarticularity. *The Hairy Ape* contains this device perhaps more consciously than any other of O'Neill's plays, but it appears in all of them. Yank mutters about "driven' t'roo," and "gettin' da speed," and "dat belongs. . . ," when he isn't silently assuming the posture of Rodin's *The Thinker*. But in all his plays the characters confess that they cannot express exactly what they mean, and part of the detective work that the plays ask of their audiences is to supply the significance to the words that the characters do use to suggest their meaning. In some cases this device works well. In *Desire under the Elms*, for instance, the constant rep-

etition of the words "it" and "something" by the characters leads them finally to equations between "it" and Eben's mother's spirit; for the audience,
there is a magic moment for each of them as he makes the connection between "it" and the very farm itself, that is the source of the contention
among them. Audiences leave a good production of *Desire under the Elms*
feeling that they have been intellectually productive. In many cases, of
course, the device did not work well, and indeed, O'Neill too often expected
audiences to bring order to his own internal chaos. In *Strange Interlude*,
with all the elaborate machinery of the "aside" to aid him in that play, in
The Great God Brown, with the help of the putatively fruitful convention
of the mask, O'Neill still cannot contrive any clear statement of the signfic-
ance of the play as a whole, either for the characters or to the audience. In
other plays O'Neill demanded less of his audience and settled for something
that was good enough: *Ah, Wilderness!* for instance, makes the moderate
and premasticated statement that while youth has its adventures and its
formless yearnings, middle-age has, if not its own enchantments, its own
contentments.

Usually, however, it is not a clear statement, but the inability to make
one, that sums up the thesis of an O'Neill play. "Stammering," says Edmund
in *Long Day's Journey into Night*, is his kind of eloquence. Indeed, the last
scene of that play works a series of variations on the theme of eloquence
versus inarticularity. Edmund, for instance, launches into a long description about the hypnotic effect of feeling a oneness with nature while settled
in the rigging of a ship under sail. His father is impressed with the speech,
and tells his son that he has "the makings of a poet." Edmund laughs, and
then sneers at his own eloquence. He picks up the pun available in the word
"makings" that his father had used, from the word's slang reference
to the "makings" of a roll-your-own cigarette, and asserts that he hasn't got
the "makings" at all. Like a man who wants to borrow, not only the tobacco
but also the papers, and a match as well, he hasn't got the makings; he's only
got the habit.

Edmund's parable of the roll-your-own cigarette is O'Neill's objective
correlative that gives to the vague concept of inarticularity a local habita-
tion and a name. There are others in other plays that are equally apt, such
as the nickel-in-the-slot player piano in *Great God Brown*, though of course
there are others that while equally concrete, are very conventional: gold,
secret hoards of money, treasure maps are offered as concrete images of the
lust for them, especially in the plays of the part of his career before 1934, in
which all the players are inflamed with the drive to possess, to dominate, to
achieve *Ubermenchheit*, to swallow the world as the only alternative to
being swallowed by it.

In the plays of the second part of his career O'Neill continued the attempt to find an objective correlative for the very idea of vagueness itself,
and many of the objects that he used themselves admit of indistinct limita-
tion. Among the more concrete are the references to limits or boundaries—

walls, fences, cages, and the kinds of edges or boundaries mentioned here before as examples of histrionic ambivalence. Characters often mention a feeling of being "caged in," and in *Desire under the Elms*, the two older sons destroy a gate as they leave to look for gold in California. Horizons in the early one-act plays and in *Beyond the Horizon* are often presented as suggestive of far away adventures. The south sea islands are described in *Differ'nt*, in *Beyond the Horizon*, and most strikingly in *Mourning becomes Electra*, as an objective correlative for social and sexual freedom, a freedom that the characters reject in favor of a life in New England for the same reason that Ephraiam Cabot gives up a farm in the west, that is, in Iowa, in order to come back to New England; only in New England is life painful and difficult enough to make it worth living.

Even less concrete among these concrete evocations of the vague are the "little formless fears" that are named in the stage directions for the third scene of *Emperor Jones*. Still more lacking in boundary is the sea. In perhaps half of his plays the sea is mentioned as a vague thing, and as both a threat and a temptation. In *Anna Christie* "dat ol' davil sea" is regularly evoked from the first line of the play to the last as an objective correlative for a kind of malicious fate, a home-brew nemesis. And in a dozen plays or more, characters run away to sea, or say that they would like to. In other plays ghosts, very often merely metaphorical ghosts, are presented with the same double suggestion as the sea, as a threat and an attraction. Ghosts appear to crazed characters, but not to the audience, in a number of the early one-act plays, and thereafter characters who feel themselves haunted by vague memories or unspecified guilt mention the word "ghosts" to mean specifically what Ibsen meant by the word, a thing that belongs, not to the present, but to the past. Eben's mother's influence in *Desire under the Elms* is called her "ghost." Various characters who sober up in *The Iceman Cometh* are told that they look like ghosts. Tyrone says in *Long Day's Journey into Night* that his wife has gone back to morphine, she'll soon be a ghost to them again. Sure enough, her last entrance is as spooky as O'Neill can contrive it.

Haze and whiteness, ice, moonlight, blanching or monochromatic lighting effects, are often features of the setting and stage directions in O'Neill's plays. One of the early one-acts published with his plays of the sea in 1918, "Ile" — that's a New-Englandism for oil, that is, whale oil — is set in a ship that has been locked in the arctic ice all winter. The blankness, the whiteness of the view, drives the captain's wife, who has come along on the whaling voyage, insane. *Emperor Jones* opens in a white room, a marked contrast to the succeeding scenes and their darkening gloom. More striking still are the blanched scenes set in moonlight, as those in *Moon of the Caribees*, in *Beyond the Horizon*, in *Desire under the Elms*, in *The Hairy Ape*, in *Dynamo*, in *Strange Interlude*, in *Lazarus Laughed*, in *The Great God Brown*, in *Mourning becomes Electra*, in *Ah, Wilderness!* and of course, in *A Moon for the Misbegotten*, in which the last two acts are played out in moonlight. The moon in all these scenes, and the moonlight, are described in the dialogue as giving an unreal quality to the scene, making what happens there seem parenthetical to the realities of the other scenes of the plays. It is a commonplace of stage designers that flat blue-white lighting reduces all colors to shades of grey, and reduces all shapes from a life-like three dimensions to a hieroglyphic two dimensions.

The most famous image of the vague in O'Neill is vague itself: the fog. It is always a danger in the early sea plays and in *Anna Christie*. It appears with obsessive frequency in the dialogue of *Long Day's Journey into Night*, and it appears in the plays between these two over and over again, sometimes merely metaphorically, in some banal comment that drunkenness or a hangover has made a character feel foggy. A play called *Fog* that O'Neill wrote before he enrolled in George Pierce Baker's seminar is about a businessman and a poet and their debate about the meaning of life while floating together in a fog-bound lifeboat near a threatening iceberg. Later in *Bound East for Cardiff*, the fog is mentioned time and again, and the foghorn blows outside while inside a sailor is dying. As he dies, the fog lifts. In *Anna Christie*, Mat comes to Anna like a gift from the fog, in a lifeboat from a wrecked ship. All during the play the fog is cited as a danger to the barge in particular and to shipping in general.

The fog is seductive and threatening at the same time. Everyone in *Long Day's Journey into Night* says so. It is literally foggy. The foghorn groans throughout the last act. We are told that the night before it sounded like a beached whale, and that Tyrone snored like a foghorn. The fog is cold and clammy. The characters claim that it makes them uncomfortable. However, we are also told by each of the characters that he likes the fog. It hides, obscures them from the world, and obscures, softens the world for them. It's like the "poetical bunk" from Dowson or Baudelaire that they are all quoting, or the sentimental memories that some of them evoke: it makes the present reality vague. Edmund speaks to himself and of people like him as "fog-people."

The vague is partly evident in the plays of O'Neill merely as a writer's problem, but it is also specifically embodied in enough different ways that it must be acknowledged as a force within the dramatic conflicts. The vague not only bothers O'Neill the way it bothers students in composition courses, but also in the same way that the sea, the horizon, the fog bother his characters: it is both seductive and threatening.

Let me recite here as an instructive parable a resume of one scene from Ibsen's *Peer Gynt*, in which Peer, in the course of a series of adventures with Norse folk-figures, runs into the Great Boyg in a scene that is to be played in total darkness. The Great Boyg is a monster that blocks Peer's road. It has no qualities at all. It is invisible and untouchable, but it has a voice. It convinces Peer that he cannot go through the Great Boyg, for if he tries that, the Great Boyg might swallow him up. He is told that he must go around, and he does so; in going around he confirms his own commitment to a rule of life that he had learned in the previous scene, to reject the dictum, "to thine own self be true," in favor of a new one, "to thine own self be enough." "Enough" becomes one of the catch-words of the Gyntian philosophy of life. Your average hack writer, as I drew the moral from Ibsen's episode here, will settle for "enough" and will be well paid for going around to it. But your true artist will never settle for anything but the word that is exactly right, will take his chances with the Great Boyg, wrestle it in its lair, and go through — or disappear entirely, swallowed up.

O'Neill wrote to George Pierce Baker in 1913 that he wanted to be "an artist or nothing"; that is, he was conscious of the odds and the consequences of a struggle with the Great Boyg, and that he accepted them. Every time he wrote a play, he wrestled with the Great Boyg, always in danger of being swallowed whole, like an amoeba's breakfast. Each play displays not a method for making a play, but an experiment to find a method by which the great enemy of the plastic power of art, the formless and unformable, may be conquered by being embodied in art. Some of these experiments were, of course, unmitigated failures. Some of the failures contain partial victories, small breakthroughs. And some are not failures, but triumphant successes.

For O'Neill, writing was a circular struggle. And here we teeter on the brink of psychology: anything that sounded to O'Neill as if it conveyed what he wanted to say sounded to O'Neill like slick, melodramatic bunk. Anything that sounded true, honest, and sincere to him was so vaguely stated, so ambivalently staged, that audiences were justifiably baffled. In such a struggle, to produce any articulate results was to give evidence against one's own artistic purity, evidence that implied that one had gone around, had settled for "enough." O'Neill produced his most articulate results when he had nothing to fear from such suspicions of himself, in a play like *Desire under the Elms* in 1924 when he was happy, successful, famous, on the verge of getting rich, and in 1939, when he had nothing to lose, facing a degenerative and only vaguely diagnosed disease which steadily increased the unsteadiness of his hands. As it became more and more difficult simply to perform the mechanical task of putting what he had in his head on the page, he became less hypercritical of what he put there. The results are the crown of his career: *The Iceman Cometh, Hughie, A Touch of the Poet, Long Day's Journey into Night,* and *A Moon for the Misbegotten.*

In *Long Day's Journey into Night* and in *A Moon for the Misbegotten,* O'Neill puts every character in both plays in exactly the same position as the one sketched above for O'Neill as a writer. Jamie Tyrone, for instance, cannot find a way to say what is in his heart. He keeps shifting back and forth, between protestations of affection for his brother or for Josie Hogan, and expressions of contempt for himself. He wants to tell his brother, to tell Josie, that he loves them. But he is suspicious of himself. He knows himself to be a liar. He knows that lies, like lines in a play, are eloquent bunk. Thus he is suspicious of all eloquence, including his own. To assume that because some false explanations are glib, that therefore all glib explanations are false, is an invalid converse proposition, but it is one that Jamie, and to some extent O'Neill too, live by, speak by. Every time Jamie finds a way to say what he feels, his words come out so clearly that they sound like lies. If the words come out couched in phrases that sound true and sincere, they come out so badly stated that they do not communicate what he feels. In *Long Day's Journey into Night* Jamie is drunk enough to smash his way through this circular dilemma, but in *A Moon for the Misbegotten*, the whole tragic tension of the final acts of that play lies in Jamie's inability to break out of that circle.

It is to embody that struggle, often pictured by O'Neill not in the form of a circle, but as an attempt to break through a wall, to cross a boundary, or as a search in the formless, in the distance, the night sky, the sea, or most characteristically, in the fog, that all these images of the vague in the dialogue and the settings of his plays serve. A simple list of these devices may not do much to make the texts of the plays seem any more powerful than they do already, but such an enumeration can demonstrate where actors find the means to make these plays, many of which are notoriously more effective on the stage than in the study, the compelling vehicles that they are. As actors demonstrate again and again, there is genuine power in the spectacle of a character risking everything on one chance, his last chance or his only chance, that he may, with only the frail reed of the American vulgate as a weapon, go through, not around, and either fail, be swallowed up in formlessness, or else win, that is, simply make himself understood.

The O'Neill-Faulkner Connection   Susan Tuck*

Eugene O'Neill is associated with such European giants as Strindberg, whom the American dramatist praised in his Nobel Prize acceptance speech and from whom he borrowed ideas about the love/hate relationship between men and women; Ibsen, who taught him much about the presentness of the past; Nietzsche, whose *Also Sprach Zarathustra* was the young O'Neill's bible; Freud, whose writings on the primacy of sex and the unconscious were to influence significantly the playwright's own dramas; and Jung, whose theories about archetypes O'Neill would use as early as *The Emperor Jones* (1920).[1]

William Faulkner has been compared to Balzac, whose *La Comédie humaine* was an inspiration for his own novels with their similarly recurring characters; to Dostoevsky, whose psychological insights and compassion for human suffering Faulkner greatly admired; with Dickens, from whom the Southerner learned a great deal about the grotesque and the art of carica-

---

*This essay is dedicated to eminent O'Neill scholar Horst Frenz, to whom all O'Neillians are indebted.

ture; to the Southwest humorists, whose macabre and extravagant humor he exhibited in his own tall tales; and with Hardy, whose Wessex landscapes may have served as a model for Faulkner's Yoknapatawpha.

Why, then, juxtapose William Faulkner and Eugene O'Neill? Although recognized as the father of the American theatre, O'Neill's considerable influence on this country's greatest novelist has been largely ignored. What did the South's quintessential spokesman find in the plays of a dramatist who worshipped the sea and declared that man lived on "hopeless hopes?" Seminal to answering that question is an early article in which Faulkner noted "that art is preeminently provincial: i.e., it comes directly from a certain age and a certain locality," but hastened to point out this rule did not apply to O'Neill: "[T]he most unusual factor about O'Neill is that a modern American should write plays about the sea. We have had no salt water traditions for a hundred years."[2] Faulkner was obviously familiar with more than the sea plays, however, for he remarked that *The Emperor Jones* had played to enthusiastic audiences

> and *The Straw* and *Anna Christie* are playing in New York this winter. These last two are later plays, not of the sea, but the thing that makes them go is the same that made *Gold* and *Diff'rent* go, that made the 'Emperor Jones' rise up and swagger in his own egoism and cruelty, and die at last through his own hereditary fears: they all possess the same clarity and simplicity of plot and language. (p. 88)

Important in this essay is the sense that Faulkner had been aware of O'Neill for some time and indeed had been following his work, for he remarks, "[O'Neill] is still developing; his later plays *The Straw* and *Anna Christie* betray a changing attitude toward his characters, a change from detached observation of his people brought low by sheer circumstance to a more personal regard for their joys and hopes, their sufferings and despairs" (p. 88).[3] Faulkner revealed a knowledge of O'Neill's personal life as well, noting that the dramatist had been to sea and knew its hardships, although "he is not physically strong, having congenitally weak lungs" (p. 88).

There are a number of ways Faulkner could have become acquainted with O'Neill's work. When he lived in New York for two months in 1921, he worked in a book store, thus giving him easy access to O'Neill's plays in print by that time.[4] Moreover, while in New York, Faulkner stayed a few blocks from MacDougal Street in Greenwich Village where the Provincetown Players had already produced fifteen of O'Neill's plays; having been a member of a theatre group at the University of Mississippi and author of at least one play, it is likely Faulkner would have taken advantage of his proximity to such dramas. Moreover, Faulkner's trips to New York were not limited to the period of early O'Neill productions. Faulkner had the opportunity to see two of O'Neill's most talked-about creations, *Strange Interlude* and *Mourning Becomes Electra*, for he was in New York in 1928 when the controversial stream-of-consciousness play was making headlines and again in 1931 when the Aeschylean trilogy was on Broadway.

Even when Faulkner went abroad he would have been confronted with the name O'Neill. When he left for Europe in 1925, it was with the hope that he might be "discovered" there. Though the trip did nothing to enhance his own career, it gave him ample opportunity to learn that Eugene O'Neill had acquired an international reputation. By the time Faulkner arrived in Paris in July 1925, *The Emperor Jones* and *The Hairy Ape* had been translated into French and *L'Empereur Jones* had been produced at the Odéon. When Faulkner traveled to England in early October 1925, Jonathan Cape had published all O'Neill's plays to date and various productions had been staged in London, among them *In the Zone, Diff'rent,* and *Ile* in 1921 and *Anna Christie* in 1923. When Faulkner arrived in London, a censorship controversy over *Desire Under the Elms* was being widely debated in newspapers and theatre journals, which were full of articles about O'Neill and his daring "sex drama." The British uproar surely would have caught the fledgling novelist's attention, for he, too, fervently believed an artist must be free to create what he pleased. At this same time, Paul Robeson in *The Emperor Jones* was receiving brilliant reviews for his performance at the Ambassadors Theatre. Although Faulkner did not stay long in England, he could not have missed London's reaction to the man whom one well-known British critic called "the most original and impressive dramatist in America."[5]

Reading O'Neill's plays and attending performances were not the only ways in which Faulkner might have familiarized himself with the dramatist, for mutual friends and acquaintances provided another opportunity. Drama critic Stark Young, a native of Faulkner's hometown in Mississippi, knew both men well, and Faulkner would often stay with Young when he visited New York. It seems highly unlikely that O'Neill would not have been mentioned by Young, who was actively involved in reviewing plays in the early twenties and would direct *Welded* in 1924. An even more likely connection was Saxe Commins. Arthur Gelb, O'Neill's biographer, recollected, "The major link between Faulkner and O'Neill was Saxe Commins. Mr. Commins was not only their editor but he also acted as close friend and confidant. He told me many times about conversations he had had with O'Neill about Faulkner, and Faulkner about O'Neill, but I don't think he ever managed to bring them together."[6]

It is to Faulkner's fiction, of course, that we must turn for evidence of the novelist's indebtedness to O'Neill. A few years after his essay on the playwright, Faulkner wrote a handful of impressionistic sketches for *The Double Dealer* — a "little" magazine that flourished in New Orleans between 1921 and 1926 — and short stories for the *Times-Picayune*.[7] In his article on O'Neill, Faulkner had commented admiringly on the dramatist's ability to convey the force of language and the power of dialect, so it is perhaps not surprising that these tales contain numerous experiments with speech patterns of various nationalities and types. Faulkner tried his hand at slang, sea language, broken Italian-American, street "jive," and black dialogue. We also find here pervasive echoes of themes that appear over and over in O'Neill's early dramas: the sailor's love/hate feelings for life on the sea; man's attempt to belong, to find his place; and the black man's misery and victimization.

"The Sailor" (Jan.-Feb. 1925) immediately suggests O'Neill's *Glencairn* plays. In only three paragraphs, Faulkner succinctly outlines the irresistible pull of the sea for a sailor who has just arrived on land and rejoices at being on solid ground once more:

> Ah, to have pavement under my feet again, instead of a motionless becalmed deck — motionless as a rock thrust up from the sea's bottom, with the very pitch starting from the seams and shrouds and canvas heavy and dead in a breathless noon. Or plunging and tacking off the bitter Horn! Icy and stiffened the gear, and cold-blisters like boils on every man's hands. But here is a stationary world: she don't pitch and groan and boom, not she! nor, scuppers under, race the howling gale. (*NOS*, p. 7)

By the second paragraph, the sailor's tone is milder and he comments, "Ah, lads, only fools go to sea — unless it be for to change women occasionally." The mention of women loosens his tongue, he describes the different women a sailor can meet, and as he talks we sense his wanderlust returning. By the third and final paragraph, he is eager to go to sea once more: "A sound footing is good, and wine and women and fighting; but soon the fighting's done and the wine is drunk and women's mouths don't taste as sweet as a man had thought, and then he'll sicken for the surge and the sound of the sea, and the salt smell of it again."

Most typically O'Neillian are the sketch's circular movement and the ambivalence the sailor feels toward the sea. "The Sailor" owes a good deal to *Bound East for Cardiff* (1916), in which Driscoll and the dying Yank discuss the hardships of their lives on the sea but confess an inability ever to leave it. Like them, Faulkner's sailor is "bound" to sea life, tied to an existence of harsh — but ever alluring — sea voyages. "The Sailor" is reminiscent, too, of *The Long Voyage Home* (1917), with Olson's poignant revelation of the longing for land a sailor often endures: "I mean all time to go back home at end of voyage. But I come ashore, I take one drink, I take many drinks, I get drunk, I spend all money, I have to ship away for other voyage."[8] But Olson never finds out whether life on land is what he imagines, for he is shanghaied and carried to yet another ship.

"White folks says, and nigger does," intones the black in "The Longshoreman" (Jan.-Feb. 1925), a brief sketch that echoes *The Emperor Jones*, which Faulkner had written about so admiringly in 1922. As he goes about his work, the black man's mind wanders: "[A]h, God, the light on the river, and the sun; and the night, the black night, in this heart. Oh, the black night, and the thudding drums sultry among the stars. The stars are cold, O God, and the great trees sailing like ships up the rivers of darkness, brushing the ancient stars forever aside, in vain" (*NOS*, p. 9). The repetition of the blackness of the night and the darkness of the forest suggest *The Emperor Jones* with its "wall of darkness dividing the world . . . and the river spread out, brilliant and unruffled in the moonlight."[9] Compare Faulkner's "giant trees sailing like ships" with O'Neill's description of tree limbs that entwine to form an enclosed space "like the dark, noisome hold of some ancient vessel" (vi, p. 198). The "thudding drums" in Faulkner's sketch also suggest *Jones*, in which the incessant beat of the tom-tom throbs throughout. Like Brutus Jones's journey, the longshoreman's reverie is symbolic and has archetypal significance; the black race undertakes the voyage, not just one individual.

"The Longshoreman" also reminds us of *All God's Chillun Got Wings* (1924). Not only does Faulkner allude twice to the hymn that gave O'Neill's play its name, but like the dramatist he repeatedly uses opposing elements to emphasize the dichotomy between black and white: night and day, hot and cold, prison and freedom. Faulkner associates blacks with warmth and spontaneity, whites with sterile mechanization and rigidity, just as O'Neill at the beginning of *All God's Chillun* portrayed the whites "awkward in natural emotion" while the blacks were "frankly participants in the spirit of Spring" (I, i, 301).

In "The Kid Learns" (May 31, 1925) Faulkner tells the story of a young street tough who is killed because he tried to protect a girl from another hood:

> Why, say, here she was again beside him, with her young body all shining and her hair that wasn't brown and wasn't gold and her eyes the color of sleep; but she was somehow different at the same time.
> "Mary?" said Johnny, tentatively.
> "Little sister Death," corrected the shining one, taking his hand. (*NOS*, p. 91)

Little sister Death will appear again in *The Sound and the Fury* on the day Quentin commits suicide, and for that reason alone this passage is significant, foreshadowing an image Faulkner would use later. Little sister Death is worth commenting upon in relation to O'Neill as well, for the playwright had used the figure of a lovely woman to presage death in *Bound East for Cardiff* when Yank, the supposedly hardened, insensitive sailor, sees a "pretty lady dressed in black" (*Seven Plays*, p. 50) just before he dies. Like Faulkner's Johnny, Yank's life has been a hard one, "one ship after another, hard work, small play, and bum grub; and when we git into port, just a drunk endin' up in a fight, and all your money gone, and then ship away again, never meetin' no nice people; never gittin outa sailor town, hardly, in any port; travellin' all over the world and never seein' none of it without no one to care whether you're alive or dead" (*Seven Plays*, p. 46). Similarly, Johnny's life is an inescapable struggle to survive on the street. Both characters are trapped in the lives they lead; rough, perhaps not particularly admirable on the surface, they are humanized by death in the form of a beautiful woman.

Space does not permit a detailed discussion of other stories from this early period, though O'Neillian echoes persist. For example, "Yo Ho and Two Bottles of Rum" (Sept. 27, 1925), a tale of greed, murder, insanity, and the sea, is reminiscent of *Gold* (1921). The use of cage imagery in "Home" (Feb. 22, 1925) is unmistakably from *The Hairy Ape* (1922); Faulkner's vagabond wonders, "How much longer would he be free, to walk the earth and drink the sun—be uncaged? Perhaps tomorrow he would clasp steel bars like a caged ape, panting for freedom" (*NOS*, p. 30). *The Hairy Ape* may also have served as a model for the desperate black in "Sunset" (May 24, 1925) who searches vainly to find a "place" and who discovers, like Yank Smith, that he belongs in death alone. In these apprenticeship sketches, Faulkner was struggling to find his voice, and we see O'Neill as a formative influence who helped to shape the future novelist's ideas and techniques.

Faulkner's major fiction bears evidence of O'Neill as well.[10] Critics often wonder how he could write two rather unremarkable novels—*Soldier's Pay* (1926) and *Mosquitoes* (1927)—then suddenly produce a masterpiece the magnitude of *The Sound and the Fury* (1929), with its highly innovative stream-of-consciousness technique. *Strange Interlude* (1928), called a "novel in dramatic form" of "revolutionary length" by O'Neill,[11] was also extremely inventive in having the characters speak their thoughts aloud. As noted earlier, Faulkner had the opportunity to see this highly publicized production in New York; an experimenter in form, it is quite likely he would have been impressed by O'Neill's radical approach to the exploration of man's subconscious. Significant was Faulkner's plan to use different colors of type in *The Sound and the Fury* to indicate different times in the flow of events; Boni and Liveright's March 1928 edition of *Strange Interlude* used blue and black inks to distinguish between dialogue and inner thoughts, suggesting Faulkner borrowed that idea.

The influence of *Strange Interlude* is found as well in Faulkner's *Requiem for a Nun* (1951). Temple Drake and Nina Leeds are extraordinary women, larger than life, who have an enormous capacity for creation and destruction. Femmes fatales who dwarf the inadequate males surrounding them, they are nearly mythic embodiments of the Female. The curious form of *Requiem*—half-play, half-novel—also suggests *Strange Interlude*, whose novelistic aspects have long been recognized.

As I Lay Dying (1930), called a tour de force by its author, was another radical departure in the tradition of the novel. Critics were astounded by the fifty-nine interior monologues and fifteen highly eccentric characters that make up the book. In reality this is a collection of voices, for each speaker steps forward, spotlighted as it were, delivers his "lines," and returns to the wings as another "actor" tells his story.[12] It is likely Faulkner was given the idea for the novel's form and a good deal of its technique by expressionist drama in general and *The Emperor Jones* specifically. We find in the book many qualities of expressionism: distortion, a dream-like quality, nightmarish images, grotesque characters, and a rapid sequence of episodic, disconnected *Stationen*, or brief scenes, that often shift with cinematic speed. *The Emperor Jones* and *As I Lay Dying* share all these characteristics. Moreover, both are archetypal journeys that reveal man's innermost thoughts and fears. Nature is alive, antagonistic, and distorted, in the play a "brooding and implacable" forest (ii, 187), in the novel a furious river of "lazy alertness" that is "dimpled monstrously."[13] There is in both a confounding of the senses and a refusal to distinguish between animate and inanimate, human and animal, for the alien landscapes objectify the characters' own grotesquely distorted souls. The strutting Brutus Jones and the banana-eating Bundrens blend the humorous and the horrible, making us laugh at their cartoon-like personalities at the same time we recognize their anguish.

Expressionist elements are found as well in *Sanctuary* (1931), in, for example, the kaleidoscopic scenes that move swiftly and chaotically with little regard for logical sequence. Consider, too, the novel's beginning, an ostensibly realistic scene — two men looking at each other over a stream — that is exaggerated and deliberately made unreal. They stare at each other for two hours, during which time a bird that is both artificial and real makes a sound "meaningless and profound."[14] One of these men is Popeye, a mechanical creature with the "vicious depthless quality of stamped tin," eyes like "two knobs of soft black rubber" (p. 4), and a face "like a mask carved in two simultaneous expressions" (p. 5). Comic yet unnervingly malevolent, Popeye is a marionette who suggests the exaggerated, mannequin-like characters of expressionist writers. O'Neill in particular utilized such figures. For example, in *The Emperor Jones*, Jeff — the first phantom to confront Jones — throws a pair of dice, "picking them up, shaking them, casting out with the rigid, mechanical movements of an automaton" (iii, 191); the actions of the prisoners in scene four "are those of automatons — rigid, slow and mechanical" (p. 194); and in scene five "there is something stiff, rigid, unreal, marionettish" about the buyers at the slave auction (p. 196). Later, the witch doctor will dance with absurd, jerky, and uncontrollable steps. And in *The Hairy Ape* the elite on Fifth Avenue are a "procession of gaudy marionettes, yet with something of the relentless horror of Frankensteins in their detached, mechanical unawareness" (v, 236). O'Neill's mechanical figures and Faulkner's puppet-like Popeye reveal man's alienation from his very self.

O'Neill turned to the alienation of the black man in *All God's Chillun Got Wings* (1924), creating one of the first unstereotyped roles for a black by considering him an individual in his own right. The uproar occasioned by this production was of international proportions; when audiences learned a white actress was to kiss a black man's hand, there was pandemonium: hate mail, death threats to O'Neill from the Ku Klux Klan, and an injunction from the mayor of New York City forbidding children to act in the play. As a Southerner who saw racial hatred on a day-to-day basis and had grown up in a town that was the scene of several lynchings, Faulkner would have been intrigued by O'Neill's controversial drama about black Jim Harris and white Ella Downey. Indeed, *Light in August* (1932) tells a similar story in the relationship between Joe Christmas and Joanna Burden, and the parallels between the novel and O'Neill's play are numerous.

In *All God's Chillun* a black friend of Jim asks, "Is you a nigger or isn't you? Is you a nigger, Nigger? Nigger, is you a nigger?" (I, ii, 311). Jim Harris spends a lifetime trying to answer that question. Even as a child, he hated his skin color and confessed to Ella, "I been drinkin' lots o' chalk 'n' water tree times a day. Dat Tom, de barber, he tole me dat make me white, if I drink enough" (I, i, 304). As an adult, Jim will metaphorically continue to drink chalk water in an effort to change his color. He has white aspirations to become a lawyer, although time and again he fails the examinations. He marries a white wife, whom he idolizes, yet the way he shows his love is to become her "black slave" (I, iii, 318), eventually devoting his entire life to her care.

Joe Christmas, too, must answer "is you a nigger or isn't you?" While Harris is externally black but internally white, Christmas is externally white but internally black:

> At night he would lie in bed . . . sleepless, beginning to breathe hard. He would do it deliberately, feeling, even watching, his white chest arch deeper and deeper within his ribcage, trying to breathe into himself the dark odor, the dark and inscrutable thinking and being of Negroes, with each suspiration trying to expel from himself the white blood and the white thinking and being.[15]

Placed in an orphanage because his grandfather suspected a black father for the illegitimate baby, Joe runs for fifteen rootless years, sometimes living with blacks, sometimes with whites, at home with neither. Faulkner once remarked that Joe's tragedy was "he didn't know what he was, and so he was nothing."[16] Like Jim Harris, he is incapable of self-definition.

Ella Downey and Joanna Burden are white women who have relationships with black men. The reason they do so is identical, their motivation determined by a sense of superiority. At least to some extent, Ella marries Jim to bolster her own ego, shattered because she was abandoned by her white lover. To be with Jim makes her conscious of a sole virtue: her whiteness. Though she seems at times to have genuine love for Jim, Ella can never forget his color, a color she has been brought up to despise. As she looks at a portrait of Jim's father, for example, she mocks: "It's his Old Man — all dolled up like a circus horse! Well, they can't help it. It's in the blood, I suppose. They're ignorant, that's all there is to it" (II, i, 330). Janus-faced Ella is loving one minute, the next "mean, vicious . . . break[ing] out harshly with a cruel, venomous grin: 'You dirty nigger!' " (II, ii, 337).

Called a "spinster" at forty, Joanna continues her affair with Christmas after she learns of his black blood because she believes she can assert her superiority and rescue an inferior from his oppression. Although she works on behalf of black colleges and employs only black lawyers, in the midst of their lovemaking Joanna calls out, "Negro! Negro! Negro!" (p. 227). Like Ella, Joanna has a "dual personality" (p. 205) and cannot forget a lifetime of prejudice.

In addition to resemblances among the characters, *All God's Chillun* and *Light in August* utilize a similar technique. O'Neill and Faulkner favored repetition, often repeating an image, motif, or phrase over and over again, and in play and novel the colors black and white effectively and insistently recur. O'Neill carefully arranges blacks and whites in distinct groups, emphasizing their separateness. On the day Jim and Ella marry, for example, whites and blacks "hurry to form into two racial lines on each side of the gate, rigid and unyielding, staring across at each other with bitter hostile eyes" (I, iv, 319). The connotations of the two colors are played upon throughout; for example, Jim declares, "All love is white," and Ella calls black Jim "the only white man in the world" (I, iii, 317; I, iii, 314). Even the music is significant, and on the day Jim and Ella marry, an organ grinder plays "Old Black Joe." The inanimate, too, is symbolic, and a primitive ebony Congo mask assumes the dimensions of an actual character.

Like Jim Harris, Joe Christmas sees the white world as completely different from the one blacks inhabit. Walking from a black shantytown — cabins "shaped blackly out of darkness" in a "black hollow" — to a white neighborhood, Joe senses the "cold hard air of white people." Suddenly, the glow of streetlights is white, there are white houses, white porches, and in "a lighted veranda four people [sit] about a card table, the white faces intent and sharp in the low light, the bare arms of the woman glaring smooth and white above the trivial cards" (p. 100). Christmas can never possess this white world, however, for his invisible blackness follows him everywhere. Faulkner repeatedly refers to him as a shadow, appropriate for a white black whose clothes — white shirt, black trousers — symbolize his double identity. When Joe and Joanna make love, they struggle as though in a "black thick pool" of "black waters" or a "black abyss" (p. 228). Throughout the novel are innumerable references to Joe's "black blood," and on the last day of his life a "black tide creep[s] up his legs, moving from his feet upward as death moves" (p. 297). Just before he is killed, there are over a dozen references to the conflict between his white and black blood (p. 393), and as he is castrated "pent black blood," a "black blast," gushes out of his body (p. 407). Jim Harris finds his "place" in sacrifice, Joe Christmas in death.

All God's Chillun and *Light in August* offer the most extended parallels between an O'Neill play and a Faulkner novel, though other possibilities suggest themselves. For example, in *Mourning Becomes Electra* (1931) O'Neill showed that man's past was inescapable, just as Faulkner would do in *Absalom, Absalom!* (1936). American epics that have the tone and scope

of Greek tragedy, play and novel reveal the past as a web that traps generation after generation and history as a nightmare from which man struggles
to awake. How much does *Absalom* owe *Mourning*? There is no definitive
answer, just as there is no real "proof" that *Light in August* was inspired by
All God's Chillun, that *The Sound and the Fury* owed its technique to
Strange Interlude, or that *As I Lay Dying* was written with *The Emperor
Jones* in mind. Evidence is very strong, however, and indicates Faulkner
never forgot the dramatist who had impressed him at an early age with the
sense of the sea and the force of language. A recent book of recollections
about Faulkner adds one more fact to what we know about the novelist's
familiarity with the playwright. "O'Neill had the right idea in *The Great
God Brown*," Faulkner remarked in the thirties. "Those masks he used for
his characters made a small play into a big one."[17] Such a comment, years
after the play was produced, indicates Faulkner was still following the innovative work of Eugene O'Neill.

Notes

1. Dates following O'Neill's plays refer to production.

2. William Faulkner, "American Drama: Eugene O'Neill," *The Mississippian*, Feb. 3,
1922; rpt. *Faulkner: Early Prose and Poetry*, ed. Carvel Collins (Boston: Little, Brown, 1962),
p. 87. Subsequent references will be included parenthetically within the text.

3. Faulkner's comments about *Anna Christie* are particularly interesting because the
play had not yet appeared in print at the time he wrote his essay. Since the play had been
performed in New York in November 1921 and Faulkner had been in the city at the time, it is
possible he had attended a performance.

4. Plays in print by the fall of 1921 were: *Thirst; The Web; Warnings; Fog; Recklessness;
Bound East for Cardiff; Before Breakfast; The Moon of the Caribbees; The Long Voyage
Home; In the Zone; Ile; Where the Cross Is Made; The Rope; Beyond the Horizon; Diff'rent;
The Straw; Gold*. For data on publication see Jordan Y. Miller, *Eugene O'Neill and the Ameri-
can Critic: A Bibliographical Checklist*, 2nd ed. (Hamden, Conn.: Shoe String Press [Archon],
1973). See also Joseph Blotner, *William Faulkner's Library: A Catalogue* (Charlottesville: Univ.
Press of Virginia, 1964), p. 126. Blotner records that friend Phil Stone ordered for Faulkner *The
Moon of the Caribbees* and *Gold*. While *Gold* was available in a single volume, *Caribbees* had
been published only in a collection that included *Ile; Where the Cross Is Made; The Rope; In
the Zone; Bound East for Cardiff;* and *The Long Voyage Home*. In later years Faulkner would
acquire the 1932 Modern Library edition of *Nine Plays* that included *The Emperor Jones; The
Hairy Ape; All God's Chillun Got Wings; Desire Under the Elms; Marco Millions; The Great
God Brown; Lazarus Laughed; Strange Interlude; Mourning Becomes Electra*.

5. St. John Ervine, "The Emperor Jones," *The Observer* [London], Sept. 13, 1925.

6. Personal letter from Arthur Gelb to Susan Tuck, June 25, 1980. Gelb is not alone in
believing the two men never knew each other personally. Dorothy Commins, Saxe Commins'
widow, wrote in a letter to me (June 25, 1980), "As far as I know they never met. That may be
due to an innate shyness in each of them. These men guarded their privacy as few men I know in
literature." Malcolm Cowley, a friend of both writers, agreed with Mrs. Commins (June 27,
1980). Well-known Faulkner scholar Cleanth Brooks admitted he did not know if the men had
ever been introduced but added: "I'm sure in my own mind that Faulkner did know about
O'Neill and must certainly have read some — maybe most — of O'Neill's plays. He may have seen
a number of them on the stage" (June 28, 1980). Finally, the letters of Stark Young are filled

with references to O'Neill and to Faulkner, but at no time is there a suggestion they were acquainted with each other. See *Stark Young: A Life in the Arts. Letters, 1900–1962*, 2 vols., ed. John Pilkington (Baton Rouge: Louisiana State Univ. Press, 1975), esp. pp. 148, 1155–56, 1263. I wish to thank Mr. Brooks, Mrs. Commins, Mr. Cowley, and Mr. Gelb for permission to quote from their letters to me.

7. Carvel Collins has arranged these early pieces in one volume under the title *New Orleans Sketches* (New York: Random House, 1968). Subsequent references will be included parethentically within the text and abbreviated *NOS*.

8. Eugene O'Neill, *Seven Plays of the Sea* (New York: Random House [Vintage], 1972), p. 73. Subsequent references will be included parenthetically within the text and abbreviated *Seven Plays*.

9. Eugene O'Neill, *Plays* (New York: Random House, 1955), ii, 187. This three-volume edition will be used throughout with subsequent references included parenthetically within the text.

10. See my articles on O'Neill and Faulkner in *The Eugene O'Neill Newsletter*, 4 (Winter 1980), 19–20; and 5 (Winter 1981), 10–16.

11. Louis Sheaffer, *Son and Artist* (Boston: Little, Brown, 1973), p. 199.

12. The dramatic aspects of *As I Lay Dying* were recognized by the Yale School of Drama in March 1982, when Faulkner's novel was produced as a two-and-a-half hour play.

13. William Faulkner, *As I Lay Dying* (1930; rpt. New York: Random House [Vintage], 1957), p. 134.

14. William Faulkner, *Sanctuary* (1931; rpt. New York: Random House [Vintage], 1958), p. 4. Subsequent references will be included parenthetically within the text.

15. William Faulkner, *Light in August* (1932; rpt. New York: Random House [Modern Library], 1959), p. 197. Subsequent references will be included parenthetically within the text.

16. *Faulkner in the University*, ed. Frederick L. Gwynn and Joseph L. Blotner (Charlottesville: Univ. of Virginia Press, 1959), p. 72.

17. Ben Wasson, *Count No 'Count: Flashbacks to Faulkner* (Jackson: Univ. Press of Mississippi, 1983), p. 113.

CONTRIBUTORS

STEVEN F. BLOOM is assistant professor of English and coordinator of the communication arts program at Emmanuel College in Boston. He is the author of several articles on O'Neill.

JACKSON R. BRYER is professor of English at the University of Maryland. He is the editor of "*The Theatre We Worked For*": *The Letters of Eugene O'Neill to Kenneth Macgowan* (1982). Among his other publications are *The Short Stories of F. Scott Fitzgerald: New Approaches in Criticism* (1983) and *Dear Scott/Dear Max: The Fitzgerald-Perkins Correspondence* (1971).

STEVEN E. COLBURN teaches at the University of Alabama and is completing a full-length study of the poetry of Anne Sexton.

FRANK R. CUNNINGHAM is associate professor of English at the University of South Dakota; his articles and reviews have appeared in *Modern Drama, Sewanee Review, Literature/Film Quarterly, Saturday Review*, and the *New York Times Book Review* among other publications.

PETER EGRI is professor of English at Budapest University. His books include *Hemingway, James Joyce and Thomas Mann, Dream, Vision and Reality*, and many others.

B. S. FIELD, JR., teaches in the English department at Wayne State University. He is an editor of the drama anthology, *Stages of the Drama*.

ELLEN KIMBEL is assistant professor of English at the Pennsylvania State University (Ogontz). She has published essays on the American short story and Willa Cather, and she lectures on film history as well as on literature.

MICHAEL MANHEIM, professor of English at the University of Toledo, published a full-length study of the Shakespearean history play in 1973, and is the author of *Eugene O'Neill's New Language of Kinship* (1982) and a wide variety of articles.

LAURIN R. PORTER teaches drama and modern literature at the University of Texas at Dallas. She is currently completing a book entitled *Possessors Dispossessed: The Late Plays of Eugene O'Neill*.

CARL E. ROLLYSON, JR., teaches in the university studies/weekend college program of Wayne State University. He has published articles on Faulkner, Styron, Mailer, O'Neill, and Arthur Miller.

JUNE SCHLUETER teaches modern drama at Lafayette College. She is the author of *Metafictional Characters in Modern Drama* (1979), *The Plays and Novels of Peter Handke* (1981), and is working on a book on Arthur Miller. ARTHUR LEWIS, a graduate of Lafayette College, has worked on Eliot and O'Neill and directed a production of Pirandello's *Six Characters in Search of an Author*.

LISA M. SCHWERDT teaches at Purdue University. She has published in *Modern Fiction Studies, Irish Literary Supplement*, and *Abstracts of English Studies*.

JOSEPH S. TEDESCO is associate professor of English at St. Bonaventure University. He is at work on a book length study of the tragicomic art of George Bernard Shaw.

SUSAN H. TUCK, associate instructor in English at Indiana University, Bloomington, a frequent contributor to the *Eugene O'Neill Newsletter*, is completing a full-length study of O'Neill and Faulkner. With Horst Frenz, she edited *Eugene O'Neill's Critics: Voices from Abroad* (1983).

INDEX

DATE DUE